THE ASTROLOGY FILE

THE ASTROLOGY FILE

SCIENTIFIC PROOF OF THE LINK
BETWEEN STAR SIGNS AND
HUMAN BEHAVIOUR

Gunter Sachs

ORION

First published in 1998 by Orion Books Ltd
Orion House, 5 Upper St Martin's Lane, London WC2H 9EA

A CIP catalogue record for this book is available
from the British Library.

ISBN 0 75281 789 2

Printed and bound in Great Britain by
Butler and Tanner, Frome and London

CONTENTS

The author will donate his share of the book's proceeds to the Mirja-Sachs-Foundation Munich. The charity will use the full funds, without any cost deduction, for the support of needy children all over the world.

FOREWORD
BY GUNTER SACHS

Like salmon swimming to their spawning grounds, astrology has made its unerring yet enigmatic way across the ages. It is different from its esoteric sisters, the crystal ball, the pendulum, the Tarot cards and other gizmos used to peer into the future, but like them it has grown up shrouded in mystery rather than illuminated by the light of science.

No amount of criticism or doubt, no coolly reasoned argument has shaken people's belief in the existence of an astrological force. To the gambler at the casino gaming table, the giggling teenager in Shanghai, the lady chatting with her friends in a Viennese coffee house, even to the captain of industry, statesman or dictator wrestling with a critical decision, proof of its validity is as irrelevant as proof of the existence of God is to a priest.

The shrewd, oracular saying 'The stars incline, they do not compel' places astrology in the happy position of never being wrong: when a prediction comes true it is due to the inclination of the stars. If it doesn't, it is because we have chosen to ignore stellar influences.

Throughout history, astrology has swung between what is and what seems to be. Never proved or disproved. Attacks by churchmen and scientists have been razor-sharp. Astrologers' weapons have been few and far between. Despite the support of great minds like Kepler or Paracelsus and the harshest criticism from preachers and professors, there is still no definite answer to the question: hocus-pocus or reality? There has never been incontrovertible proof.

Then came the dawn of the computer age. With it came all the paraphernalia, databases and government-operated super-computers which made it possible to explore the mystery and to answer at least one fundamental question: Does the star sign under which a person is born have any influence on that person's nature?

One clear, starry New Year's Night in the Swiss mountains, I discussed the problem with my friend Claus Jacobi. He laughed and said: 'That might be just the sort of challenge you love.' I took up that challenge.

Following an inspirational event in Key West with unexpectedly fortunate results, which I describe in Chapter 1, I first went in search of people with ideas. I managed to win over my two collaborators Hanswerner Schwenk and Markus Gohr, as well as Claus Jacobi, to my cause. None of us knew much about astrology.

We drew up a few guidelines:

Our aims were:
- for the first time in the long history of astrology to examine by means of a broadly structured scientific study the possible effect of star signs on human behaviour;
- not to prove that there is such a thing as astrology above and beyond mythology, but to investigate whether it exists, allowing for an open result;
- to publish our study even if it failed to prove the existence of non-mythological astrology. That would also have been of interest;
- to base our research exclusively on empirical data and not to interview any astrologers;

- to examine and explain scientifically any factors which might distort our statistical results;
- to indicate as significant any noticeable deviations from expected results which could not be explained as pure chance ('Significance', *see* page 43);
- to have our calculations and their results checked by a suitable neutral authority such as a university.

We commissioned the Institut für Demoskopie, Allensbach, one of the leading European public research institutes, to conduct a representative survey of attitudes and consumer behaviour according to star sign. This is included in the appendix as a separate entity.

For the benefit of devotees of astrology, at the end of each individual analysis we compared our results with what astrologers had to say. Likewise with many of the statistics brain teasers. These are clearly distinguished from the statistical sections under the heading 'The Astrological Angle'.

To coordinate the collection and evaluation of data we set up the 'Institute for Empirical and Mathematical Research into the Truthfulness of Astrology concerning Human Behaviour and Predisposition' – IMWA for short.

We needed to have access to the vast quantities of information stored in databases in the industrialized nations. First of all we approached the keepers of the public records of Switzerland, which are by far the most accurate in the whole of the West. Since 1850 regular censuses have provided detailed information about the state, structure and distribution of the population. Since 1875 even the hour of birth of every single Swiss citizen has been recorded.

We also had the support of public authorities, insurance

companies and publishing houses in other countries, i.e. Great Britain and Germany.

In order to check our data analysis and our calculations, we enlisted the help of the Institute of Statistics at Munich's Ludwig-Maximilian University.

As the months went by, we built up an extremely extensive database containing millions of individual statistics about the birth dates of criminals and traffic offenders, couples marrying and divorcing, sick people and suicides, working people and those interested in astrology. While respecting the rules on data protection, all the organizations participating in the project arranged members of these particular groups under star signs according to their dates of birth. The units so created were then adjusted for any factors which might have biased a statistical comparison – such as seasonal birth rate rises or the different lengths of time covered by the star signs.

The adjusted data, arranged according to star sign, formed the basis of our research. Do Pisces commit more traffic offences than Geminis? Do more Scorpios than Taureans choose to commit suicide? In theory, the average proportions should always be about the same.

But was this really the case? Or did the twelve star signs behave in significantly different ways? If this was true, then the stars really do influence human nature. Or might there also be some other factor at work? We looked into that possibility too.

I should point out that in the course of this project we were only able to look at star signs (i.e. Sun signs). Astrologers might consider this inadequate, since they take many other aspects and concepts into account: planets, Moon, houses, ascendants and so on. Collecting and processing this kind of information must remain no more than speculative for the time being. After early results indicating that star signs exerted some influence over human behaviour, I published articles on the subject in several 'serious' German and Swiss newspapers and magazines in the hope of finding more sources of information for our study.

It was as though I had opened the flood gates. I was engulfed by torrents of abuse and insults. 'Stick to what you're best at, playboy – chasing good-looking women!' I never imagined what academics could come up with. Time and again they accused me of getting my terminology confused. I studied mathematics at university in French-speaking Switzerland. The fact that the sums were right did not seem to interest my correspondents.

When I published a second article about our survey of 350,000 marriages, people wrote to me by the hundred. Our calculations were incorrect, they claimed, since so many marriages between two star signs were classic cases of self-fulfilling prophesies. Men and women who believe in astrology go to marriage bureaux with the firm intention of finding an Aries partner, or scan the personal ads in search of a Libra lady. Maybe. But none of these smart alecs could say how many such cases there were. We examine this phenomenon in our chapter on marriage. Hopefully, nobody will accuse us of making self-fulfilling prophesies of suicide, which we also researched. Surely no one could suggest that there are such people as suicide counsellors?

Some of our critics even lectured us about precession of the equinoxes – the slow shift of the earth's axis resulting in a change of position of the star signs. This, they claimed, would render our research irrelevant.

Not so: we were taking snapshots and simply reporting on

what they showed, so did not need to concern ourselves with geophysical phenomena.

'The scientist's challenge is all about proving new theories wrong', Francis Crick, British Nobel prizewinner and discoverer of the molecular structure of DNA, once said to me. I think he was even more far-sighted than I ever imagined.

When we came to evaluate our first, extremely large, set of data, it showed astonishing differences between the star signs. These were so surprising that we decided to run a cross-check. We shuffled all the birth dates like a pack of cards, whisked them in the computer like batter in a blender and then split the mixture into twelve piles.

This created twelve artificial star signs, twelve groups that were totally different from the actual star signs. These were evaluated in exactly the same way. Lo and behold, between these twelve fictitious star signs there were no notable behavioural differences, no more than slight deviations which, in contrast to those seen among the genuine star signs, were of no statistical significance. For more information about this impressive thought-provoking experiment turn to page 203!

At the same time, for some investigations, where the numbers surveyed permitted, we split the data into different samples. As the testing period was spread over a longer time, in this case from 1987 to 1994, we were able to examine the years 1987–1990 and 1991–1994 separately.

We then grouped together the odd and even years and finally looked at each year separately, which confirmed the results for the whole period. The so-called sensitivity analysis revealed that the results could be reproduced. *Per aspera ad astra!*

Altogether, over a period of two years we looked at ten

different aspects of life. Each of these ten surveys showed significant differences between specific star signs, some greater than others, but in any case far more than could be explained away as pure chance.

When our job was finished, after the computers had processed millions of data sets, we had statistical proof that there is a correlation between star signs and human behaviour in all the fields of activity researched, star signs had a definite influence over how we humans behave. How pronounced the correlation might be, or how much of it comes from the stars, we do not know. All we know is that it does exist.

The vehemence with which opponents of astrology defend their position will continue. But so will mathematics and astrology.

Allow me to end with an allegory:

When there is water coming through the ceiling, we know that there is a lot more water in the world: we may see it in a little puddle from an overturned vase, a rain-flooded room or a pipe that bursts and releases a whole reservoir of water.

We have proved the existence of a few 'astro-drops'. The question is: how many more drops are out there?

ASTROLOGY THROUGH THE AGES
BY CLAUS JACOBI

'It was on the 28 August 1749 at the stroke of twelve noon, that I came into the world at Frankfurt on the Main. The constellation was auspicious: the Sun was in Virgo and at its culmination for the day. Jupiter and Venus looked amicably upon it, and Mercury was not hostile. Saturn and Mars maintained indifference. Only the Moon, just then becoming full, was in a position to exert adverse force, because its planetary hour had begun. It did, indeed, resist my birth, which did not take place until this hour had passed.'

(Translated by John Oxenford from Goethe's autobiography.)

This was how the sixty-year-old Johann Wolfgang von Goethe described his arrival on earth. In later years astrologers taught him to 'value very highly' the 'good aspects' of this event.

Astrology is based on the assumption that the position of the heavenly bodies influences events here in earth. The Universe, or macrocosm, is reflected in the fate and character of each individual human being – the microcosm. For thousands of years, astrology had been considered a science. Several centuries ago it then became widely regarded as superstition. It has continued to influence our destiny in both of these capacities.

Whether we humans came down from the trees or were expelled from paradise: the heavens have always fascinated us – and helped us to survive, hunt, roam, sow, wonder at and pray. Nomadic peoples used the positions of the stars to guide them on land, seafarers at sea. The position of the Sun taught farmers about the cycles of growth and decay, while hunters observed the changing sky to gauge weather conditions. And at last a home for the gods had been found.

World history, as we know it, began less than 10,000 years ago. Five fertile river valleys were the cradle of earliest civilization: the Nile, Euphrates, Tigris, Indus and the Yellow River. On their muddy banks *Homo sapiens* invented the bicycle and government, constructed the plow and the pyramids, created idols and laws, bronze and calendars.

All these early cultures venerated the Sun, Moon and stars, for their influence on the earth was evident, they brought night and day, harvest, drought and rain. They appeared to be close by and were observed to discover their secrets.

Astrology's birthplace appears to have been in Mesopotamia, the country between Euphrates and Tigris, present day Iraq. Cuneiform tablets from the library of the Chaldean king Assurbanipal, who ruled in the seventh century BC, indicate origins in the third millennium BC in the Sumerian city states south of Babylon. In the Chaldean Empire observation and interpretation of the stars were perfected to such an extent that the word 'Chaldean' became synonymous with 'astrologist', as in the Old Testament (Daniel 1).

A celestial religion was established in Babylon. For the Chaldeans, the heavens provided a stage for the adventures and heroic deeds of their gods. Sunrise and sunset, the waxing and waning of the Moon, the fire of the fixed stars and planetary orbits were proof of divine existence, divine power, passion and intention.

Babylonian priests recorded the motion of the stars, drew

celestial charts, which were passed on from one generation to the next, and attempted to interpret the will of the gods from planetary positions. They attempted to calculate these constellations in advance to forecast the fate of rulers and the empire.

Thus in Babylon, the two major human needs were united, to be separated thousands of years later; religion and science joined forces. Astrology became synonymous with astronomy. The study of the stars and the belief in their influence were inseparable.

Already in Babylonian times, particular characteristics were ascribed to the individual planets – including the Sun and the Moon, but no Uranus, Neptune and Pluto which had not yet been discovered. These planets did not wander all over the heavens, rather their orbit remained within a narrow belt around the firmament. This was divided into twelve segments, each named after a nearby constellation of stars. This was the origin of the signs of the zodiac. Each planet was later assigned two houses, the Sun and the Moon one each.

In the beginning, astrologers were only concerned with predictions about kings and kingdoms; cities and tribes; wars; epidemics and natural disasters. In his excellent book *Geschichte der Astrologie* (History of Astrology) Wilhelm Knappich quotes these early Babylonian predictions:

- 'If, when the Moon rises, it appears to be wearing a tiara, the king will come to power.'
- 'When the fiery light of Venus illuminates the breast of Scorpio, then rain and floods will ravage the land.'

Personal astrology, with its focus on individual character and destiny based on the constellation at the time of birth, probably arose only towards the end of the Babylonian empire in the sixth century BC, presumably already then under Greek influence. The term horoscope itself definitely derives from the Greek, from *hora* (time) and *skopos* (observer). The oldest known horoscope dates back to 412 BC.

After the sixth century BC, the disbelieving century of Buddha and Pythagoras, Confucius and (reputedly) Laotse, the bold notion that the earth is floating in space gained acceptance. Astrological knowledge spread far beyond the borders of Babylon to China, Persia and India, Egypt and Greece, the Roman Empire and Scandinavia. It was often passed on by traders or invaders travelling to foreign countries, to develop independently as in China or later among the Mayas in Mexico.

Each culture contributed something to astrology. The Talmud contains astrological references. The transmigration of souls was integrated in Indian astrology, while the Persians included the moment of conception in their astrological calculations.

In Egypt, where the pharaoh was said to have come from the lap of the sun god and to return there after death, and the calendar had been invented 3,000 years BC, daily oracles remind one of the horoscopes in the popular press today, such as: 'Do not leave the house today: Whoever is born on this day will die this day of an infection'.

In China, where the lunar year is observed, there are also signs of the zodiac named after animals, but these had different names and no fixed dates. When the appearance of several comets caused anxiety in the Chinese Empire, the emperor forbade sexual relationships between astrologers and public servants or citizens, to prevent the precipitous expansion of astrological knowledge. 'The censors must see to this,' ordered the emperor.

Astrology also plays a role in Christian tradition. The pilgrimage of the three wise men was to the Star of Bethlehem, beneath which the saviour would be born. Uncommon celestial events – such as eclipses of the Sun or Moon – have always fascinated star gazers most. They have been compared with a wild boar swallowing the Moon, a snake the Sun. In the fifth century BC, the Greek historian Herodotus wrote about Egyptian astrologers: 'If a miracle occurs they take careful note of its outcome, and if a similar occurrence ever takes place in future, they think it must end the same way.'

In Greece itself, astrology was adapted to the thought structures of Hellenistic philosophy. Deities became natural forces. The spheres of the fixed stars encircled the world of Aristotle. Everything from colours to numbers was assigned to a star. Astrology was especially important to medicine. Each organ was assigned a planet, each part of the body a sign of the zodiac.

The art of astrology spread from Athens to Rome, where its influence was extremely strong. Roman emperors, from Tiberius, through Nero and Vespasian, to Marcus Aurel all had court astrologers even if they did place a temporary ban on astrology in the Empire, arousing the protest of Cicero, Tacitus and Seneca.

Caesar's legions took Taurus as their emblem. Augustus had a silver coin stamped with Capricorn. During chariot races in the imperial stadium each of the twelve stables bore a zodiac symbol; the seven lanes of the race track were dedicated to the seven known planets, as were the seven days of the newly created week.

Then there appeared upon the scene a man of exceptional talent who integrated all the astronomical, astrological and geographical knowledge of his age: Claudius Ptolemaeus – better known as Ptolemy – of Alexandria. A child of both Greek and Egyptian culture, he was born in about AD 100 and lived until about AD 160. He was the creator of the Ptolemaic system. This theory places the Earth at the centre of the Universe. The Sun, Moon and planets were thought to circle around the Earth. Ptolemy's system is, therefore, known as geocentric – earth-centred.

People accepted this illusory geocentric model for almost fifteen hundred years (although the Greek Aristarchos of Samos had already claimed in about 250 BC that the Earth turned 'in a circular movement around the Sun').

Ptolemy's masterpiece consisted of thirteen volumes and was entitled *Syntaxis mathematica* (also known by the Arabic abbreviation *Almagest*). It effectively defined astrology until the late Middle Ages. The contents included calculations of planetary orbits and the oldest known star catalogue, listing 1,028 heavenly bodies.

Ptolemy's second extensive work, *Geographike hypegesis* comprises eight books, six with longitude and latitude charts and an index of 8,000 geographical locations. This index is the most ancient source of many geographical as well as ethnological names – Friesians, Lombards, Saxons and Sudetens for example.

The Egyptian mathematician's third multi-volume work devoted to astrology – with additional essays on acoustics and optics – is the *Quadripatitum* or *Tetrabiblos* – meaning a book in four parts. The four books deal with the nature of the stars, their movements, and their effects on both terrestrial events and individual human beings. *Tetrabiblos* had been defined as a 'scientific basis of astrology as the physical state of the cosmos'. For centuries, the work was regarded as the astrologer's bible. The man who was perhaps the most important scientist of his age proved to be the most enduring of all astrologers.

'Mortal as I am,' he wrote, 'I know that I was born for only one day. But when I see the stars circling in their orbits, then my feet no longer touch the ground. I climb up to Zeus to feast on ambrosia, the food of the gods.'

Ptolemy imagined the cosmos as a kind of interlocking machine. In his book *The Sleepwalker* Arthur Koestler took the idea to its logical conclusion. He describes a vehicle in which 'the seven passengers, Sun, Moon and the five planets needed a machinery of not less than thirty-nine wheels to move through the sky.'

A thousand years later, Alphonso X of Castile, known as Alphonso the Wise, was initiated into the Ptolemaic system. Confronted with its intricacies he remarked: 'If the Almighty had consulted me before he embarked upon the Creation, I should have recommended something simpler.'

Ptolemy's work was deeply rooted in the Hellenistic system, from the mathematics of Pythagoras to the philosophy of Aristotle, tutor to Alexander the Great. But, after Ptolemy, Europe was overtaken by a new religion – Christianity. The Church deeply mistrusted and was opposed to astrology. Christians felt astrology was suspiciously pagan and cast doubt on both the omnipotence of God, and the free will of human beings.

When Christianity became the official religion of the Roman Empire in AD 380, that great Father of the Church, Saint Augustine (AD 354–430) launched a devastating attack on astrology. Born in Tagaste, North Africa, the son of a pagan father and a Christian mother, Augustine had studied astrology as a young man.

But 'by the grace of God', he had recognized and rejected 'the perfidious prophesies of the astrologers and their godless foolishness'. Astrology, he asserted, directly opposed our free will. With characteristic passion he called it *'fornicatio animae'* – fornication of the soul. When Emperor Justinian I banned astrology in AD 533, many astrologers fled from Rome to Persia (now modern Iran).

As Christianity established itself in Europe, astrology's role diminished. Meanwhile it was attracting growing interest in the Arab world. There, the techniques of observing and interpreting the stars were further developed and refined. Although the Koran forbad the worship of the Sun and Moon, this in no way diminished Arab enthusiasm for astronomy and astrology. They produced new calculations, formulated new interpretations, built new observatories. Most importantly, they added a strong dose of Islamic fatalism to astrology: each individual destiny appeared to have been predetermined. Harun Al Rashid (*c.* 763–809) was Caliph of Baghdad, ruling over a vast empire. This legendary figure inspired the fictional Caliph in *One Thousand and One Nights*, and was a contemporary of Charlemagne. Al Rashid was one of the most noteworthy patrons of this branch of astrology. Later the Ottomans integrated the crescent Moon and star in their flag.

Astrology found its way back to Europe via Sicily and Spain in the heart of the Middle Ages and with renewed vigour. A period of unrest followed the demise of the Carolingian dynasty and many people sought reassurance in the stars. The new millennium only deepened their uncertainty.

Gerbert of Aurillac (*c.* 940–1003) became Pope Sylvester II at this time. He accepted astrology as a natural science, although he rejected the idea of natal charts. The universities of Paris, Padua, Bologna and Florence installed chairs in astrology – astronomy was studied as a complementary science.

The great German scholar Albertus Magnus (c. 1200–1280) correlated the healing powers of plants to the influence of the planets and zodiac signs. Like his disciple, St Thomas Aquinas (1225–1274), he believed that the stars influenced earthly events. Both men, however, were convinced that our capacity for independent thinking was more than a match for the forces of destiny. Another deep thinker, the Scottish scholar Michael Scot (c. 1175–1234) was also well acquainted with astrology and advisor to the Holy Roman Emperor, Frederick II. The tomb of Piero d'Abano, who served the French King Philip the Fair (1268–1314), actually bore this epitaph: 'He was so skilled in astrology, that he was accused of sorcery.' The rigid line between science and mysticism had yet to be drawn.

With the dawning of the Renaissance, astrology became ever more firmly established. The West rediscovered antiquity, according more importance to the values of ancient Greece and the Roman Empire. Humanists attempted to revive the love of learning and regarded theology with scepticism.

These were times of tumultuous change. Columbus had discovered America; Vasco da Gama had sailed around the Cape of Good Hope and Ferdinand Magellan circumnavigated the globe, only to be killed by natives in the Philippines. Seafarers were the astronauts of their times.

What times these were!

Erasmus of Rotterdam, in the words of Arthur Koestler, 'laid the egg of the Reformation' and Martin Luther incubated it. Luther nailed his theses to the church door in Wittenberg. The Borgia pope mistreated his beautiful daughter Lucretia, and married her off four times. Before having her beheaded, Henry VIII made the six-fingered Anne Boleyn the mother of England's Virgin Queen, Elizabeth. Curiously enough, this outstanding woman was born under the sign of Virgo the Virgin.

Creativity burgeoned all over Europe. Leonardo da Vinci designed a flying machine and painted the *Mona Lisa*. Michelangelo created the *Pietá*. Dürer drew like an angel. Dante wrote his *Divine Comedy*, Cervantes *Don Quixote* and Machiavelli *The Prince*. The Spanish historian and poet Diego Hurtado de Mendoza wrote that 'The influence of the firmament over the success of human enterprise was rarely doubted at this time', while German writer Hermann Kesten affirms: 'Astrologers were the great puppet-masters of the century, the powerful of this world dangled on their strings.'

Court astrologers cast horoscopes for kings, queens, princes and bishops. Pope Paul III (1468–1549), for example, is described by the German historian Leopold von Ranke as a man 'full of talent and spirit' and 'penetrating intelligence'. Yet he had profound belief in the stars. According to Mendoza: 'Paul III never held an important meeting of the consistory, nor set out on any journey without choosing the day, without having observed the constellation. An alliance with France was deemed unseemly because the natal signs of King and Pope were not compatible.'

The French Queen Catherine de Medici (1519–1589), spouse of Henry II and mother of Charles IX appointed her astrologer Michel de Notre Dame (1503–1566) personal physician to her son. Under the now famous name of Nostradamus, the astrologer issued vague, rhyming prophesies for as far ahead as the year 3000. Even today many people attach some credence to these visionary revelations.

Hardly any sovereigns chose to rule without an astrologer's advice, while any doctor willing to practise without at least some astrological knowledge was rare indeed. One of the greatest of these was Philippus Aurelius Theophratus Bombastus von Hohenheim, better known as Paracelsus. He established natural healing; introduced chemical remedies; discovered zinc; used arsenic to combat syphilis; believed in astrology and insisted that every doctor should have some astrological knowledge.

Paracelsus claimed: 'The Sun, Moon and all the planets are in Man, likewise all the stars and the entire chaos . . . the body draws the heavens towards it . . . The whole is a great, divine order.'

There were countless legends about astrological predictions coming true. One astrologer foretold that Prince Henry of Portugal (1394–1460) 'was destined to make great and nobel conquests, but above all he is destined to discover things hidden and secret from other men.' Was this a self-fulfilling prophecy? Henry the Navigator, as he was known, discovered new shores long before Columbus, exploring the unfamiliar coasts of Africa. For forty years this great adventurer searched for what Ptolemy had once referred to as the *Promentorium Sanctum*, the land beyond the known seas.

But perhaps the greatest discovery of all – and one which was to change the world – took place at Frauenburg in East Prussia. To be precise, this momentous event took place in the north-west tower of the ramparts surrounding the town's hilltop cathedral.

Here, on 24 May 1543, the canon of the cathedral, Nikolaus Koppernigk of Torun lay dying. He was seventy years old. For thirty years he had lived in the three-storey tower with its panoramic views over a freshwater lagoon – the *Frisches Haff*. At night he could see the stars which inspired him. The old man had been laid low by a brain haemorrhage. Arthur Koestler poignantly recounts how the first completed copy of his only published scientific work arrived from the printer just hours before he died. *De revolutionibus orbium coelestium – On the Revolutions in the Heavenly Spheres* was placed upon his bed so that he could hold the book, although by now his mind was wandering. The work was dedicated to Pope Paul III, a believer in astrology. Its publication had been delayed for nearly three decades.

Through his observations and calculations, Copernicus, as he is better known, recognized that the Sun, not the Earth, was at the centre of our planetary system. The Sun did not revolve around the Earth, but the Earth around the Sun – exactly like other planets. Only the Moon orbited the Earth. The distance between the Earth and the Sun was negligible compared with the distance from the fixed stars and planets. Our Universe was heliocentric, that is, centred on the Sun – rather than geocentric, or Earth-centred.

For thousands of years, humanity had believed a nonsense. The Copernican model of the Universe finally superseded Ptolemy's geocentric theory. The geocentric conception was replaced by a heliocentric conception of the world. As a result, theology, astronomy and astrology, the church and science saw their theories fall apart. Another century would pass before a new truth would prevail.

Surprisingly enough, it was an astrologist who reported Copernicus' astronomic findings, even before he himself did so. This was his pupil Hans Joachim von Lauchen, a brilliant and impetuous young man. He was born in Tyrol, former Rhaetia and called himself the Rhaetian. In 'The Discoverers', Daniel J. Boorstin alleges his father, a doctor, was beheaded for sorcery. One thing appears certain, that his son completed his studies at the University of Wittenberg with a work in which he concludes that astrological predictions were not forbidden under Roman law.

In 1539, at the age of 25, he became Copernicus' pupil and a year later 'Narratio Prima' was printed, a report of the not yet published 'Book of Rotations by the learned and excellent mathematician, the honourable Dr Nikolaus von Thorn, canon of Ermland'.

Works published by the Rhaetian aroused little interest at first – exactly like Corpernicus' book, the first edition of a thousand copies was never sold out, and it was only reissued four times in 400 years. Findings from Ermland on the fringes of western civilisation did not appear about to cause a sensation.

Some twenty years after the death of Copernicus, Galileo Galilei (1564–1642) was born. He was to present a new vision of the Universe to a sceptical world. Galileo is now regarded, along with Sir Isaac Newton, as one of the fathers of modern physics. He began his career as a professor at the universities of Pisa and Padua. Galileo later became the respected court mathematician and philosopher at the Florentine court of the Grand Duke of Tuscany. He made improvements to the telescope, which had been invented by a Dutch spectacle-maker, Hans Lippershey. With this new tool at his disposal he discovered the mountains of the Moon; the starry realms of the Milky Way; the four largest moons of Jupiter, and the rings of Saturn. In 1632, the great man publicly declared his support for the Copernican hypothesis of a Universe centred around the sun, a theory condemned by the Church. Thereupon, he was arrested by the Inquisition. Despite retracting his statement, he was condemned to indefinite house arrest. Sadly, for such a great visionary, he was blind during the last five years of his life. His last words: '*Eppur si muove!*' – 'But it does move!' are almost certainly apocryphal, but nevertheless they have become one of the most widely quoted statements about Galileo's perception of the Universe.

It was an astrologer who encouraged Galileo in his support of Copernicus and who, like Galileo, was to gain worldwide fame as an astronomer. Johannes Kepler (1571–1630), wrote to Galileo in Rome: 'Have faith, Galileo, and come forward!'

Kepler was born in Weil, Germany, into a modest Protestant family. It was twenty-eight years since the death of Copernicus. He studied theology and mathematics before being appointed as a teacher of astronomy at the Protestant school in Graz, Austria. This post carried the grandiose title 'Mathematicus of the Province', but the job was poorly paid. Kepler supplemented his paltry salary by publishing calendars with astrological predictions. He was lucky with his first edition, forecasting bitter cold and a Turkish invasion. Six months later he wrote to his university teacher, Michael Maestlin: 'But the way, so far the calendar's predictions are proving correct. There is an unheard-of cold in our land. In the Alpine farms people are dying of the cold. It is reliably reported that when they arrive home and blow their noses, the noses fall off . . . As for the Turks, on January 1 they devastated the whole country from Vienna to Neustadt, setting everything on fire and carrying off men and plunder.'

Around 1600, Johannes Kepler became assistant to the

Danish astrologer and astronomer Tycho Brahe (1546–1601). They must have made an odd couple – one a pauper, the other a rich and eccentric aristocrat. Tycho Brahe came from a noble old Danish family. When part of his nose was sliced off during a student duel, he replaced the missing piece with a gold and silver alloy. He made annual predictions for the Danish royal family, while pouring scorn on 'foolhardy astrologers': 'Many of them know nothing at all about the stars (one is ashamed to write it down).' Although it was really beneath the dignity of an aristocrat, he planned to publish a polemic: *Contra Astrologos pro Astrologia* – 'Against astrologers, for astrology', because he felt that charlatans were severely damaging what he himself regarded as a science.

Tycho Brahe became one of the foremost astronomers of his time, recognized for his observations and calculations. However, half a century after Copernicus' death, Brahe did not subscribe to the Copernican theory of the Sun as the centre of the Universe. In fact, until his own death, he remained convinced that the Sun revolved around the Earth. Brahe entered the service of the Holy Roman Emperor, Rudolph II. The castle of Benetek, north-east of Prague, was placed at his disposal so that he could continue his studies. It was there that Johannes Kepler joined him as his assistant. Their relationship was only to last eighteen months. On 13 October 1601, Brahe was invited to dine with a certain Baron Rosenberg in Prague. As a gentleman, Brahe thought it bad manners to leave the table in order to relieve oneself. This was to prove fatal, for as Kepler noted, he 'held back his water beyond the demands of courtesy', until his bladder and kidneys failed. He fell into a delirium, and died eleven days later. Johannes Kepler succeeded him as Imperial Mathematicus.

Kepler's views on astrology were mixed. 'That the sky does something to Man' was self-evident to him, but, he admitted, 'I know not enough with certainty that I should dare to predict with confidence any specific thing.' He was wary of making ill-considered statements: 'There are many astrologers who enjoy and believe in such games, thus any who gladly and with open eyes wish so to do, may make use of their time and effort; philosophy and thus also true *astrologia* is evidence of God's work and not at all a foolish thing, which I for my part will not dishonour.' Like Tycho Brahe, Kepler saw many astrologers as a danger to astrology.

In his book *Wallenstein*, German writer Golo Mann affirms that there 'was never a fortuneteller who took more seriously his responsibilities' as 'the most famous of all interpreters of natal signs'. Despite – or maybe because of – this, in 1608 Kepler was asked to cast a horoscope for a twenty-four-year-old 'Bohemian gentleman'. It is not known whether Kepler knew the man's identity. However, on a copy of the horoscope he kept for himself, he noted the name 'Waltstein' in his secret script, but nobody knows when he wrote it. In fact, his client was Albrecht Wenzel Eusebius von Wallenstein, the future general, who was then a very young officer in the service of the Hapsburgs.

Kepler predicted that Wallenstein (1583–1634) would lead both a fortunate and dangerous life. He forecast marriage to a rich widow in 1608. 'Anno 1609', Wallenstein later scribbled in the margin of the horoscope, 'in May I was married to a widow, as described here.' He had married Lucretia von Vickov, a widow, who died only five years later – leaving him vast estates in Moravia, and making him a very wealthy man.

In December 1624 the Thirty Years' War had already

begun. Wallenstein had been made Duke of Friedland. Once more he turned to Johannes Kepler, asking him to revise and extend the horoscope drawn up sixteen years before. Since Kepler's prophecies had indeed come true, although not precisely on the date predicted (marriage in 1609 instead of 1608), Wallenstein asked whether his calculations of the exact time of birth might have to be revised. Wallenstein observed that clocks 'were not always right'. And so Kepler got back to work. His corrected version revealed some changes. For example, the Moon had moved to a new house of the horoscope. At best, this indicated an improvement in 'social status'. Wallenstein was to rise to become the most powerful military commander of the Thirty Years' War. Kepler saw his star continuing to shine brightly in the sky. But after the year of glory the second horoscope suddenly darkened. It forecast 'dreadful disorder over the land' in March 1634, then broke off completely. On 25 February 1634 Wallenstein was murdered. Johannes Kepler died in 1630 four years before his startling prediction came true.

In 1628 he had become the official Friedland mathematician. He left the three Kepler's Laws to posterity – concerning the planets and their elliptical orbits. In fact, he the great astronomist, was Wallenstein's historically important astrologist, not Seni, who became famous thanks to Schiller's (1759–1805 German poet, dramatist and historian) drama.

Wallenstein and Kepler were dead. But the Thirty Years' War continued to devastate the whole of Europe. According to Swedish reports 1,700 fortresses, 1,500 towns and 17,000 villages were flattened in the course of the conflict. About fifty per cent of the German population were killed, and half the national wealth destroyed. The end of the war in 1648 marked the birth of the absolutist state. It also marked a turning point for natural sciences. People began to believe that scientists could solve all the mysteries of the world. René Descartes (1596–1650) philosopher and mathematician, asserted that nature obeys strict mathematical laws. Descartes' most famous statement: 'I think, therefore I am' encapsulated the spirit of the Age of Reason. There was little room for belief and even less for superstition, magic, alchemy or metaphysics. Logic and empirical knowledge became the icons of a new era.

Christianity prevailed, somewhat weakened, but astrology began to lose credibility. It was ridiculed, derided, reviled and forbidden. In his *History of Astrology*, Wilhelm Knappich speaks of astrology's 'catastrophic set-back'. In 1666, astrology was officially excluded from the French Academy of Science. In 1682, Louis XIV, the Sun King, outlawed the printing and distribution of astrological almanacs. In Italy in 1688, the Curia, or Papal Court in Rome forbade astrological literature altogether. The German Empire outlawed fortune-telling in 1699. And by 1756 Maria Theresa, queen of Hungary and Bohemia, issued a decree declaring that 'no calendar shall henceforth contain any astrological prediction or superstitious conjecture'.

'What in this day and age is more contemptible than astrology, stargazing, the writing of calendars and natal charts?' asked Abias Trew, professor of mathematics at Altdorf University in the mid-seventeenth century. According to the theologian Johann Amos Comenius, astrology was a 'black art' and astrologers 'star swindlers'. 'Nostradamus and the most ridiculous quack doctors are, compared to these fools, very reasonable men,' Voltaire (1694–1774) wrote scornfully of Persian astrologers. And even the good-hearted philosopher Gottfried Wilhelm Leibnitz (1646–1716) considered that 'the art of astrological prediction' was based on 'sheer deception', which he found despicable.

For the second time since the birth of Christ, Europe had consigned astrology to the scrap heap. The 'royal art' had also suffered a decline between 400 and 800, a period sometimes known as the 'Dark Ages', when Christianity was at its height, and satisfied the human longing for the supernatural and resurrection. Rationalism and enlightenment were now called for. Truth was perceived to lie in the natural sciences. Belief in progress superseded belief in the stars.

The future belonged to independent scientific research. Once astronomy was the underling of astrology. Now the two disciplines parted company. New possibilities, new methods, new observations, new attitudes, new hypotheses and a new *Zeitgeist* spelt progress. Astrology, it seemed, had no place in this brave new world.

Copernicus' heliocentric theory contributed decisively to this decline – despite the fact that it had taken over a hundred years to find acceptance. As late as 1831, Pope Gregory XVI graciously advised: 'Let the Earth turn'. And Galileo was only officially pardoned by Pope John Paul II in 1992. By the eighteenth century, the Church was no longer in a position to influence such matters. The natural sciences were the new masters of the world. Copernicus was one of their heroes, and he had effectively pulled the rug from under the astrologers' feet. The more his heliocentric principle was scrutinized, the more astrology was exposed to ridicule. How could anyone take seriously a doctrine whose basic assumption stated that the Sun and the planets revolved around the Earth? Worse still: seven planets (Mercury, Mars, Venus, Saturn and Jupiter, plus the Sun and Moon) had been at the heart of astrology from the beginning. Astronomers were to discover three more: Uranus in 1781, Neptune in 1846 and Pluto in 1930.

How did this affect omniscience of the known planets? Another problem arose with the precession of the equinoxes. This means that as the Earth's axis shifts over time, the signs of the zodiac – as seen from our planet – appear to move further and further away from their original constellations. The Sun no longer enters the constellation of Aries, for example, on 21 March – although two thousand years ago it did. Astrologers, however, still divide the zodiac into twelve equal sections, and use the traditional dates. Since they believe this is symbolic, it does not actually matter where the Sun is today. The stars and signs are part of a greater unity, and do not exert any measurable effects in a literal way. With the dawn of the Enlightenment in the eighteenth century, astrology stood before the ruins of its reputation and credibility. Its temple was destroyed, its teachings branded as superstition. It was laid low, but still alive. Its greatest minds set about picking up the pieces and putting them back together again. Interpretations and empirically established figures and methods dating back thousands of years were re-examined. The question was not which heavenly body revolved around which, but where the Sun and planets stood at any given moment. Moreover, a Capricorn was a Capricorn, whether in Finland or Tierra del Fuego. The system was modified and amplified to embrace each new astronomical finding.

Even now, open-minded thinkers did not deny their interest in astrology, although they did not identify themselves with it. When Schiller was struggling with Wallenstein's astrological inclinations, which went too far for his own taste, his friend Goethe offered a helping hand. In a letter dated 1798 he wrote: 'Experience tells us that the nearest constellations have a decisive influence on weather, vegetation and so on; we can only progress outwards step by step and it is impossible to say where the effect ends. Indeed, astronomers find everywhere disturbance of one constellation by another. Thus the philosopher is inclined to accept only things that are far removed.'

More than one hundred years later a newspaper published a daily horoscope for the first time. These are now printed by the million every day. But that was in 1899. The twentieth century had begun, and with it came astrology's second renaissance. Once again, people were ready for stargazing, as they had been in the Middle Ages. World War Ì, the 'mother of all disasters', changed the face of Europe for ever. It engendered World War II and set the stage for monsters like Stalin, Hitler and Mao. Scientists split the atom, cloned living creatures and began to explore the frontiers of space. Christian values gradually declined, and belief in science began to falter. Every advance seemed to bring new dangers. It was the perfect moment to sow the astrological seed.

Following World War I, controversial new theories such as psychoanalysis and anthroposophy became linked with astrology. Swiss psychiatrist and psychologist Carl Gustav Jung (1875–1961), for example, saw in astrological symbolism 'archetypes' of the soul. World War II created further chaos across the whole of Europe. It is not surprising, therefore, that popular interest in esoteric subjects burgeoned. It was to become a vast industry embracing everything from UFOs to reincarnation, Eastern meditation techniques to alternative medicine. And astrology took pride of place at the forefront of this unprecedented fascination with the unknown. People believed in it, charlatans profited from it, intellectuals fought for it. Once again an attempt was made to capture the spirit of the heavens.

Astrology can be divided into six main streams, as outlined by Solange de Mailly-Nesle in her book *Astrologie*:

- Esoteric and spiritual astrology, a form of belief in spiritual guidance.
- Empirical or pragmatic astrology, focusing on predictions, such as newspaper and computerized horoscopes.
- Scientific astrology, which seeks to prove the bases of astrology by scientific methods, so far without producing generally accepted scientific evidence.
- Reformed astrology which uses new technology to achieve more precise interpretations.
- Symbolic and psychological astrology which seeks to rehabilitate astrological symbolism with the aid of psychoanalytic techniques.
- Global astrology, dealing with history and nations, meteorology, the environment and natural disasters.* This is often called 'mundane' astrology – meaning 'of the world'.

The more the effects of cosmic forces on earthly events was researched by scientists, the more astrology was re-admitted to the realms of possibility. The fact that the ebb and flow of the tides is caused by the Moon's magnetism added weight to the argument. Astrology blossomed independently of religion or political systems. It flourished in democracies and dictatorships. The immortal singer, Caruso, and a son of the great Queen Victoria liked to hear what the stars foretold. In 1941, the Nazi regime outlawed astrology and threw

*Cf: Solange de Mailly-Nesle, *Astrologie*, Cologne, p. 83ff

astrologers into concentration camps. Even so, as the war neared its end, Heinrich Himmler commissioned one such prisoner, the astrologer Wilhelm Sulff, to cast Hitler's horoscope to ascertain whether a *putsch* was likely.

Half a century later, Nancy Reagan brought astrology to the White House. In his book *For the Record*, President Ronald Reagan's former Chief of Staff, Donald T. Regan, recalls:

Practically every major move or important decision was agreed with a woman in San Francisco who cast horoscopes. Shortly before the President was shot in an assassination attempt in 1981, this astrologer prophesied that 'something bad' would happen to Ronald Reagan. The First Lady always referred to the woman as her 'friend'. Although I never met this clairvoyant, she had such a significant influence on my work and on affairs of state that in the end I kept an appointment calendar in different colours on my desk. The 'good' days were marked in green, 'bad' days in red and the 'uncertain' days in yellow. I needed this *aide memoire* to know the opportune moment to send the President of the United States from one place to another, to plan a public appearance for him or to initiate negotiations with a foreign power.

According to the 1989 *Guinness Book of Records*, Elizabeth Teissier is the most widely read astrologer in Europe. She has cast horoscopes for the King of Spain, and several Presidents of France. Even Boris Yeltsin appears to have leanings towards the supernatural. It is said that he has received treatment from a faith healer and believes in the stars. His former press attaché, Vozhchanov, confirmed these rumours when he told the *Sunday Times* in London: 'Yeltsin is very superstitious. In making personal decisions he is influenced by his horoscope. For example, when the water is exposed to bad rays, he does not go fishing.'

But not everyone is convinced by astrology. In 1975, 180 scientists – including 18 Nobel Prizewinners – signed a declaration condemning astrology, claiming that it contributed to 'the increase in irrationalism and hostility to culture'. And one of the co-founders of space medicine (medical questions relating to space flight), the astronomer Professor Hans Haber, was convinced: 'The stars do not lie, because they have nothing to tell us.'

It seems to be an eternal controversy. The American banker James Pierpoint Morgan (1837–1913), who consulted the New York astrologer Evangeline Adams about planetary influences over the stock exchange, laconically observed that 'Millionaires don't believe in astrologers, billionaires keep them on the payroll'. And this was at a time when a million was still a million.

Who is right? Perhaps the truth lies somewhere in between. When the US President Dwight D. Eisenhower fell ill in 1957, I was a young correspondent reporting from his ranch in Gettysburg. One evening I was standing around with one of the medical experts who had been summoned there. We were surrounded by Black Angus cattle. As we gazed up at the starry sky, the conversation naturally turned to astrology. I asked this man of science what he thought of it. I have forgotten his name, but not his answer: 'If there is as much to astrology as its supporters believe, there would be no need for any other science. And if there is as little to it as its opponents claim, astrology would not have existed for 6,000 years.'

STATISTICS OF THE STARS

It's just human nature. When we see the remarkable results of a statistical study, we are sometimes in too much of a hurry to interpret them in a certain way, and fail to ask whether there are other possible explanations. For the purposes of this book we have taken great care not to offer simplistic explanations where there could be other, more complex ones. Nor have we claimed a connection which is not backed up by statistical evidence.

To start with, we should like to deal with a few basic statistical concepts which we shall come across again and again in the following chapters. Let us forget about star signs for the moment and turn our attention to that old favourite, the imaginary game of dice used to torment all students of statistics at their very first lecture.

According to the elementary rules of the theory of probability, if we roll a correctly manufactured dice 600 times, we can expect each of the six sets of spots to come up 100 times, given that one sixth of 600 is 100. We call this the mathematical expectation.

But even if the dice is perfectly made, in real life hardly any number will be thrown exactly 100 times. One number will perhaps fall only 90 times, while other numbers will come up 108 or 114 times. If, for example, the number 5 is thrown 110 times, we call this the actual value. In this case the actual value is 10 per cent above the mathematical expectation (110 against 100).

The bigger the difference between actual value and mathematical expectation, the smaller the influence of chance. But where is the limit? At what point does chance seem doubtful? When the number 5 appears 122 times in 600 throws? or 139 times? At what point can we say with probability verging on certainty that there is something wrong with the dice? When, in 600 throws, the number 5 comes up 183 times? Or 194 times? Might it not appear 600 times? The dice has no memory.

Using the methods of mathematical statistics, we can establish criteria as to which deviations between mathematical expectations and actual values can be taken as being conditional on chance and which not. In this case the law of large numbers applies: the more often the dice is thrown, in other words the larger the sample size, the more accurate the evidence.

It would go beyond the scope of this book to explain the methods in minute detail, especially as they require profound mathematical knowledge, and use terms such as 'normal distribution', 'Gaussian distribution curve', 'variance' and 'standard deviation'.

For our purposes, we can make do with the practical application of these statistical methods for our investigation, and we would ask any full-blooded mathematicians among our readers to forgive us for certain simplifications. These are intended to help towards better understanding, without in any way distorting the respective results.

An example to illustrate the effect of large numbers: if the number 5 comes up 120 times with 600 throws of the dice, there is the same probability that with 60,000 throws the number will appear 10,200 times. In the 600-throw test the deviation of the actual value from the mathematic expectation is 20 per cent, with 60,000 throws, it is only 2 per cent. A larger sample size narrows the relative deviation between expectation and actual values.

Whether one person would have the patience to roll a dice 60,000 times is open to question. In a scientific journal published in Zurich in 1882, a researcher by the name of Wolf described an experiment involving 20,000 throws. For us, it is relevant to the theory of the Gaussian distribution curve of probability density which states:

The greater the population, the smaller the relative deviation between mathematical expectation and actual value which can be explained as being due to chance.

Statisticians have developed certain procedures, such as evaluating and indicating the probability of an element of chance in the deviation between mathematical expectation and actual value.

In practice:

- If the probability of chance elements in the deviation is no more than 5 per cent, or in a ratio of 1:20, the deviation is described as significant.
- If the probability is no more than 1 per cent, or in a ratio of 1:100, the deviation is described as highly significant.

Of course, these definitions are purely conventional. As a rule, the available data and the purpose of the research will determine the level of significance.

When, for example, a study aims to find out whether people with particular jobs are more likely to suffer from certain diseases and only 500 cases are available, researchers would, of necessity, have to be satisfied with a relatively low level of significance. However, if the purpose were to test the tensile strength of climbing ropes, a level of significance of 5 or even 1 per cent would not be enough. Testing the safety of climbing ropes – especially if one had the freedom to choose the length of the experimental run – demands a higher, in other words a stricter level, before ropes from a specific production run could be given the seal of quality.

Once again, the rule applies: the greater the population the more meaningful the result.

For our enquiry, which involved extremely large sets of data, we decided on the following definitions: we would indicate the deviation between actual value and mathematical expectation as being:

- slightly significant, if the probability of chance elements in the deviation were no more than 5 per cent, or in a ratio of 1:20;
- significant, if the probability of chance elements in the deviation were no more than 1 per cent, or in a ratio of 1:100;
- highly significant if the probability of chance elements in the deviation were no more than 0.1 per cent, or in a ratio of 1:1000.

This means that we have set considerably stricter standards than is usual in statistical investigations. In the tables included in the following chapters, we have indicated the levels of significance as follows:

*	=	slightly significant
* *	=	significant
* * *	=	highly significant

In the graphs, the columns showing astrological signs with significant values are printed in a black background. Unremarkable deviations from the mathematical expectation are printed in white. The appropriate individual tests examine whether the deviation observed is significant in either direction.

In the two investigations into illness and choice of job we have not shown slight significances. These are merely marked by the words 'noteworthy cases'. The size of the sample for these two analyses was so large and so many individual evaluations were necessary, that a 'multiple test problem' could not be excluded.

This phenomenon often leads to more significant deviations than statisticians are prepared to recognize.

There are two more terms that we shall meet time and again in the following chapters, the so-called chi-square test of goodness of fit and the chi-square test of independence. As an illustration, we shall again make use of the tried-and-tested dice example.

If a dice is rolled 600 times, we could produce the following table:

Score on dice	Number of dice
1	90
2	81
3	106
4	93
5	134
6	96
total	600

To test whether this result can be explained by chance, the first thing statisticians will usually do with such a one-dimensional distribution is carry out the chi-test of goodness of fit which essentially tests in a global and general way whether or not the deviations are within acceptable limits. The whole table is tested in an arithmetical operation with a view to finding out whether the resulting distribution corresponds with the assumed uniform distribution (null-hypothesis) which demonstrates any significant correlation.

- If it does, in other words if the deviations between the actual distribution and mathematical expectation can easily be explained by pure chance, no further delving is necessary. Even if the separate values were analysed, no significant deviations are likely.
- If it does not, that is to say when the hypothesis of a uniform distribution is rejected, it is worth analysing the separate deviations and determining which of them can be labelled as significant and which not.

In the case of the dice example represented by the table on the opposite page, the chi-square goodness of fit test would show that the null hypothesis is rejected. Additional analyses would reveal that, compared with the mathematical expectation of 100, number 5 is significantly over-represented and the number 2 slightly significantly under-represented.

The chi-square test of independence is applied when we are presented with two sets of data to be evaluated together. The results are produced on a two-dimensional contingency table which shows how often each possible paired combination occurs.

Here, too, we take an example from the realm of dice: we

throw a red and a blue dice simultaneously and take note of the pairs of spots. After 3,600 throws we have a two-dimensional distribution with 6 × 6 fields, which shows how often, for example, the red dice shows 2 spots at the same time as the blue dice shows 5 spots.

Provided that neither dice is loaded and neither exerts any magical force over the other, the mathematical expectation in the 36 fields of our table is 100 (3,600 ÷ 36 = 100) for each possible pairing of numbers.

red dice shows	blue dice shows						total
	1	2	3	4	5	6	
1	98	121	89	95	117	104	624
2	108	78	91	93	115	106	591
3	105	110	86	111	77	96	585
4	91	81	130	107	92	120	621
5	97	121	106	91	91	103	609
6	105	80	102	90	101	92	570
total	604	591	604	587	593	621	3600

The hypothesis that neither dice influences the other, i.e. that the numbers of spots on each dice are completely independent of one another, is proved with the aid of the chi-square test of independence. The actual two-dimensional frequency table is compared with the expected frequency, assuming that the two factors are independent of one another. Only if the independence test shows that there is a strong probability of a connection between the two factors is it worth the effort of carrying out a closer analysis of the individual fields of the table.

As far as our own research was concerned a typical example of a two-dimensional distribution was the question:

Do brides born under a particular star sign more frequently go to the altar with bridegrooms of a particular star sign?

The chi-square test of independence suggested that it was worth testing for particular significant differences. You can see the results in the chapter entitled 'Who marries whom?'

Finally, two words about terminology. The data used was taken from Swiss, German and British databases. However, this is of no relevance to our results. In our findings we thus sometimes refer to female or male persons.

In this book, we are occasionally confronted with complicated facts. In order to bring these home to the reader we have tried to use easily understandable language. We ask the statisticians, who always encouraged us to express ourselves in correct technical terms, to forgive us for not always doing so. We do try to respect their suggestions and wishes, but sometimes we are obliged to simplify complicated concepts. This is comparable to a gourmet menu which uses the words *Fruits de terre en robe de chambre à la Duc d'Arcangues*' to describe what we usually refer to as 'potatoes'.

For the sake of simplicity, instead of 'those belonging to a specific sign of the zodiac', we often use the term 'star signs'.

1

WHO BUYS ASTROLOGICAL LITERATURE?

'World literature is the result of the fortunate combination of the twenty-six letters of the alphabet.'

Shawn G. Custer

Millions of people have believed in the power of the stars for thousands of years. All over the world today more than a billion horoscopes are printed every week.

A representative survey recently found that 92 per cent of all British people know their star sign. Meanwhile, nobody knows whether or not there is anything at all to astrology, and that is precisely what I wanted to find out. But I did not know how to approach this age-old puzzle.

I was on a photo-shoot at Key West, Florida. Following a visit to the weather-beaten Colonial House, where Ernest Hemingway wrote *In Another Country*, I had a flash of inspiration.

I came across twelve volumes of a series of books on astrology in a local bookshop. There was one book for each sign of the zodiac. In theory, each book must sell at the same rate as all the others. But suppose they didn't. This would indicate that people born under some star signs are more – or less – interested in astrology than others.

This in turn would validate the assumption that people

born under different signs behave differently – one of the fundamental principles of astrology.

Early next morning, with my heart in my mouth, I made two phone calls to Germany. I asked my friend Rolf Heyne, the Munich publisher, whether he could let me have the sales figures for his series of astrology books – *Zodiac Signs*. Yes he could. He faxed them to my office. Then I asked Mr Bosse, responsible for birth rates at the Federal Office of Statistics in Wiesbaden if he would be kind enough to send me the birth figures – we really needed to know how many Arians or Librans were alive in each year. He, too, surprised me by agreeing immediately.

Then came the Night of the Thousand Numbers – more than 300,000 sales figures from the astrology books plus the birth statistics since 1950.

Using a rudimentary pocket calculator – it was night-time by now – I and my assistant 'Mouse' Birling worked out the not very difficult, but multi-digit sum. It was a hell of a job – but before midnight we knew for certain: the deviations between the buying habits of the various star signs were so much greater than the mathematical expectation, that even I could guess that they included some runaway exceptions.

Later, the statisticians at Munich University confirmed highly significant deviations between ten of the twelve star signs (*see* table, page 56). The influence of star signs on human behaviour was obviously proven – at least as far as buying horoscope books were concerned. Eureka!

So, we surmised, it was reasonable to assume that star signs behaved differently in other aspects of life – one of the basic principles of astrology. It was certainly a first step – but we were just at the beginning of a long journey. There was yet another interesting twist to the story of the astrology books. The buying habits of faithful followers of astrology had enabled us to produce a piece of evidence that suggested astrology – at least at this point – was not merely a matter of belief.

ANALYSIS

In order to test statistically whether people born under the twelve signs of the zodiac displayed different buying habits, we needed the sales figures for the books over a longer period. We had four years of sales figures at our disposal.

We also needed a so-called relevant population, namely a group of possible purchasers of this type of book, and that involved rather more complex methods.

We based our research on people born in Germany between 1950 and 1979. The Federal Office of Statistics holds extensive and reliable data on the numbers of people born over this period, classified under months of birth.

To make sure that the distribution of the population by month of birth in the years 1950–1979 did not differ significantly from that of older citizens, we compared it with reliable data from the years 1920–1935. There proved to be no differences of any consequence. In order to counter objections that statistical accuracy could be affected by including years with an exceptionally high birth rate, or those where the contraceptive pill caused a slump in the numbers of babies born, we arranged the birth dates in different groups. For example, we extracted the years 1959–1965 or

1966–1979 and repeated our calculations. The deviations we found were unremarkable.

Of course, not everyone born between 1950 and 1979 is still alive and therefore among potential book buyers. Naturally, the death rate is higher among people born in 1950 than among those born in 1979. We also took this into account. The figures were adjusted using a table of 'Age-specific mortality rates and life expectancy' drawn up by the Federal Office of Statistics. With the aid of these figures, we were able to determine the probability of survival for people born in each separate year. This allowed us to produce accurate statistics of how many people born in the respective years are still alive.

After taking life expectancy figures into consideration, we arrived at a relevant population of people born between 1950 and 1979. This population totalled 23,879,258 men and women.

Naturally, the births are not classified by star signs but by calendar month, so we had to convert calendar months into star signs. According to the period covered by each sign, (e.g. Aquarius: 21 January to 19 February) we transferred the figures for the month to the two relevant signs of the zodiac. This also allowed for the peculiarities of leap years. Finally, we obtained the following division of the relevant population (see opposite page).

This table shows the very pronounced seasonal nature of the birth rate. While, for example, Arians and Geminis each account for nearly 9 per cent of the relevant population, only 7.44 per cent are Sagittarians.

Over the four-year period 1991–1994, the Heyne publishing house in Germany sold 313,368 books in its paperback *Zodiac Signs* series.

	Population		
Star signs	Number of births for years 1950 - 1979	Percentage of births for years 1950 - 1979	Actual sales of Heyne's *Zodiac Signs* by unit
Aries	2.139.460	8,96 %	26.799
Taurus	2.047.972	8,58 %	24.966
Gemini	2.146.536	8,99 %	25.675
Cancer	2.035.639	8,52 %	27.528
Leo	2.047.455	8,57 %	25.735
Virgo	2.019.327	8,46 %	25.307
Libra	1.868.883	7,83 %	24.865
Scorpio	1.829.677	7,66 %	27.062
Sagittarius	1.777.207	7,44 %	24.831
Capricorn	1.923.268	8,05 %	25.443
Aquarius	2.022.631	8,47 %	27.527
Pisces	2.021.203	8,46 %	27.630
	23.879.258	100,00 %	313.368

In the table on page 54, we compare the proportion of individual volumes within the overall sales figures with the proportion of star signs in the relevant population.

Let's take a closer look at the right hand side of the table: the deviation for Aries is shown as minus 0.41 per cent. That is the deviation found between the actual value (8.55 per cent) and mathematical expectation (8.96 per cent).

As the proportion of Aries in the relevant population is 8.96 per cent, one might have expected that the proportion of Aries books within the overall sales figures would be 8.96 per cent. Therefore 28,076 Aries books would have been sold. In actual fact, however, only 26,799 books (or 8.5 per cent) about the star sign Aries were sold, in other words 4.5 per cent fewer than might have been expected.

Conversely, in the case of Scorpio: the percentage of Scorpios in the population, 7.66, might be expected to purchase 24,011 Scorpio books, when the actual total sold was

Who buys how many astrology books?

Star signs	Number of births between 1950 - 1979	Percentage of births for years 1950 - 1979	Actual book sale of Heyne's Zodiac Signs	Actual book sale of Heyne's Zodiac Signs in per cent	Percentage difference from expected result
Aries	2.139.460	8,96 %	26.799	8,55 %	-0,41 %
Taurus	2.047.972	8,58 %	24.966	7,97 %	-0,61 %
Gemini	2.146.536	8,99 %	25.675	8,19 %	-0,80 %
Cancer	2.035.639	8,52 %	27.528	8,78 %	+0,26 %
Leo	2.047.455	8,57 %	25.735	8,21 %	-0,36 %
Virgo	2.019.327	8,46 %	25.307	8,08 %	-0,38 %
Libra	1.868.883	7,83 %	24.865	7,93 %	+0,11%
Scorpio	1.829.677	7,66 %	27.062	8,64 %	+0,97 %
Sagittarius	1.777.207	7,44 %	24.831	7,92 %	+0,48 %
Capricorn	1.923.268	8,05 %	25.443	8,12 %	+0,07 %
Aquarius	2.022.631	8,47 %	27.527	8,78 %	+0,31 %
Pisces	2.021.203	8,46 %	27.630	8,82 %	+0,35 %
	23.879.258	100,00 %	313.368	100,00 %	

27,062. So almost 13 per cent more Scorpio books were sold than we could have assumed, given the proportion of Scorpios in the relevant population (*see* table, page 56).

Are these simply haphazard deviations of the sort one can expect any time and anywhere? Or is it highly probable that such deviations cannot be explained as pure chance?

To find out, we passed our data on to the Institute of Statistics at Munich's Ludwig-Maximilian University and asked them to test these deviations for their significance.

First, they ran a chi-square goodness of fit test (*see* page 45). This initial test was to investigate whether the hypothesis of the equal proportion of sales was tenable. Or, to put it more simply, given the deviations could we still assume that people born under every star sign were equally interested in horoscope books? Or were the deviations between actual and expected sales figures so high that they could not be put down to pure chance? If this were so, then the hypothesis of equal distribution would not stand up. We would then have to assume that there was some correlation between people's star signs and their interest in astrology.

The test produced the following result: the probability that the actual value came about purely by chance is less than 1 in 10 million. Based on our pre-established level of significance (*see* page 44), the influence of pure chance could be statistically excluded. The next stage involved testing each individual star sign to see whether the deviations between actual values and mathematical expectations were significant or not.

It is remarkable that ten out of twelve star signs showed highly significant deviations.

Who buys how many astrology books?

Star signs	Number of births for years 1950 - 1979	Percentage of births for years 1950 - 1979	Actual sales of Heyne's *Zodiac Signs* by unit	Expected sales, by unit, based on percentage of population	Deviation from expected figure, in percent (see graphic)	Degree of significance
Aries	2.139.460	8,96 %	26.799	28.076	-4,55 %	*** -
Taurus	2.047.972	8,58 %	24.966	26.876	-7,11 %	*** -
Gemini	2.146.536	8,99 %	25.675	28.169	-8,85 %	*** -
Cancer	2.035.639	8,52 %	27.528	26.714	+3,06 %	*** +
Leo	2.047.455	8,57 %	25.735	26.869	-4,22 %	*** -
Virgo	2.019.327	8,46 %	25.307	26.500	-4,50 %	*** -
Libra	1.868.883	7,83 %	24.865	24.525	+1,38 %	neutral
Scorpio	1.829.677	7,66 %	27.062	24.011	+12,71 %	*** +
Sagittarius	1.777.207	7,44 %	24.831	23.322	+6,47 %	*** +
Capricorn	1.923.268	8,05 %	25.443	25.239	+0,81 %	neutral
Aquarius	2.022.631	8,47 %	27.527	26.543	+3,71 %	*** +
Pisces	2.021.203	8,46 %	27.630	26.524	+4,17 %	*** +
	23.879.258	100,00 %	313.368	313.368		

* slightly significant   ** significant   *** highly signficant

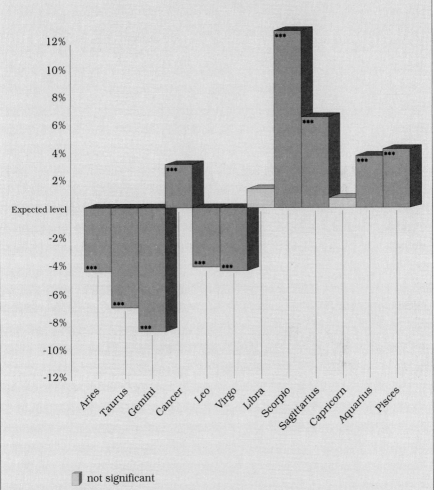

Deviation of actual sales from expected sales in percent

Actual sales: 313.368

not significant

significant   * slightly significant   ** significant   *** highly significant

Cancer, Scorpio, Sagittarius, Aquarius and Pisces customers actually bought *more* books than the mathematical expectation, with Scorpio showing an especially pronounced deviation.

Sales to customers born under Aries, Taurus, Gemini, Leo and Virgo were *lower* than expected, with Gemini showing the largest deviation (*see* table, page 56).

Provided we do not doubt the validity of statistical science in general, one thing is for sure: there is some kind of definite correlation between being born under a particular star sign and buying astrological literature.

SUMMARY
The subject of the investigation was sales of the paperback series *Zodiac Signs*. The survey was based on data relating to the sale of 313,368 books in the period 1991–1994 divided into star signs. We observed ten highly significant deviations. The influence of chance elements on the observed deviations can be excluded with odds of 1:10,000,000.

THE ASTROLOGICAL ANGLE

Since similar statements of probability recur in the summaries at the end of each chapter, we shall explain them briefly:

The result of the chi-square test tells us that the probability that there is no correlation between star signs is infinitesimal, namely 1 in 10 million. In other words, practically null. Impressive proof that some kind of correlation *does* exist between star signs and buying habits.

Although, for practical purposes any ratio above 1 in a thousand is barely statistically relevant, since it has even less effect on the results achieved, we show them anyway.

In *Keywords in Astrology*, Hajo Banzhaf and Anna Haebler describe the character of Scorpio – the sign buying the most astrological books – as follows:

> Scorpio is the sign of the profound and the extreme. Its archetype is the magician, its shadow the vampire. Nothing is less appealing to Scorpios than superficiality and mediocrity. Theirs is the world of the enigmatic. They are Faustian individuals, whose urge to explore draws them irresistibly to the obscure, the mysterious and the concealed, to society's taboos, . . . their yearning to uncover mysteries and their courage can lead them into danger. Profound and analytical. Astute and unyielding in the search for ultimate wisdom. Will confidently speak out where others would prefer to remain silent.*

According to this profile, Scorpios seem to be predestined to take an interest in the mysteries of astrology. The author of *The Astrology File* was born under the sign of Scorpio.

Keywords in Astrology has this to say about Geminis, whose books had the lowest sales:

Strengths: Well-considered, systematic, concentrated

* Hajo Banzhaf & Anna Haebler, *Schlüsselworte zur Astrologie*, Munich 1996, p. 56 ff

behaviour guided by a rational approach, analytically proven ideas with negligible emotional involvement. . . . Resourceful, highly logical and emphatically intellectual.*

Hardly the sort of person inclined to delve into the occult.

Now we were faced with the kind of brainteaser you find in the up-market weekend supplements:

We had based our calculations of book sales on information provided by the publishers, and assumed that books were mainly purchased one at a time.

However, there must be customers who buy all twelve books at once. The question then is whether such buyers noticeably affect our results.

Yes, they do, and in a curious way: *en bloc* sales affected the results by increasing the levels of significance for eight signs (Taurus, Gemini, Cancer, Leo, Virgo, Scorpio, Aquarius and Pisces) and reducing them for two (Aries and Sagittarius). In theory, 80 per cent *en bloc* sales would even move Sagittarius from the negative to the positive field. The two runaway and highly significant results (Scorpio and Gemini) would achieve even higher levels of significance. Certainly a rather academic exercise in logic. If the share of *en bloc* sales were around 20 per cent, which according to our research would be very high, our levels of significance would be virtually untouched.

Among the marginal groups, whose buying habits are not recorded, are people who believe in astrology but buy a book about a star sign other than their own, perhaps to find out more about a friend, or as a gift for that same friend. Then there are the kleptomaniacs who cannot grab the book for

* Hajo Banzhaf & Anna Haebler, *Schlüsselworte zur Astrologie*, Munich 1996, p. 47

their own sign without being spotted and so shoplift the nearest volume, or foreign tourists who do not appear in the relevant population.

All these groups have one thing in common: their buying habits have a negligible effect on the research, and to some degree cancel each other out.

2

WHO MARRIES WHOM?

'If there is such a thing as Heaven on Earth, it is a happy marriage.'

Marie von Ebner-Eschenbach (1830–1916)

The family is older than recorded history. It is found all over the world, and honoured by every religion. According to that fine historian Will Durant, the family 'is the heart of civilisation'. And the heart of the traditional family is marriage.

Marriage has always been the subject of both praise and scorn. 'The greatest blessing on earth, when husband wife are united in true harmony', sang the poet Euripides 2,400 years ago. His contemporary and fellow bard, Xenarchos, meanwhile claimed mockingly: 'Happy are the cicadas, for their females are dumb.'

Johann Wolfgang von Goethe declared: 'Marriage is the beginning and the pinnacle of all culture.' But Goethe also criticized marriages which, he felt, 'spoil the most tender of relationships'. Did this great writer take his own advice? No, he got married.

As well as monogamy, polygamy – or multiple marriage – exists among tribal peoples, and in the Orient. It may take the form of polygyny (where one man has several wives), or polyandry (one woman with several husbands).

Sometimes there is a distinction between main and secondary marriages. 'Complete freedom from matrimonial ties (promiscuity) has not been observed anywhere,' a major German reference book stated in 1978. However, people have come a long way since then.

Today, for example, many British citizens have begun to have serous misgivings about the value of matrimony. According to official annual statistics, the number of marriages fell from 385,490 in 1950 to 291,069 in 1994. And this is the pattern which prevails all over the Western world.

Nevertheless, the motives which drive two people to enter into that most intimate relationship seem to be unchanged: love and passion; the desire to have children; the longing for happiness and security; and sometimes perhaps even the attraction of a dowry – even though canny Scots warns us: 'Never marry for money, it's cheaper to borrow'.

Do star signs influence our choice of partner? Or perhaps the question should be: are marriages really made in Heaven?

ANALYSIS

Astrologers claim that people are predisposed to be attracted by one another. Similarly, your star signs may be incompatible – and any relationship fraught with difficulties. So we set out to discover whether this was a mistaken belief, or if there was actual proof, according to strict mathematical and statistical criteria.

In carrying out our research into the influence of star signs on the choice of marriage partners, we had the co-operation of the Swiss Federal Office of Statistics. Their Population Development Department has recorded every marriage in Switzerland since 1987, plus the birth dates of both partners.

The data made available to us covered all marriages between the years 1987 and 1994, involving 717,526 men and women. They could be classified under their star sign according to their date of birth. We put together a 12 × 12 field table (*see* page 66) showing 144 possible combinations, 'star sign of bride/star sign of bridegroom'.

If we assume that a person's star sign has no influence whatsoever over his or her choice of partner, the number of marriages would be evenly distributed over the 144 potential combinations. Admittedly, we have to take account of the fact that the number of people of marriageable age differs from one sign to another. Since, over the course of the year, the birth rate is particularly high in spring and particularly low in autumn, people born under Aries in March or April will be over-represented in marriage statistics, while Scorpios born in October and November will represent an unusually small proportion.

As the next step, we drew up tables of mathematical expectations (*see* page 70). Let's take as an example the combination of Taurus woman/Aquarius man.

Marriages: actual combinations 1987 - 1994

MEN	Aries	Taurus	Gemini	Cancer	Leo	Virgo	Libra	Scorpio	Sagittarius	Capricorn	Aquarius	Pisces
					WOMEN							
Aries	3154	2925	2952	2738	2862	2737	2578	2404	2317	2622	2788	2932
Taurus	2828	2843	2692	2698	2553	2577	2585	2445	2271	2574	2654	2697
Gemini	2895	2844	2973	2694	2708	2620	2576	2438	2343	2544	2745	2798
Cancer	2634	2626	2684	2554	2546	2511	2288	2284	2156	2340	2628	2694
Leo	2862	2602	2626	2589	2561	2511	2355	2282	2120	2444	2464	2666
Virgo	2615	2601	2560	2481	2426	2542	2324	2267	2114	2353	2464	2516
Libra	2572	2467	2585	2447	2489	2339	2331	2094	2086	2278	2429	2466
Scorpio	2405	2288	2299	2338	2271	2211	2120	2065	1924	2179	2313	2467
Sagittarius	2510	2295	2275	2204	2227	2134	2024	1931	1994	2023	2261	2188
Capricorn	2636	2606	2549	2412	2441	2410	2248	2217	2067	2494	2533	2605
Aquarius	2813	2544	2777	2565	2682	2602	2409	2213	2227	2525	2812	2735
Pisces	2906	2765	2740	2670	2597	2502	2377	2466	2248	2452	2757	2738

Marriages: expected combinations 1987 - 1994

MEN	Aries	Taurus	Gemini	Cancer	Leo	Virgo	Libra	Scorpio	Sagittarius	Capricorn	Aquarius	Pisces
					WOMEN							
Aries	3021	2890	2918	2796	2794	2732	2596	2494	2380	2652	2838	2898
Taurus	2875	2750	2777	2661	2659	2600	2471	2374	2265	2524	2701	2759
Gemini	2945	2817	2844	2726	2723	2663	2531	2431	2320	2586	2767	2825
Cancer	2740	2621	2647	2537	2534	2479	2355	2262	2159	2406	2575	2629
Leo	2753	2633	2659	2548	2546	2490	2366	2273	2169	2417	2587	2641
Virgo	2678	2562	2587	2479	2477	2422	2301	2211	2110	2351	2516	2570
Libra	2616	2502	2527	2421	2419	2366	2248	2160	2061	2297	2458	2510
Scorpio	2460	2353	2376	2277	2275	2225	2114	2031	1938	2160	2311	2360
Sagittarius	2385	2282	2304	2208	2206	2158	2050	1969	1879	2095	2241	2289
Capricorn	2674	2558	2583	2475	2473	2418	2298	2208	2107	2348	2512	2566
Aquarius	2828	2705	2732	2618	2615	2558	2430	2335	2228	2483	2657	2714
Pisces	2857	2733	2759	2644	2642	2584	2455	2359	2251	2508	2684	2741

We know that of the 358,763 women getting married, a total of 31,406 were born under the sign of Taurus. That represents 8.754 per cent of all brides. We also know that of the 358,763 men getting married, 30,904 were Aquarians, i.e. 8.614 per cent of all bridegrooms.

To arrive at the mathematical expectation for the Taurus woman/Aquarius man combination, we multiply the two percentages: 8.754% × 8.614% = 0.754%. Under normal circumstances, we might therefore expect that at 0.754 per cent of all wedding ceremonies a Taurean woman and an Aquarian man exchanged their vows, making the mathematical expectation for this combination 2,705. In actual fact, between 1987 and 1994, the total number of marriages of couples born under these signs was only 2,544.

Statisticians talk about expectations under the null hypothesis. This means that the values formulated in our two-dimensional tables are based on the assumption that the bride's star sign (characteristic 1) and the bridegroom's star sign (characteristic 2) are independent of one another.

In this way, we calculated the mathematical expectation and deviations for all 144 fields of the tables. As assumed, we found some very minor and also some very striking differences from the mathematical expectation.

Up to this point we had been moving in the realms of relatively simple mathematics. Now it was time to look into the deviations in the 144 fields, using the ingenious methods of statistics. The questions we were asking were: which results could be explained as chance? And which were so pronounced that they should be regarded as significant or even highly significant?

Having formulated the questions, we showed our two 144-field tables, i.e. the one giving the actual values, and the other giving the mathematical expectations, to the statisticians at the University in Munich, Germany.

They ran a so-called chi-square test of independence (*see* page 46) on the two-dimensional table of actual marriage. The question was: Can the hypothesis be sustained that the bridegroom's star sign (characteristic 1) is completely independent of that of his partner (characteristic 2) and vice versa? The test of independence revealed that there was only the infinitesimal 0.00018 per cent (1 in 55,555) chance that this null hypothesis would hold good. Statistically, therefore, the claim that certain star sign combinations marry more often than others can be called highly significant.

This made it worth the effort of undertaking separate analyses, on a field-by-field basis, of the deviations between actual values and mathematical expectations.

The study proved that in 25 of the total 144 possible combinations there were significant, or at least slightly significant, deviations between the actual values and mathematical expectations (*see* tables pages 72–73).

Marriages between the following star signs were significantly, or slightly significantly, *higher* than expected:

Man	*Woman*
Aries	Aries**
Taurus	Taurus*
Taurus	Libra**
Gemini	Gemini*
Leo	Aries*
Virgo	Virgo**
Libra	Libra*
Scorpio	Pisces**
Sagittarius	Sagittarius**

Sagittarius	Aries**
Capricorn	Capricorn***
Aquarius	Aquarius***
Pisces	Scorpio**

* = slightly significant ** = significant *** = highly significant

It is extraordinary that among these thirteen star sign combinations, between whom there is obviously a special attraction, there are no less than eight pairings where both partners were born under the same sign.

The following combinations were significantly, or slightly significantly, *less* than expected:

Man	*Woman*
Aries	Scorpio*
Taurus	Gemini*
Taurus	Leo*
Cancer	Aries*
Leo	Aquarius**
Scorpio	Gemini*
Sagittarius	Pisces*
Sagittarius	Capricorn*
Aquarius	Scorpio**
Aquarius	Taurus***
Pisces	Virgo*
Pisces	Libra*

These pairs are less likely than expected to walk up the aisle together.

In the case of 25 of the 144 possible star sign combinations, the deviations between the respective actual values and mathematical expectations are so great that we can no longer talk about chance. There seems to be an inexplicable force at work which has a special influence on emotional ties between people born under certain signs of the zodiac.

But is this really anything to do with star signs? In an attempt to answer this question we carried out a fascinating experiment. Selecting random days scattered across the whole year we created a fictitious 'sign of the zodiac'. We thus 'manufactured' twelve artificial 'star signs' and, once again, 144 possible pairings.

We subjected these newly created signs to exactly the same calculations we had done before with the genuine ones. Now we were on tenterhooks to see whether significant deviations between actual values and mathematical expectations might show up here as well.

Lo and behold! Overall, the chi-square test of independence showed that no significant degree of dependence could be proved. The deviations came within the bounds of the statistical norm.

This remarkable result shows that star signs clearly are of particular importance when it comes to choosing a partner. The scientific study carried out by our Institute into the possible influence of star signs in the choice of a marriage partner entitles us to assume that such a connection does exist. For more information turn to pages 203/204!

SUMMARY
The subject of the investigation was the correlation between star signs and marriage. The population for the survey was based on data relating to 358,763 marriages between 1987 and 1994, divided according to the star signs of each partner. Among the 144 possible pair combinations we observed 25 significant deviations. The influence of chance elements on the observed deviations can be excluded with odds of 1:50,000.

THE ASTROLOGICAL ANGLE

In the following section, we should like to familiarize the reader with the most extraordinary phenomenon we came across in our research. One of the basic principles of astrology states that star signs belonging to the same element harmonize with one another. The twelve signs of the zodiac are assigned to the following elements:

Fire: Aries, Leo and Sagittarius
Air: Aquarius, Gemini and Libra
Earth: Taurus, Virgo and Capricorn
Water: Cancer, Scorpio and Pisces

Marriage

MEN		WOMEN				
		Aries	Taurus	Gemini	Cancer	Leo
Aries	Actual Marriages	3154	2925	2952	2738	2862
	Expected Marriages	3021	2890	2918	2796	2794
	Significance/Diff.	** +133	+35	+34	-58	+68
Taurus	Actual Marriages	2828	2843	2692	2698	2553
	Expected Marriages	2875	2750	2777	2661	2659
	Significance/Diff.	-47	* +93	* -85	+37	* -106
Gemini	Actual Marriages	2895	2844	2973	2694	2708
	Expected Marriages	2945	2817	2844	2726	2723
	Significance/Diff.	-50	+27	** +129	-32	-15
Cancer	Actual Marriages	2634	2626	2684	2554	2546
	Expected Marriages	2740	2621	2647	2537	2534
	Significance/Diff.	* -106	+5	+37	+17	+12
Leo	Actual Marriages	2862	2602	2626	2589	2561
	Expected Marriages	2753	2633	2659	2548	2546
	Significance/Diff.	** +109	-31	-33	+41	+15
Virgo	Actual Marriages	2615	2601	2560	2481	2426
	Expected Marriages	2678	2562	2587	2479	2477
	Significance/Diff.	-63	+39	-27	+2	-51
Libra	Actual Marriages	2572	2467	2585	2447	2489
	Expected Marriages	2616	2502	2527	2421	2419
	Significance/Diff.	-44	-35	+58	+26	+70
Scorpio	Actual Marriages	2405	2288	2299	2338	2271
	Expected Marriages	2460	2353	2376	2277	2275
	Significance/Diff.	-55	-65	* -77	+61	-4
Sagittarius	Actual Marriages	2510	2295	2275	2204	2227
	Expected Marriages	2385	2282	2304	2208	2206
	Significance/Diff.	** +125	+13	-29	-4	+21
Capricorn	Actual Marriages	2636	2606	2549	2412	2441
	Expected Marriages	2674	2558	2583	2475	2473
	Significance/Diff.	-38	+48	-34	-63	-32
Aquarius	Actual Marriages	2813	2544	2777	2565	2682
	Expected Marriages	2828	2705	2732	2618	2615
	Significance/Diff.	-15	*** -161	+45	-53	+67
Pisces	Actual Marriages	2906	2765	2740	2670	2597
	Expected Marriages	2857	2733	2759	2644	2642
	Significance/Diff.	+49	+32	-19	+26	-45

Total number of Marriages Analysed: 358.763

1987 - 1994

WOMEN

Virgo	Libra	Scorpio	Sagittarius	Capricorn	Aquarius	Pisces
2737	2578	2404	2317	2622	2788	2932
2732	2596	2494	2380	2652	2838	2898
+5	-18	* -90	-63	-30	-50	+34
2577	2585	2445	2271	2574	2654	2697
2600	2471	2374	2265	2524	2701	2759
-23	** +114	+71	+6	+50	-47	-62
2620	2576	2438	2343	2544	2745	2798
2663	2531	2431	2320	2586	2767	2825
-43	+45	+7	+23	-42	-22	-27
2511	2288	2284	2156	2340	2628	2694
2479	2355	2262	2159	2406	2575	2629
+32	-67	+22	-3	-66	+53	+65
2511	2355	2282	2120	2444	2464	2666
2490	2366	2273	2169	2417	2587	2641
+21	-11	+9	-49	+27	** -123	+25
2542	2324	2267	2114	2353	2464	2516
2422	2301	2211	2110	2351	2516	2570
** +120	+23	+56	+4	+2	-52	-54
2339	2331	2094	2086	2278	2429	2466
2366	2248	2160	2061	2297	2458	2510
-27	* +83	-66	+25	-19	-29	-44
2211	2120	2065	1924	2179	2313	2467
2225	2114	2031	1938	2160	2311	2360
-14	+6	+34	-14	+19	+2	** +107
2134	2024	1931	1994	2023	2261	2188
2158	2050	1969	1879	2095	2241	2289
-24	-26	-38	** +115	* -72	+20	* -101
2410	2248	2217	2067	2494	2533	2605
2418	2298	2208	2107	2348	2512	2566
-8	-50	+9	-40	*** +146	+21	+39
2602	2409	2213	2227	2525	2812	2735
2558	2430	2335	2228	2483	2657	2714
+44	-21	** -122	-1	+42	*** +155	+21
2502	2377	2466	2248	2452	2757	2738
2584	2455	2359	2251	2508	2684	2741
* -82	* -78	** +107	-3	-56	+73	-3

☐ positive ■ negative　　* slightly significant　　** significant　　*** highly significant

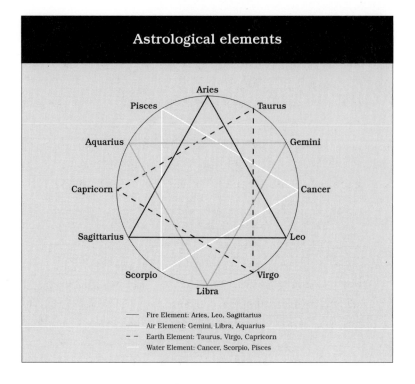

Astrological elements

Fire Element: Aries, Leo, Sagittarius
Air Element: Gemini, Libra, Aquarius
Earth Element: Taurus, Virgo, Capricorn
Water Element: Cancer, Scorpio, Pisces

Each group forms a triangle inside the circle of the zodiac, with each sign 120° from its companions. This is called a trine aspect.

We have already seen that, among the many marriages recorded, there are thirteen combinations which lead noticeably more often to matrimony. Therefore, of all 144 possible pairings, these signs feel the strongest attraction for one another.

The result was amazing: when we compared the astrological principle of the elements with our statistically-based evidence twelve of the thirteen pairs who marry most frequently belonged to the same element.

This striking result was examined, with the help of combinatorial analysis, to establish to what extent it could be explained by chance. The element of chance in this result was no more than 1 in 7,700,000.

There was another remarkable result. We have already seen how not only signs governed by the same element experience a special mutual attraction, but also how well-above-average numbers of people born under the same star sign seek each other out – namely in eight of the thirteen significant cases.

Once again we used combinatorial analysis to show the influence of chance, and once again came up with an impressive result.

The probability is less than 1 in 6,700,000 that eight of the thirteen significant star sign combinations with an above-average inclination to get married consisted of people with identical signs. Strangely enough, astrological literature is somewhat reticent on the subject of harmony between people born under the same star sign. So we felt it was even more appropriate that we should be the first to point out this curious phenomenon.

We were, therefore, able to conclude that the astrological principle of attraction between star signs ruled by the same element is spot on – and with a degree of accuracy that we can almost certainly call complete.

Likewise – although this is nowhere near so pronounced – we have the case of the twelve star combinations who, according to our calculations, are significantly *less likely* to come together. Here there doesn't seem to be much in the way of mutual attraction. In the zodiac these star signs stand in a square formation, in other words at angles of 90° or

180° to one another. Astrologers, too, tell us that they get along less well with each other.

The following star sign combinations stand in square formation:

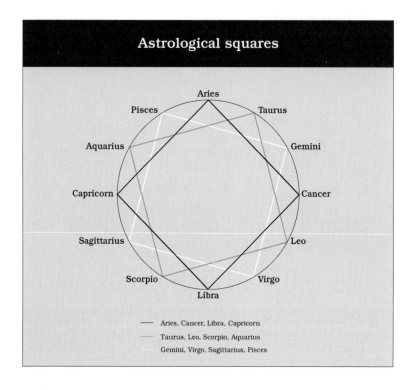

Aries/Cancer/Libra/Capricorn
Taurus/Leo/Scorpio/Aquarius
Gemini/Virgo/Sagittarius/Pisces

Of the twelve pairs that marry more rarely, six stand opposite one another in square formation. Again, using combinatorial analysis we reckoned that the element of chance in this result was excluded with odds of 1 to 433.

We also wanted to explore a third fascinating phenomenon: the self-fulfilling prophecy.

Astrologers often say that Scorpio and Pisces make good marriage partners. Meanwhile, believers in the self-fulfilling prophecy theory claim that the Scorpio man has found out which star sign will suit him best. He has heard it from a marriage guidance counsellor, or read it in an astrology book. Perhaps for one reason or another, the single Scorpio has this information in mind as he scans the personal ads looking for the ideal partner. This phenomenon certainly exists. We are simply asking how influential it is. Do believers in astrology account for such a high percentage of the population that they can noticeably affect the marriage statistics? It is worth noting that in astrological literature combinations of identical star signs are handled with extreme caution, the tendency is towards a negative or neutral, only rarely positive, assessment.

We have shown that among the thirteen combinations of significantly higher attraction there are eight pairs with identical star signs. These, as we have seen, seldom harmonize, so there can be no prophesies according to which believers in astrology can orient themselves. In this respect we would like to mention that among the twelve combinations with significantly less force of attraction there is not a single combination with identical star signs.

We took this matter one step further and approached the Institut für Demoskopie, Allensbach, Germany, to carry out a representative survey into the phenomenon.

Astrological signs and partnership

At the request of the IMWA Institute, Munich, marriages were statistically evaluated from an astrological standpoint, with some surprising results. Marriages between people born under certain star signs were far more frequent than one would expect if left to chance. At the same time, certain other combinations of star signs forged far fewer life partnerships than levels of probability might have suggested.

As a possible explanation for this state of affairs, it was assumed that certain outside influences were at work. Since there is no doubt that a considerable proportion of the population are interested in, and know something about, astrology, we could suppose that such people might choose a marriage partner or 'significant other' on astrological grounds. Just how often such guidelines are used can be seen from the lonely hearts columns in the newspapers. Advertisers often explicitly state they are looking for friends or marriage partners with specific star signs.

A survey commissioned by the IMWA Institute was carried out to discover what practical meaning the astrological factor had for marriages and stable domestic relationships. How widespread is the belief in a special kind of harmony between people with particular star signs? And how often are marriages or stable domestic relationships formed with the deliberate intent of creating a desired star sign combination?

Is there any evidence that people who believe in astrology shy away from forming relationships with particular star signs? Is it possible that the various deviations from the mathematical expectation of the marriage statistics are really something to do with prior knowledge of astrology? Or, should we assume that other factors cause these deviations?

These questions were answered by a representative public opinion poll conducted among 2,174 men and women aged sixteen and over.

The survey

The survey took place throughout Germany between 25 March and 7 April 1997. It took the form of face-to-face and 'paper and pencil' interviews, since experience shows that disruptive factors are less likely with interviews of this kind.

The questions were asked within the framework of a multi-subject questionnaire. The other themes – feelings about life in general, attitude to work, attitude to the media, company and brand awareness, political inclinations, and insurance – had nothing to do with astrology. These questions were left until the end of the questionnaire.

The questions

In order to carry out the commissioned survey, the following questions were asked. Taking account of popular parlance, the questions were framed using the term 'star signs' rather than 'Sun signs'.

a) All interviewees were asked 'Do you know your star sign?' If 'Yes', 'What is it?'
b) Interviewees who named their star sign were then asked whether they were married or in a stable domestic relationship.

c) Interviewees who named their star sign and were married or in a stable domestic relationship were asked 'Do you know your partner's star sign?' If 'Yes', 'What is it?'

d) Interviewees who named their star sign, were married or in a stable domestic relationship and knew their partner's star sign were asked 'When you decided on each other, did your star signs play a part in the decision?' Possible replies: Yes/A little/No/No information.

e) Interviewees who had named their star sign, were married or in a stable domestic relationship and knew their partner's star sign were asked: 'Do you believe that there are star signs which are particularly well-suited to each other and lead to particularly happy relationships?' Possible replies: I believe this/I don't believe this/Undecided, don't know.

f) Interviewees who replied to the previous question 'I believe this ' were asked 'are your star signs well-suited, from what you've heard?' Possible replies: Well-suited/No/Don't know.

Survey results

a) Knowledge of star sign, distribution of separate groups
Of those questioned 93 per cent knew their star sign; only 7 per cent replied 'No' to the question: 'Do you know your star sign?' Women in particular have some knowledge of astrology. Men were less well informed about star signs; 90 per cent knew their star sign.

Each group consisted of between 6 and 10 per cent of the total numbers questioned arranged separately under star signs. There are no great differences in the distribution. Those born under the sign of Sagittarius made up the smallest group. (*See* Table 1, below)

Table 1: Do you know your star sign?	
	Total sample
Yes, I know it	93 %
No, I don't know it	7 %
	100 %
If 'Yes', 'What is it?'	
Capricorn	8 %
Aquarius	7 %
Pisces	8 %
Aries	10 %
Taurus	9 %
Gemini	8 %
Cancer	7 %
Leo	8 %
Virgo	8 %
Libra	8 %
Scorpio	6 %
Sagittarius	6 %
	93 %
Total surveyed	**2174**

Distribution of star signs amongst population over 16 years old.

b) Partnership and star signs

Of those questioned who named their own star sign, 59 per cent were married and 12 per cent were in a stable domestic relationship.

c) Of the groups who named their own star sign and were also married or in a stable domestic relationship, 94 per cent were able to name their partner's star sign.

Knowledge of their partner's star sign was also evenly distributed.

d) The role of star signs in the choice of partner
The astrological aspect does not seem to be one of the main criteria in choosing a partner. Of the 1,261 of those questioned who were in a stable domestic relationship, and knew both their own and their partner's star sign, only 0.6 per cent said that star signs had had any bearing on their choice of partner (0.4 per cent of the population). The percentage among married interviewees was slightly higher (0.7 per cent) than among those who were cohabiting (0.2 per cent). (*See* Table 2 on page 83)

Clearly, fewer than 1 per cent of those questioned consciously chose their partner with astrological considerations in mind. Meanwhile there was a somewhat larger minority of 3.8 per cent of married or cohabiting interviewees who said that star signs had exerted 'a little' influence on their choice of partner. Quite obviously, even among people interested in astrology, star signs are not a decisive factor when it comes to forming intimate relationships.

The explanation of deviations in the marriage statistics by reason of astrological knowledge among the population would therefore only be valid if the deviation merely applied to 0.7 per cent of marriages.

Table 2: When you decided on each other, did your star signs play a part in the decision?			
	In total	Married	In unmarried partnership
Yes	0,6 %	0,7 %	0,2 %
A little	3,8 %	3,9 %	3,3 %
No	93,7 %	93,7 %	93,6 %
No information	1,9 %	1,7 %	2,9 %
	100 %	100 %	100 %
Total surveyed	1261	1030	231

Distribution of star signs amongst population over 16 years old.
Survey of those who can name their star sign, are either married or in a stable domestic relationship and can name their partner's star sign.

e) The assumption that certain star sign combinations are particularly well suited.

While, as a rule, star signs are not among the conscious motives for forming a relationship, a large number of those questioned did support the assumption that certain star sign combinations lead to particularly harmonious relationships. Of those who were married or in stable domestic relationships and could name both their own and their partner's star sign, almost a quarter (24 per cent) said they believed that there were star signs that were a particularly good match and formed especially happy partnerships. Young women were particularly aware of such fortunate combinations.

f) However, only 11 per cent of this group classified their own marriage or relationship as belonging to this type of auspicious union. Even so, this does not affect the wide-spread belief that certain relationships are especially favoured by the stars. (*See* Table 3, below)

Table 3: Do you believe that there are star signs which are particularly well-suited to each other and lead to particularly happy relationships?	
	In total
I believe this	24 %
I don't believe this	52 %
Undecided, don't know	24 %
	100 %
If, 'I believe this', 'are your star signs well-suited, from what you've heard?'	
Well-suited	11 %
No	5 %
Don't know	8 %
Unquestioned section of survey group	76 %
	100 %
Total surveyed	**1261**

Distribution of star signs amongst population over 16 years old.
Survey of those who can name their star sign, are either married or in a stable, domestic relationship and can name their partner's star sign.

According to the IMWA findings, those groups who belong to particularly frequent or particularly rare star sign pairings, are less likely to believe in relationships with fortuitous astrological aspects. Among those in very common star sign combinations, 20 per cent are convinced that there is a special kind of harmony between certain signs, a belief shared by 19 per cent of those in particularly rare star sign pairings. Conversely, belief in favourable aspects is more widespread among those whose relationships are unexceptional when the marriage statistics are evaluated from an astrological standpoint. Of these, 25 per cent believe in the positive influence of the stars on specific relationships. (*See* Table 4, below)

Table 4: Do you believe that there are star signs which are particularly well-suited and lead to particularly happy relationships?		
	Star sign combinations occurring with average frequency in partnerships	Star sign combinations occurring with above average frequency in partnerships	Star sign combinations occurring with below average frequency in partnerships
I believe this	25 %	20 %	19 %
I don't believe this	51 %	48 %	61 %
Undecided don't know	24 %	32 %	20 %
	100 %	100 %	100 %
If, 'I believe this', 'are your star signs well-suited, from what you've heard?'			
Well-suited	12 %	10 %	6 %
No	5 %	4 %	5 %
Don't know	8 %	6 %	8 %
Unquestioned section of survey group	75 %	80 %	81 %
	100 %	100 %	100 %
Total surveyed	1046	98	117

Distribution of star signs amongst population over 16 years old.
Survey of those who can name their star sign, are either married or in a stable domestic relationship and can name their partner's star sign.

The public opinion survey reveals an interesting distinction between belief and behaviour. A fair proportion of married people, and those in stable domestic relationships, believe that some relationships are particularly favoured by the stars. However, more than 99 per cent have quite different priorities when actively looking for a partner. Although they desire an astrologically auspicious relationship, they do not deliberately go looking for it.

3

WHO DIVORCES WHOM?

'These days you can say you have a happy marriage if you put off getting divorced three times.'

Danny Kaye (1913–1987)

For ever is a hell of a long time. That's the title of playboy Teddy Stauffer's memoirs. For decades the old charmer kept the female population of the western hemisphere holding their proverbial breath. The words 'For ever' are spoken in many US marriage ceremonies, the equivalent of the 'Till death do us part' that we vow in church. 'Mr Acapulco' dedicated his memoirs to – in alphabetical order – 'Alberta, Alice, Ampera . . . and so on, to Xaviera, Zayne and Zita'. In between are a good dozen names – a lengthy and delightful procession of feminine charm.

It seems he was ahead of his time, for the trend towards serial marriage has now caught on in all the western industrialized nations, from Switzerland to Canada.

Sixty years ago the King of England, Edward VIII, was forced to renounce the throne in order to be able to wed Wallace Simpson, a divorcee. The present Prince of Wales is himself divorced. Ronald Reagan was the first divorced President of the United States to enter the White House, and Willy Brandt was the first divorced German Chancellor to move into the Palais Schaumburg. In the West, incidentally, it is usually the wife who instigates divorce proceedings. Twice as many women as men apply to end their marriages.

Men seem somewhat inclined to go along with author and playwright Rolf Hochhuth when he says: 'No marriage is worth what the divorce is going to cost you.'

Do star signs have a serious hand in this, too?

ANALYSIS

We investigated whether the divorce rate was unusually high among certain star signs.

We were given data on all couples granted a divorce in Switzerland between the years of 1987 and 1994, with the dates of birth of both parties. This was a total of 109,030 couples.

We used exactly the same method as we did for marriages, so this time we can run through the various stages of our research a bit more speedily.

First of all, we listed the 109,030 women and 109,030 men under their respective star signs and created a table of actual values with 12×12 fields.

Then we set up a table of mathematical expectations. Given, for example, that Aries men represented 9.13 per cent of male divorcees, and Leo women made up 8.558 per cent of female divorcees, the mathematical expectation for the Aries man/Leo woman combination was $9.130\% \times 8.558\% = 0.7813\%$.

So we might have expected that 0.7813% of all the 109,030 divorces – or 852 divorces – involved this combination of star signs. In actual fact, 931 marriages between Aries men and Leo women ended in divorce, considerably

Divorces: actual combinations 1987 - 1994

MEN	Aries	Taurus	Gemini	Cancer	Leo	Virgo	Libra	Scorpio	Sagittarius	Capricorn	Aquarius	Pisces
					WOMEN							
Aries	887	866	924	815	931	803	802	718	698	775	828	907
Taurus	833	829	863	760	765	805	808	707	667	772	784	834
Gemini	902	810	891	842	837	826	780	701	705	815	837	870
Cancer	816	772	833	728	788	751	725	715	639	724	811	810
Leo	827	836	814	807	788	767	764	711	667	730	723	840
Virgo	839	780	816	754	745	773	682	661	681	714	745	771
Libra	819	774	772	734	723	723	660	651	618	676	735	719
Scorpio	743	731	748	678	677	656	631	611	598	632	689	780
Sagittarius	710	701	738	673	713	613	595	592	622	581	629	679
Capricorn	799	834	818	720	766	748	680	690	651	724	791	726
Aquarius	806	771	913	809	778	780	767	698	705	725	829	807
Pisces	902	863	835	820	820	761	718	692	690	751	812	863

Divorces: expected combinations 1987 - 1994

MEN	Aries	Taurus	Gemini	Cancer	Leo	Virgo	Libra	Scorpio	Sagittarius	Capricorn	Aquarius	Pisces
					WOMEN							
Aries	902	873	910	834	852	822	786	744	725	787	841	877
Taurus	855	827	862	790	807	779	745	704	687	745	797	831
Gemini	890	861	897	823	840	811	775	733	715	776	829	865
Cancer	826	800	833	764	780	753	720	681	664	720	770	803
Leo	841	814	848	777	794	766	733	693	675	733	784	817
Virgo	812	786	819	751	767	740	708	670	653	708	757	790
Libra	780	755	786	721	736	711	680	643	627	680	727	758
Scorpio	741	717	747	685	700	675	646	611	595	646	691	720
Sagittarius	711	688	717	658	671	648	620	586	571	620	663	691
Capricorn	811	785	818	750	766	739	707	669	652	707	756	788
Aquarius	851	824	858	787	803	775	742	701	684	742	793	827
Pisces	864	836	871	799	815	787	753	712	694	753	805	839

more than expected (*see* tables, page 89).

Now it was back to the statisticians. Their first chi-square test of independence (*see* page 46) showed that in the case of divorce, there is no significant degree of dependence between the star signs of the two partners. Quite the opposite to marriage, where we found a clear correlation. This suggested that star sign combinations who married more frequently than expected would also be among those who had a higher-than-average divorce rate – simply on the basis of the larger number of marriages.

In order to eliminate this possibility, we chose a slightly different strategy:

We already knew that in Switzerland there had been a total of 358,763 marriages and 109,030 divorces between 1987 and 1994. Based on these figures we worked out a divorce factor of 0.304. Or to put it another way: an average of 304 per thousand marriages ended in divorce between 1987 and 1994.

This calculation can then be applied individually to each of the 144 possible star sign pairings. We know, for instance, that in the eight-year period under review there were 2,605 marriages and 726 divorces between men born under Capricorn and women born under Pisces.

This makes a divorce factor of 0.279, which is considerably *lower* than the overall divorce factor of 0.304. This might be an indication that Capricorn men and Pisces women had particularly lasting relationships.

If we use this method for working out the divorce quotient for all 144 possible combinations, we can create a new table with 12 × 12 fields (*see* pages 92–93). We can then carry out the chi-square test of independence (*see* page 46) on these tables. The result shows that there is at least a slightly significant correlation between divorce and the star signs of the parties involved. The connection was, however, nowhere near as strong as it was in the case of marriage.

The analysis of deviation in specific cases revealed that there is a significantly below-average divorce rate for marriages between the following star signs. In other words, these unions obviously had special staying power:

Man	Woman
Aries	Aries
Gemini	Taurus
Taurus	Cancer
Capricorn	Pisces
Pisces	Scorpio

Conversely, the divorce rate was significantly above average among the following combinations:

Man	Woman
Aries	Leo
Gemini	Capricorn
Libra	Aries
Scorpio	Gemini
Sagittarius	Gemini

Therefore, there is an interesting – and statistically provable – correlation between divorce and the partners' star signs.

One further question fascinated us: were there any combinations of star signs who married and were also unusually devoted to one another, and thus under-represented among the divorce statistics? One might have assumed so. We tested this assumption statistically in the following way:

Divorce quotients

		WOMEN				
MEN		Aries	Taurus	Gemini	Cancer	Leo
Aries		0,281	0,296	0,313	0,298	0,325
	Significance	** -				** +
Taurus		0,295	0,292	0,321	0,282	0,300
	Significance				* -	
Gemini		0,312	0,285	0,300	0,313	0,309
	Significance		** -	* -		
Cancer		0,310	0,294	0,310	0,285	0,310
	Significance				* -	
Leo		0,289	0,321	0,310	0,312	0,308
	Significance	* -				
Virgo		0,321	0,300	0,319	0,304	0,307
	Significance	* +				
Libra		0,318	0,314	0,299	0,300	0,290
	Significance	** +				
Scorpio		0,309	0,319	0,325	0,290	0,298
	Significance		* +	** +		
Sagittarius		0,283	0,305	0,324	0,305	0,320
	Significance	* -		** +		* +
Capricorn		0,303	0,320	0,321	0,299	0,314
	Significance					
Aquarius		0,287	0,303	0,329	0,315	0,290
	Significance	* -		* +	* +	* -
Pisces		0,310	0,312	0,305	0,307	0,316
	Significance					

Total number of divorces: 109.030   Overall divorce quotient: 0,304

			WOMEN			
Virgo	Libra	Scorpio	Sagittarius	Capricorn	Aquarius	Pisces
0,293	0,311	0,299	0,301	0,296	0,297	0,309
0,312	0,313	0,289	0,294	0,300	0,295	0,309
0,315	0,303	0,288 *** -**	0,301	0,320 **** +**	0,305	0,311
0,299	0,317	0,313	0,296	0,309	0,309	0,301
0,305	0,324 *** +**	0,312	0,315	0,299	0,293	0,315
0,304	0,293	0,292	0,322	0,303	0,302	0,306
0,309	0,283 *** -**	0,311	0,296	0,297	0,303	0,292
0,297	0,298	0,296	0,311	0,290	0,298	0,316
0,287	0,294	0,307	0,312	0,287	0,278 *** -**	0,310
0,310	0,302	0,311	0,315	0,290	0,312	0,279 ***** -**
0,300	0,318	0,315	0,317	0,287	0,295	0,295
0,304	0,302	0,281 **** -**	0,307	0,306	0,295	0,315

☐ positive ■ negative   * slightly significant   ** significant   *** highly significant

For each of the 144 combinations we correlated the actual number and the expected number of marriages in the period 1987–1994, in other words, we established a quotient from actual values and mathematical expectations. To keep things simple we called this the 'marriage rate'. A marriage rate of 1.05 would mean that there were actually five per cent more marriages between the star signs in question than might have been expected.

A 'divorce rate' can be calculated in the same way. A divorce rate of 0.95 indicates that the actual divorces among these combinations was five per cent under mathematical expectation.

We then divided the marriage rate by the divorce rate. When the result is clearly more than one, this indicates enduring attraction between people born under these two star signs. We found a combination of more frequent marriages and more infrequent divorces than might have been expected under normal circumstances. Conversely, when the marriage rate/divorce rate result was obviously less than one, the indication is that there is lasting aversion – or to put it more diplomatically – a below-average chance of lasting attraction.

The tables on pages 96–97 show the result of this mathematical experiment. We have highlighted the three most enduring star sign combinations and the three pairings most likely to break up.

SUMMARY

The subject of the investigation was the correlation between star signs and divorce. The survey was based on data relating to 109,030 divorces between 1987 and 1994. With the aid of known data relating to marriages, divorce quotient could be determined for the purposes of comparison. Among the 144 possible pair combinations we observed twenty-five significant deviations. The influence of chance on the observed deviations can be excluded with odds of 1:26.

THE ASTROLOGICAL ANGLE

It is obvious that star signs play a far less significant role in divorce than in marriage. There is at least one possible explanation for this: when people decide to get married they are usually mutually motivated by feelings such as love, sexual desire, the wish to have children, or the longing for domesticity. Divorce, meanwhile, is generally triggered by the breakdown of the relationship, whatever inspired it.

There may also be another factor. Marriage involves two people moving towards one another. When there are mysterious forces working on those born under specific signs of the zodiac, they emanate from both partners, in other words from two sources. The wish to divorce, however, is usually expressed by only one partner. The forces which might have something to do with star signs are imbalanced.

Lasting attraction between

MEN	WOMEN					
	Aries	Taurus	Gemini	Cancer	Leo	Virgo
Aries	1,062	1,021	0,996	1,003	0,937	1,026
Taurus	1,009	1,031	0,968	1,054	1,013	0,959
Gemini	0,970	1,074	1,052	0,966	0,998	0,966
Cancer	0,973	1,038	1,014	1,056	0,994	1,015
Leo	1,057	0,962	1,028	0,979	1,013	1,007
Virgo	0,945	1,024	0,993	0,997	1,008	1,005
Libra	0,936	0,962	1,042	0,993	1,048	0,972
Scorpio	0,975	0,954	0,966	1,038	1,032	1,023
Sagittarius	1,054	0,988	0,959	0,976	0,951	1,046
Capricorn	1,001	0,959	0,987	1,015	0,987	0,985
Aquarius	1,050	1,005	0,955	0,953	1,059	1,011
Pisces	0,974	0,980	1,035	0,983	0,977	1,001

The three strongest, most lasting attractions occur between

1) Capricorn man and Pisces woman (1,102)
   Slightly above average attraction leading to marriage,
   but sharply below average proportion of divorces.

2) Pisces man and Scorpio woman (1,076)
   Clearly above average attraction leading to marriage,
   slightly below average proportion of divorces.

3) Gemini man and Taurus woman (1,074)
   Only average attraction leading to marriage,
   but sharply below average proportion of divorces.

		WOMEN			
Libra	Scorpio	Sagittarius	Capricorn	Aquarius	Pisces
0,974	0,999	1,011	1,004	0,998	0,978
0,964	1,026	1,032	0,984	0,998	0,974
1,012	1,049	1,024	0,937	0,983	0,984
0,964	0,961	1,037	0,968	0,969	1,015
0,954	0,979	0,990	1,015	1,033	0,982
1,048	1,039	0,960	0,993	0,995	1,003
1,068	0,958	1,026	0,998	0,978	1,036
1,026	1,016	0,988	1,031	1,003	0,965
1,028	0,971	0,975	1,031	1,063	0,973
1,017	0,973	0,982	1,038	0,964	1,102
0,958	0,953	0,969	1,041	1,013	1,033
1,015	1,076	1,004	0,980	1,018	0,971

☐ Strongest, most lasting attraction ■ Strongest, most lasting aversion

The three strongest, most lasting aversions occur between

1) Libra man and Aries woman (0,936)
   Slightly below average attraction leading to marriage,
   but sharply above average proportion of divorces.

2) Aries man and Leo woman (0,937)
   Slightly above average attraction leading to marriage,
   but very sharply above average proportion of divorces.

3) Gemini man and Capricorn woman (0,937)
   Slightly below average attraction leading to marriage,
   but sharply above average proportion of divorces.

We wondered: are there star signs for whom the risk of divorce is unusually high?

- Among men, there was no star sign which significantly deviated from the average risk of divorce.
- Among women, however, there was one significant deviation: Gemini. Here, the likelihood of divorce is significantly higher for every man. The husband with a Gemini wife is faced with an above-average risk of divorce.

This chapter shows that Gemini women figure in three of the twenty-five combinations most likely to divorce. Astrological literature confirms that women born under this sign are generally restless and always looking for change.

Note: The author of this book has been married for twenty-eight years to a Gemini woman who has never been divorced. He hopes, that whatever the stars may say, things will stay that way.

4

WHO IS SINGLE?

'Only in solitude is life enjoyed to the full.'
August Graf von Platen (1796–1835)

Errol Flynn cruised the seven seas beneath the black sails of his black yacht 'Zaca'. This famous film star of the 1930s and 1940s sailed alone, without a girlfriend, or even a dog, for company. He threw rum barrels at customs officials and other uninvited visitors in the world's most far-flung harbours. It was certainly not lack of success, but a strong desire for freedom that turned everyone's fantasy pirate into the world's most envied bachelor.

It seems Flynn was ahead of his time.

Fewer and fewer people are getting married, more and more of them are choosing to remain single. Increasing individualism is at the root of both trends. Individualism, which at the beginning of the last century was called 'egoism', endeavours to put the interests of the individual before those of society at large.

The number of single-person households in Great Britain is about 27 per cent.

They can do it because they can afford it, since being a loner is the most expensive lifestyle in terms of accommodation, motoring and taxation.

There are more unattached people in cities than anywhere else.

More and more men and women are reluctant to surrender their freedom, in order to share their lives with, and take responsibility for, others – possibly 'until death do them part'.

More and more people dream of enjoying liberty and the leisure for self-realization, even though there is a price to be paid. A survey of women between the ages of twenty-five and fifty, for example, revealed that singles have three times less sex per week than married women.

'The strong man is mightiest alone', said eighteenth-century poet Friedrich von Schiller. The Berlin-born painter Max Liebermann put it another way when the group of artists known as the 'Association of Eleven' split up: 'If I can do it myself, why should I rely on anyone else?'

Does this kind of pride impel men and women to go it alone? Are people born under certain star signs, which astrologers claim have an exceptional desire for freedom and strong self-awareness, more inclined to live alone than others?

ANALYSIS

Our question was: Are people born under certain star signs more ready for commitment and therefore more likely to marry? On the other hand, are there some who are inclined to give the register office a wide berth?

Switzerland's most recent census (1990) covered the entire population, divided into males and females with exact birth dates.

We were therefore able to classify the whole population according to star sign.

From the marriage statistics, we took the numbers of married people born under each star sign, again divided into men and women. Then, in order to examine their readiness for commitment more closely, we compared the two sets of data.

For example, the marriage statistics told us that 8.76 per cent of married women were born under the sign of Taurus. From the 1990 census, we know that 8.95 per cent of women aged between eighteen and forty were Taureans.

Limiting the population to the eighteen-to-forty age group may seem rather arbitrary, since, of course, there are women who marry before the age of eighteen and after the age of forty. However, this simplification can be justified from the point of view of methodology. The birth-rate over the course of the year has remained unchanged for decades. Only in more recent years, since around 1985, has the birth-rate noticeably shifted from season to season. However, those born since that date are not yet of marriageable age, so, for practical purposes, we can base our study on a relatively constant birth-rate over the course of the year.

When we compared the numbers of marriages with the 'relevant marriageable population', it became clear that certain star signs are rather more prepared to commit themselves to matrimony (*see* tables, pages 102–105).

Who is keen to marry? (men)

Star signs	Number of births for years 1954 - 1976	Percentage of births for years 1954 - 1976	Actual marriages 1987 - 1994	Expected marriages 1987 - 1994	Deviation from expected figure, in percent (see graphic)	Degree of significance
Aries	119.253	9,22 %	33.009	33.085	-0,23 %	neutral
Taurus	114.184	8,83 %	31.417	31.679	-0,83 %	neutral
Gemini	116.041	8,97 %	32.178	32.194	-0,05 %	neutral
Cancer	107.592	8,32 %	29.945	29.850	+0,32 %	neutral
Leo	107.784	8,34 %	30.082	29.903	+0,60 %	neutral
Virgo	106.006	8,20 %	29.263	29.410	-0,50 %	neutral
Libra	102.913	7,96 %	28.583	28.552	+0,11 %	neutral
Scorpio	96.894	7,49 %	26.880	26.882	-0,01 %	neutral
Sagittarius	95.651	7,40 %	26.066	26.537	-1,77 %	** -
Capricorn	107.966	8,35 %	29.218	29.954	-2,46 %	*** -
Aquarius	112.350	8,69 %	30.904	31.170	-0,85 %	neutral
Pisces	106.507	8,24 %	31.218	29.549	+5,65 %	*** +
	1.293.141	100,00 %	358.763	358.763		

* slightly significant   ** significant   *** highly significant

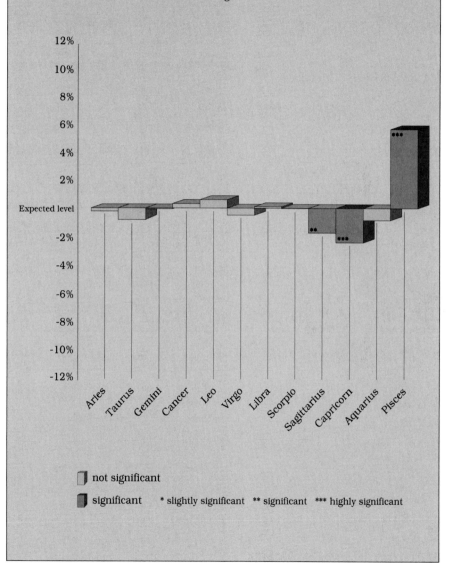

Deviation of actual marriages from expected marriages in percent (men)

Actual marriages: 358.763

Who is keen to marry? (women)

Star signs	Number of births for years 1954 - 1976	Percentage of births for years 1954 - 1976	Actual marriages 1987 - 1994	Expected marriages 1987 - 1994	Deviation from expected figure, in percent (see graphic)	Degree of significance
Aries	111.294	9,08 %	32.830	32.576	+0,78 %	neutral
Taurus	109.663	8,95 %	31.406	32.098	-2,16 %	*** -
Gemini	107.469	8,77 %	31.712	31.456	+0,81 %	neutral
Cancer	101.275	8,26 %	30.390	29.643	+2,52 %	*** +
Leo	101.735	8,30 %	30.363	29.778	+1,97 %	*** +
Virgo	101.503	8,28 %	29.696	29.710	-0,05 %	neutral
Libra	102.473	8,36 %	28.215	29.994	-5,93 %	*** -
Scorpio	90.404	7,38 %	27.106	26.461	+2,44 %	*** +
Sagittarius	89.964	7,34 %	25.867	26.332	-1,77 %	** -
Capricorn	97.940	7,99 %	28.828	28.667	+0,56 %	neutral
Aquarius	104.868	8,56 %	30.848	30.695	+0,50 %	neutral
Pisces	107.114	8,74 %	31.502	31.352	+0,48 %	neutral
	1.225.702	100,00 %	358.763	358.763		

* slightly significant ** significant *** highly significant

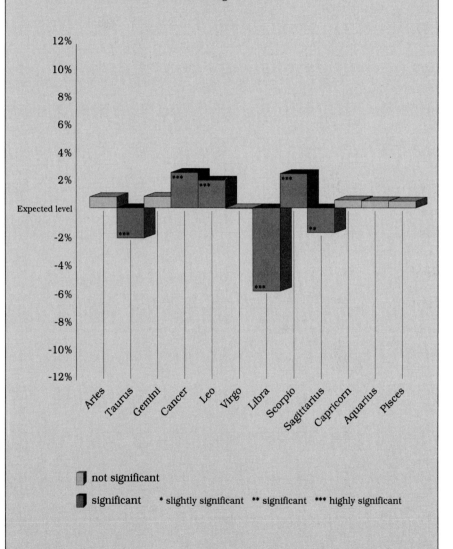

Deviation of actual marriages from expected marriages in percent (women)

Actual marriages: 358.763

12%
10%
8%
6%
4%
2%
Expected level
-2%
-4%
-6%
-8%
-10%
-12%

Aries Taurus Gemini Cancer Leo Virgo Libra Scorpio Sagittarius Capricorn Aquarius Pisces

not significant

significant   * slightly significant   ** significant   *** highly significant

We found that women born under Cancer, Leo and Scorpio, and Pisces men, showed a well-above-average inclination towards marriage, statistically highly significant.

On the other hand, highly significant numbers of Taurus, Libra and Sagittarius women seemed exceptionally reluctant to tie the knot, as are men born under Capricorn.

We then looked at the unmarried state in greater detail and from a different standpoint.

Among other questions, the census of some 6,873,000 registered citizens asked about marital status. Obviously it would make no sense to include people of all ages in an enquiry about singles. Children and young teenagers could not be taken into consideration. For young adults, staying unattached is not a deliberate decision or an expression of their ability or otherwise to sustain a committed relationship. In many instances, it is simply because they are still training for a career, their earnings are meagre, and they are not yet ready to marry and start a family. When we refer to single people, we usually mean those who are still unattached by the age of thirty or so. For this reason we confined our research to men and women between thirty and sixty-five years of age.

Without going into detail about the statistical calculations, the immediate finding was that there was a clear link between the unmarried state and star sign. The chi-square test produced a null result, meaning that we could with absolute certainty reject the hypothesis that there was no correlation between marital status and star signs.

A disproportionate number of Scorpios (highly significant) and Sagittarians (highly significant) figured among single men.

A disproportionate number of Capricorn women (highly significant) remained unattached.

There were fewer unmarried men than expected under the signs of Aquarius (highly significant) and Pisces (highly significant).

Fewer than expected Aquarius (highly significant) and Capricorn (highly significant) women stayed single (*see* tables on pages 108–111).

SUMMARY
The subject of the investigation was the correlation between star signs and the single state. The survey was based on data taken from official marriage statistics (compare Chapter 2). We also had access to figures taken from the 1990 Swiss population census, recording 2,731,766 'single' men and women. Seven significant deviations were observed.

The influence of chance elements on the observed deviations can be excluded with odds of 1:10,000.

The influence of chance elements on the observed deviations can be excluded with odds of 1:10,000,000.

Who is single? (men)

Star signs	Number of births according to 1990 census for years 1925 - 1960	Percentage of births for years 1925 - 1960	Actual singles marital status 'single' for years 1925 - 1960	Expected singles marital status 'single' for years 1925 - 1960	Deviation from expected figure, in percent (see graphic)	Degree of significance
Aries	123.552	9,13 %	21.824	22.065	-1,09 %	neutral
Taurus	117.883	8,72 %	20.752	21.053	-1,43 %	neutral
Gemini	119.923	8,87 %	21.536	21.417	+0,55 %	neutral
Cancer	112.160	8,29 %	20.338	20.031	+1,53 %	neutral
Leo	113.903	8,42 %	20.542	20.342	+0,98 %	neutral
Virgo	110.550	8,17 %	19.777	19.743	+0,17 %	neutral
Libra	107.178	7,92 %	19.291	19.141	+0,78 %	neutral
Scorpio	100.959	7,46 %	18.692	18.030	+3,67 %	*** +
Sagittarius	97.291	7,19 %	17.978	17.375	+3,47 %	*** +
Capricorn	112.382	8,31 %	19.524	20.070	-2,72 %	*** -
Aquarius	117.352	8,68 %	20.534	20.958	-2,02 %	** -
Pisces	119.478	8,83 %	20.773	21.337	-2,64 %	*** -
	1.352.611	100,00 %	241.561	241.561		

* slightly significant   ** significant   *** highly significant

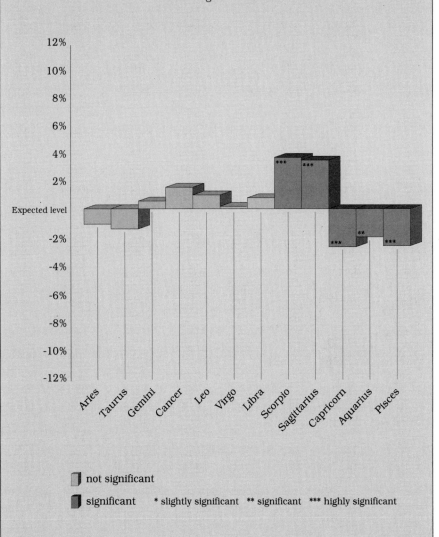

Deviation of actual singles from expected singles in percent (men)

Actual singles: 241.561

not significant

significant   * slightly significant   ** significant   *** highly significant

Who is single? (women)

Star signs	Number of births according to 1990 census for years 1925 - 1960	Percentage of births for years 1925 - 1960	Actual singles marital status 'single' for years 1925 - 1960	Expected singles marital status 'single' for years 1925 - 1960	Deviation from expected figure, in percent (see graphic)	Degree of significance
Aries	125.826	9,12 %	17.413	17.232	+1,04 %	neutral
Taurus	120.206	8,72 %	16.485	16.463	+0,13 %	neutral
Gemini	121.731	8,83 %	16.930	16.672	+1,55 %	neutral
Cancer	114.907	8,33 %	16.001	15.737	+1,67 %	neutral
Leo	116.399	8,44 %	16.141	15.941	+1,25 %	neutral
Virgo	113.034	8,20 %	15.540	15.480	+0,38 %	neutral
Libra	109.651	7,95 %	14.790	15.017	-1,51 %	neutral
Scorpio	104.013	7,54 %	14.291	14.245	+0,32 %	neutral
Sagittarius	100.579	7,29 %	14.033	13.775	+1,87 %	neutral
Capricorn	111.992	8,12 %	14.885	15.338	-2,95 %	*** -
Aquarius	119.628	8,67 %	15.921	16.384	-2,82 %	*** -
Pisces	121.199	8,79 %	16.452	16.598	-0,88 %	neutral
	1.379.165	100,00 %	188.882	188.882		

* slightly significant   ** significant   *** highly significant

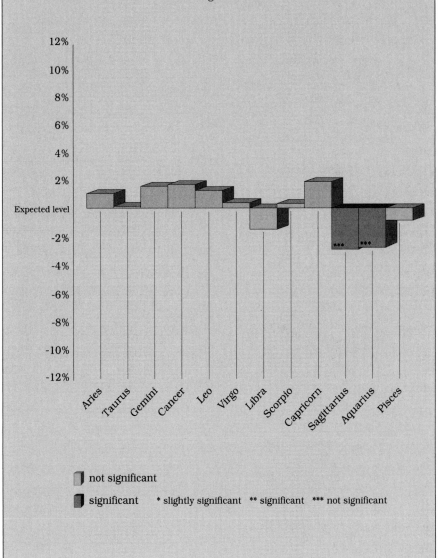

Deviation of actual singles from expected singles in percent (women)

Actual singles: 188.882

12%
10%
8%
6%
4%
2%
Expected level
-2%
-4%
-6%
-8%
-10%
-12%

Aries Taurus Gemini Cancer Leo Virgo Libra Scorpio Capricorn Sagittarius Aquarius Pisces

not significant

significant   * slightly significant ** significant *** not significant

THE ASTROLOGICAL ANGLE

If we compare the results of our investigation of single people with the marriage statistics, it is striking just how little agreement there is between the two sets of data.

Only Pisces men, who appear to be unusually keen on marriage, are under-represented among the unattached.

It is also difficult to record the statistics of all single people. It is certainly problematic to classify only unmarried people between the ages of thirty and sixty-five as 'unattached', because the term can also be applied to those who are widowed, divorced or separated. Even so, we thought it was only right to record in this book a tendency which, at first sight, seems almost contradictory when compared to the marriage statistics.

5

WHO STUDIES WHAT?

'In the early days of our youth, at a time when we yet lack insight, we each decide on an occupation. Thus most men are already shackled to an occupation and a way of life before they are able to judge which would best suit them.'

Marcus Tullius Cicero (106–43 bc)

When someone asked the young Mark Twain what he would be when he grew up he replied: 'At the age of eight I wanted to be a chimney-sweep, at fourteen I wanted to be Napoleon. Since then my ambitions have grown and grown.'

Not all children can be so precise.

'What do you want to be when you grow up?' It's the kind of question that gets on your nerves. When you are very young you can still get away with telling people you want to be an engine-driver. Later it gets harder. An honest answer, like 'I don't know' is a big disappointment to your aunts and uncles. But once they have finished secondary education, many twenty-year-olds are faced with a difficult choice: which university or college course can they or should they begin.

In Great Britain, for example, in 1960 there were about 320,000 students in higher education. Since then their numbers have increased five fold.

Now there are almost 1.6 million young people at British universities and colleges.

The largest groups are studying law, economics and social sciences.

According to research by the Ministries of Culture in the various German states, the total number of budding graduates will have shot up to around two and a half million by the year 2010.

If the worst comes to the worst, they only have to remember the words of Goethe's *Faust*:

> I have pursued, alas, philosophy,
> Jurisprudence, and medicine,
> And, help me God, theology,
> With fervent zeal through thick and thin,
> And here, poor fool, I stand once more,
> No wiser than I was before.

As yet no one studies what is written in the stars. But do students' star signs have some influence on their choice of subject? We were eager to find out. After considerable debate the Universities Clearing House opened up the archives of student applications, academic subjects, and, of course, the all-important star signs.

ANALYSIS

We gathered extensive information on university candidates and their choice of subjects. We examined statistics relating to students applying to the Universities Clearing House for the winter semester 1994/95; the summer semester 1995; and the winter semester 1995/96. Every year around 100,000 students apply to this organization for places on degree courses for which there is restricted entry.

We evaluated data relating to 100,082 applicants for the winter semester 1994/95; 31,337 for the summer semester 1995; and 99,617 for the winter semester 1995/96.

The total of 231,026 applicants were divided according to star signs and according to their desired degree subjects in ten restricted-entry disciplines:

- Architecture
- Business management
- Biology
- Law
- Medicine
- Psychology
- Pharmaceutics
- Veterinary medicine
- Economics
- Dentistry

Our statistical starting point was the same as that for our marriage survey. Having tested whether star sign X was more or less likely to choose star sign Y as a marriage partner, we were now about to discover whether star sign X was more or less likely to choose degree course Y.

The more critical reader might well protest that this analogy is unconvincing. Marriage is a reciprocal choice, but in this case, while the student does indeed choose the subject, the subject does not choose the student. This subtle difference, however, is irrelevant from a statistical point of view.

By now, we are familiar with the investigation procedure:

		Archi-tecture	Business management	Biology
Aries	Actual Applicants to Study	2017	3663	1070
	Expected Applicants to Study	1982	3618	1066
	Significance/Difference	+35	+45	+4
Taurus	Actual Applicants to Study	1997	3798	1105
	Expected Applicants to Study	2049	3740	1103
	Significance/Difference	-52	+58	+2
Gemini	Actual Applicants to Study	1962	3707	1078
	Expected Applicants to Study	1964	3586	1057
	Significance/Difference	-2	* +121	+21
Cancer	Actual Applicants to Study	2152	3746	1061
	Expected Applicants to Study	2064	3769	1111
	Significance/Difference	* +88	-23	* -50
Leo	Actual Applicants to Study	1929	3639	1065
	Expected Applicants to Study	1944	3550	1046
	Significance/Difference	-15	* +89	+19
Virgo	Actual Applicants to Study	1904	3428	962
	Expected Applicants to Study	1891	3452	1018
	Significance/Difference	+13	-24	* -56
Libra	Actual Applicants to Study	1871	3368	1009
	Expected Applicants to Study	1886	3444	1015
	Significance/Difference	-15	-76	-6
Scorpio	Actual Applicants to Study	1723	3103	966
	Expected Applicants to Study	1726	3151	929
	Significance/Difference	-3	-48	+37
Sagittarius	Actual Applicants to Study	1742	3151	962
	Expected Applicants to Study	1743	3182	938
	Significance/Difference	-1	-31	+24
Capricorn	Actual Applicants to Study	1666	2988	930
	Expected Applicants to Study	1708	3118	919
	Significance/Difference	-42	** -130	+11
Aquarius	Actual Applicants to Study	1811	3416	984
	Expected Applicants to Study	1836	3352	988
	Significance/Difference	-25	+64	-4
Pisces	Actual Applicants to Study	1896	3381	1008
	Expected Applicants to Study	1877	3426	1010
	Significance/Difference	+19	-45	-2

Law	Medicine	Psychology	Pharma-ceutics	Veterinary medicine	Economics	Dentistry
4869	3601	2278	768	444	584	635
4975	3555	2395	741	448	580	569
* -106	+46	** -117	+27	-4	+4	** +66
4985	3712	2600	775	435	624	573
5144	3675	2476	766	463	600	588
* -159	+37	** +124	+9	-28	+24	-15
4857	3426	2475	681	451	559	557
4931	3523	2374	734	444	575	564
-74	-97	** +101	* -53	+7	-16	-7
5136	3680	2526	772	468	591	630
5183	3703	2495	772	467	604	592
-47	-23	+31	0	+1	-13	* +38
4986	3453	2245	758	424	551	504
4882	3488	2350	727	440	569	558
* +104	-35	-105	* +31	-16	-18	-54
4836	3500	2154	680	406	546	601
4748	3392	2286	707	428	554	543
+88	* +108	** -132	-27	-22	-8	** +58
4988	3375	2231	703	436	522	466
4736	3384	2280	705	427	552	541
*** +252	-9	-49	-2	+9	-30	*** -75
4387	3065	2026	664	385	514	523
4333	3096	2086	645	390	505	495
+54	-31	* -60	+19	-5	+9	+28
4396	3110	2060	640	443	548	478
4376	3127	2107	651	394	510	500
+20	-17	-47	-11	** +49	+38	-22
4311	3165	2067	612	413	522	501
4288	3064	2064	638	386	500	490
+23	+101	+3	-26	+27	+22	+11
4494	3253	2353	687	431	522	513
4610	3294	2219	686	415	538	527
* -116	-41	** +134	+1	+16	-16	-14
4673	3328	2387	733	392	554	523
4712	3367	2296	701	425	549	538
-39	-39	** +91	+32	* -33	+5	-15

▢ positive ■ negative   * slightly significant   ** significant   *** highly significant

We created a two-dimensional table of 12 × 10 fields of the twelve star signs and the ten degree courses. Here we listed the already-known actual values of the star sign-subject combinations.

Using the chi-square test of independence (*see* page 46), we determined whether we could sustain the hypothesis that the choice of studies was completely independent of star sign. The odds were less than 1 in 10,000,000, that is to say we could safely assume a correlation between choice of degree course and star sign.

As a next step, in order to discover which degree subject showed particularly significant deviations from the distribution of the population under review, we also carried out a chi-square test of goodness of fit (*see* page 45).

We had taken 'potential university entrants' as the population of our study. That is, people born in Germany between 1966 and 1976, classified by star sign.

Results showed that for psychology, medicine, law, business management and architecture, there was a highly significant deviation between the distribution of university applicants and that of potential university entrants. The deviations for dentistry and pharmaceutics were significant.

After this preliminary investigation, it seemed worth our while to do a detailed analysis. Following the usual routine, we worked out the mathematical expectation for each of the 120 fields of our table and then compared them with the actual values. The deviations between actual values and mathematical expectations were tested for their level of significance. Two of these deviations were highly significant, ten were significant and fifteen slightly significant.

This means that almost one in four star sign-subject combinations showed significant deviations from the distribution expected, if in fact there is no correlation between star sign and choice of academic subject.

You can clearly see preferences for certain subjects and antipathy towards others from the tables on pages 116 and 117.

So our study demonstrated there is a definite statistically provable correlation between star sign and choice of degree course.

Two other aspects interested us: who is most strongly drawn towards an Alma Mater? And which star signs are under-represented among university candidates?

When we compared the distribution of star signs among applicants for university places and potential university entrants born between 1966 and 1976, as the table on page 120 shows, we found the following:

The number of students born under Taurus, Cancer, Libra and Sagittarius and applying for university entrance was greater than expected.

Conversely, Aries, Gemini and Capricorn candidates were under-represented.

SUMMARY
The subject of the investigation was the correlation between star signs and the choice of degree course. The survey was based on data relating to 231,036 university applicants. Among the ten subject areas there were twenty-seven significant deviations. The influence of chance elements on the observed deviations can be excluded with odds of 1:10,000,000.

Who is keen to study?

Star sign	Number of births for years 1966 - 1976	Percentage of births for for years 1966 - 1976	Actual applicants to study	Expected applicants to study	Deviation from expected figure in percent (see graphic)	Degree of significance
Aries	674.142	9,12 %	19.929	20.782	-4,28 %	*** -
Taurus	644.898	8,72 %	20.604	19.880	+3,51 %	*** +
Gemini	678.693	9,18 %	19.753	20.922	-5,92 %	*** -
Cancer	645.425	8,73 %	20.762	19.896	+4,17 %	*** +
Leo	644.432	8,71 %	19.554	19.866	-1,59 %	neutral
Virgo	623.665	8,43 %	19.017	19.225	-1,10 %	neutral
Libra	575.727	7,78 %	18.969	17.748	+6,44 %	*** +
Scorpio	564.443	7,63 %	17.356	17.400	-0,25 %	neutral
Sagittarius	545.710	7,38 %	17.530	16.822	+4,04 %	*** +
Capricorn	586.155	7,93 %	17.175	18.069	-5,21 %	*** -
Aquarius	608.864	8,23 %	18.464	18.769	-1,65 %	neutral
Pisces	603.662	8,16 %	18.875	18.609	+1,41 %	neutral
	7.395.816	100,00 %	227.988	227.988		

* slightly significant   ** significant   *** highly significant

Deviation of actual applicants to study from expected applicants to study in percent

Actual applicants to study: 227.988

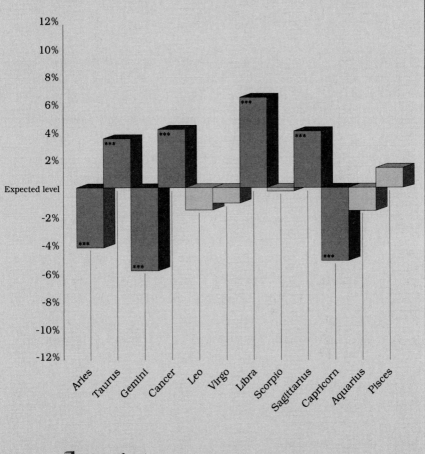

THE ASTROLOGICAL ANGLE

We were amused by some of the inconsistencies we found. Why are so many Virgos attracted to medicine and dentistry, while relatively few opt for biology?

Does it have something to do with the liking for healthy competition that astrological literature attributes to Virgo?

Other results are also well in line with the traits of particular star signs. So it comes as no surprise that Libras with their sense of justice and their talent for balanced judgement are significantly over-represented among law students.

And if there is some mysterious force that drives people born under particular signs towards or away from certain academic disciplines, it is only natural that psychology, a subject on which opinions are dramatically divided, should show the most frequent deviations. No doubt as a choice of degree course, psychology is much more closely bound up with the nature of the student's personality than, for example, the sort of courses that qualify people to earn a steady living. Business management or pharmaceutics, for example, showed only very slightly significant deviations.

6

WHO DOES WHICH JOB?

'Man's greatest problem is to know how properly
to achieve his place in Creation.'

Immanuel Kant (1724–1804)

One of the most important stages in finding one's place in the
scheme of things is one's occupation. Having a trade or profession is what distinguishes us from the animals.

But what was the first-ever form of employment? Was it
the woman who diddled the hunter of a part of his kill for
extramarital services? Maybe it was precisely for that reason
that men went out hunting in the first place. We can only
guess how and why men and women first chose particular
jobs. In any case, it seems to have had something to do with
enjoyment, and special skills.

The word 'profession' used to mean a 'vocation' in the
ethical sense. It meant something different from random
gainful employment.

Meanwhile, the boundaries between 'profession' and 'job'
have become more flexible. As a rule, both provide a means
of earning a living and achieving material comfort.

'He who does not teach his child a trade is teaching him
to steal', warns an old Persian saying. And an English
proverb follows up with 'He who changes his trade makes
soup in a basket'. Article 23 of the United Nations General

Declaration of Human Rights guarantees all people freedom in their choice of occupation, including the right to choose freely between one place of employment or training and another.

Nevertheless it is becoming increasingly hard for young people to find their 'vocation'. And yet there are few things in life that afford a person so much pride as knowing that he or she is doing a good job.

'An occupation is the backbone of life', said German philosopher Friedrich Nietzsche. 'Men seldom endure an occupation in which they do not believe or which they cannot convince themselves is basically more important than all others. Women regard their lovers in the same way.'

So who does which job?

ANALYSIS

After discovering the correlation between star sign and choice of degree subject, we were interested in finding out whether there was an affinity between people born under certain star signs and particular types of trade or profession.

We based our research into this topic on the 1990 Swiss census mentioned in a previous chapter. First of all citizens were not asked to state the type of work they did, but the status they had achieved at work.

Of the 6,873 million questioned, 4,369 million replied about their professional status. The remainder who replied 'not applicable' consisted of non-earners (pensioners, housewives, young children, students and the unemployed).

Among those who did reply, we did not take into consideration apprentices, people employed in family businesses and certain others whose work status was hard to classify, but these omissions were of no consequence in terms of numbers.

Nearly 93 per cent of the respondents, exactly 4,045,170 could be placed in one of the following categories:

- Self-employed (entrepreneurs, freelancers, farmers): 486,469 people
- Executive (directors, managers, senior civil servants): 234,807 people
- Middle management (office managers, workshop managers, branch managers, supervisors, site foremen): 736,392 people
- White-collar/blue-collar workers: 2,587,502

Briefly, we followed the familiar procedure:

We created a two-dimensional table with 12×4 cells, listing the actual value for the 48 possible star sign/professional status combinations. With the help of the chi-square test of independence (*see* page 46) we first tested whether the distribution of numbers over the 48 fields was consistent with the hypothesis of independence between star sign and professional status. The probability that such independence existed was less than 1 in 10,000,000. The result was clear:

There was an obvious correlation between the two characteristics.

The individual analysis followed, first working out the mathematical expectations, then comparing the actual values with mathematical expectations, and finally testing the significance of deviations.

We soon came up with a result: comparison of actual value and mathematical expectation in a total of forty-eight fields in our table revealed fifteen highly significant and four significant deviations.

As the table opposite confirms:

There is an obvious correlation between star sign and professional status.

As well as asking citizens about their professional status, the census asked them to state their actual occupation. Those no longer in work were asked to give their last job. Although no one was obliged to answer this question, 3,590,913 people did supply information.

We limited our evaluation to the forty-seven most frequently named occupations which provided the largest population. It would not have made much sense to categorize 324 poultry breeders or 203 professional hunters according to their star signs; the numbers in the separate fields would have been far too small to be able to draw any meaningful conclusion.

In evaluating the forty-seven occupations, the chi-square test of independence (*see* page 46) showed a highly significant correlation between star sign and occupation.

The individual analysis of the 564 field tables (12 × 47 fields), showed up forty-three highly significant and thirty-four significant deviations between actual value and mathematical expectation, as well as seventy-three noteworthy cases (*see* page 45). In over a quarter of the fields there were at least slightly significant degrees of deviation. These are summarized in the tables on pages 130–137).

Who does which job? (status)

		Self-employed	Executive	Middle management	White collar/ blue collar
Aries	Actual Workers	45.437	21.490	67.898	232.204
	Expected Workers	44.453	21.455	67.287	233.964
	Significance/Difference	*** +984	+35	+611	*** -1760
Taurus	Actual Workers	42.835	20.719	64.714	220.491
	Expected Workers	42.279	20.406	63.996	222.522
	Significance/Difference	+556	+313	+718	*** -2031
Gemini	Actual Workers	43.153	21.431	66.768	224.987
	Expected Workers	43.166	20.834	65.340	227.193
	Significance/Difference	-13	*** +597	*** +1428	*** -2206
Cancer	Actual Workers	40.930	20.352	62.372	211.883
	Expected Workers	40.723	19.655	61.642	214.335
	Significance/Difference	+207	*** +697	+730	***-2452
Leo	Actual Workers	40.903	20.298	62.478	215.650
	Expected Workers	41.095	19.834	62.205	216.294
	Significance/Difference	-192	*** +464	+273	** -644
Virgo	Actual Workers	39.504	19.498	60.309	211.313
	Expected Workers	40.002	19.307	60.550	210.538
	Significance/Difference	** -498	+191	-241	+775
Libra	Actual Workers	37.716	18.420	57.909	206.098
	Expected Workers	38.683	18.670	58.553	203.599
	Significance/Difference	** -967	-250	-644	*** +2499
Scorpio	Actual Workers	36.620	17.378	54.371	193.715
	Expected Workers	36.547	17.639	55.320	192.354
	Significance/Difference	73	-261	** -949	*** +1361
Sagittarius	Actual Workers	35.414	16.788	52.940	186.277
	Expected Workers	35.306	17.040	53.442	185.825
	Significance/Difference	+108	-252	-502	+452
Capricorn	Actual Workers	38.806	18.555	58.457	212.152
	Expected Workers	39.613	19.119	59.962	208.493
	Significance/Difference	-807	-564	-1505	*** +3659
Aquarius	Actual Workers	42.384	19.744	63.531	221.253
	Expected Workers	41.976	20.260	63.539	220.931
	Significance/Difference	*** +408	*** -516	-8	+322
Pisces	Actual Workers	42.914	20.134	64.645	224.479
	Expected Workers	42.646	20.583	64.552	224.453
	Significance/Difference	+268	*** -449	+93	+26

☐ positive ■ negative * slightly significant ** significant *** highly significant

SUMMARY
The correlation between star signs and the choice of occupation was examined. The survey was based on data taken from the 1990 Swiss census relating to 4,045,170 working men and women. Of the forty-seven occupations examined, seventy-seven showed significant deviations and seventy-three 'noteworthy' cases. The influence of chance elements on the observed deviations can be excluded with odds of 1:10,000,000.

THE ASTROLOGICAL ANGLE

When interpreting the results, a degree of caution is advised. For example, the fact that people born under the star sign of Leo are significantly over-represented among senior salaried employees, while there are significantly few Leos among ordinary workers and employees suggests that Leos are born leaders.

This isn't necessarily so! The replies given to the Federal Office of Statistics in Berne were based on the respondent's own assessment. It may be that reputedly status-conscious Leos embellished their answers or, like Willy Loman in Arthur Miller's *Death of a Salesman*, over-estimated the importance of their jobs. This would, by the way, also be evidence of the influence of other star signs.

The opposite could apply to people born under Capricorn,

whom astrologers credit with orderliness and a sense of reality. Capricorns are over-represented among ordinary white- and blue-collar workers – but maybe this is only because they are under no illusions, or because they were particularly conscientious in filling out the census questionnaire.

These considerations – as well as the multiple test problem – led us to consider possible fluctuations with more circumspection and to denote slightly significant results as merely 'noteworthy'.

Readers interested in astrology will not be surprised by the evaluation of individual occupations, which shows that people born under certain star signs are significantly more likely to be found in certain professions, such as:

- creative Taureans in architecture
- art-loving Librans in interior design
- sensitive Pisceans in caring professions

Conversely, there was no confirmation of the generally accepted astrological theory that tidy-minded Capricornians are most frequently found in banking and insurance.

Among farmers there is a distinct parting of the ways according to star sign. Farming is a crowded occupation in terms of numbers, and so our results are especially meaningful. We found ten highly significant and one significant deviation among the twelve star signs.

Far more farmers than expected were born under the signs of Aries, Sagittarius, Capricorn, Aquarius and Pisces (all highly significant). Meanwhile, there was a highly significant under-representation of farmers born under Gemini, Cancer, Leo, Virgo and Libra, while Taureans were significantly under-represented.

		Farmer	Gard-ener	Florist	Baker	Tailor
Aries	Actual Workers	10289	1961	497	1566	879
	Expected Workers	9740	2026	540	1627	866
	Significance/Difference	*** +549	-65	° -43	-61	+13
Taurus	Actual Workers	8963	1878	513	1452	826
	Expected Workers	9196	1913	510	1536	818
	Significance/Difference	** -233	-35	+3	** -84	+8
Gemini	Actual Workers	8790	1933	518	1647	802
	Expected Workers	9358	1947	519	1563	832
	Significance/Difference	*** -568	-14	-1	+84	-30
Cancer	Actual Workers	8195	1812	474	1500	743
	Expected Workers	8802	1831	488	1470	783
	Significance/Difference	*** -607	-19	-14	+30	° -40
Leo	Actual Workers	8245	1793	503	1505	710
	Expected Workers	8816	1834	489	1473	784
	Significance/Difference	*** -571	-41	+14	+32	** -74
Virgo	Actual Workers	7952	1739	474	1428	732
	Expected Workers	8532	1775	473	1425	759
	Significance/Difference	*** -580	-36	+1	+3	-27
Libra	Actual Workers	7762	1725	470	1480	778
	Expected Workers	8192	1704	454	1368	729
	Significance/Difference	*** -430	+21	+16	*** +112	° +49
Scorpio	Actual Workers	7614	1585	428	1414	756
	Expected Workers	7736	1609	429	1292	688
	Significance/Difference	-122	-24	-1	*** +122	** +68
Sagittarius	Actual Workers	7855	1659	421	1274	687
	Expected Workers	7536	1568	418	1259	670
	Significance/Difference	*** +319	** +91	+3	+15	+17
Capricorn	Actual Workers	8847	1886	473	1402	772
	Expected Workers	8477	1763	470	1416	754
	Significance/Difference	*** +370	*** +123	+3	-14	+18
Aquarius	Actual Workers	10326	1912	523	1412	823
	Expected Workers	9170	1908	509	1532	816
	Significance/Difference	***+1156	+4	+14	** -120	+7
Pisces	Actual Workers	10069	1940	524	1444	824
	Expected Workers	9351	1945	519	1562	832
	Significance/Difference	*** +718	-5	+5	** -118	-8

Carpenter	Brick Layer	Painter	Fitter/Metalworker	Mechanical Engineer	Auto Mechanic	Cabinet Maker
1272	4225	2661	1234	4532	2463	469
1288	4394	2724	1298	4559	2489	464
-16	° -169	-63	-64	-27	-26	5
1167	3970	2486	1252	4224	2394	444
1216	4148	2572	1226	4305	2350	438
° -49	*** -178	° -86	+26	° -81	44	6
1215	4096	2514	1206	4221	2415	457
1237	4221	2617	1247	4380	2391	445
-22	*** -125	** -103	° -41	*** -159	+24	+12
1159	3628	2469	1137	4022	2306	420
1164	3971	2462	1173	4120	2249	419
-5	*** -343	+7	° -36	** -98	+57	+1
1161	3805	2607	1202	4090	2220	412
1166	3977	2465	1175	4127	2253	420
-5	*** -172	** +142	+27	-37	-33	-8
1157	4059	2475	1201	4041	2257	419
1128	3848	2386	1137	3994	2180	406
+29	*** +211	° +89	° +64	+47	+77	+13
1071	4006	2452	1138	3794	2085	438
1083	3695	2291	1092	3834	2093	390
-12	*** +311	*** +161	+46	-40	-8	** +48
1036	3711	2291	1044	3636	1943	348
1023	3489	2163	1031	3621	1976	368
+13	*** +222	*** +128	+13	+15	-33	-20
963	3518	2160	928	3608	1915	372
996	3399	2108	1005	3528	1925	359
-33	** +119	° +52	° -77	° +80	-10	+13
1198	4047	2347	1186	4094	2090	361
1121	3824	2370	1130	3968	2166	403
** +77	*** +223	-23	° +56	** +126	-76	° -42
1188	4089	2407	1187	4338	2346	401
1212	4136	2564	1222	4292	2343	436
-24	-47	** -157	-35	+46	+3	° -35
1282	4167	2468	1269	4506	2369	452
1236	4218	2615	1246	4377	2389	445
° +46	-51	** -147	+23	** +129	-20	+7

positive ■ negative ° noteworthy case ** significant *** highly significant

		Carpenter/ Furniture Maker	Architect	Architectural Draughtsman/ Woman	Bank Clerk
Aries	Actual Workers	3335	1552	1521	462
	Expected Workers	3242	1551	1554	476
	Significance/Difference	° +93	+1	-33	° -14
Taurus	Actual Workers	3067	1569	1542	448
	Expected Workers	3061	1465	1467	449
	Significance/Difference	+6	** +104	° +75	-1
Gemini	Actual Workers	3126	1543	1546	474
	Expected Workers	3114	1490	1493	457
	Significance/Difference	+12	+53	+53	+16
Cancer	Actual Workers	2887	1428	1406	453
	Expected Workers	2930	1402	1405	430
	Significance/Difference	° -43	+26	+1	° +22
Leo	Actual Workers	2914	1451	1402	439
	Expected Workers	2934	1404	1407	431
	Significance/Difference	-20	+47	-5	+8
Virgo	Actual Workers	2857	1396	1400	417
	Expected Workers	2839	1359	1361	417
	Significance/Difference	+18	+37	+39	+
Libra	Actual Workers	2790	1277	1236	413
	Expected Workers	2726	1305	1307	400
	Significance/Difference	+64	-28	° -71	° +12
Scorpio	Actual Workers	2671	1205	1186	373
	Expected Workers	2575	1232	1234	378
	Significance/Difference	° +96	-27	-48	-5
Sagittarius	Actual Workers	2549	1158	1137	372
	Expected Workers	2508	1200	1203	368
	Significance/Difference	+41	-42	-66	+3
Capricorn	Actual Workers	2797	1286	1389	405
	Expected Workers	2821	1350	1353	414
	Significance/Difference	-24	-64	+36	-9
Aquarius	Actual Workers	2937	1405	1521	431
	Expected Workers	3052	1460	1463	448
	Significance/Difference	° -115	-55	° +58	° -17
Pisces	Actual Workers	2984	1437	1453	440
	Expected Workers	3112	1489	1492	457
	Significance/Difference	° -128	-52	-39	° -16

Insurance Broker	Marketing	Tax C'sul- tant	Company Owner	Book- Keeper	Computer Scientist	Computer Programmer	Post Office Official
995	410	436	10190	2317	1507	989	948
996	398	465	10137	2409	1498	1042	938
-1	+12	-29	+53	° -92	+9	-53	+10
925	387	440	9667	2306	1415	972	880
941	376	439	9571	2274	1415	984	886
-16	+11	+1	+96	+32	0	-12	-6
955	417	474	9698	2345	1530	988	853
957	382	446	9739	2314	1440	1001	902
-2	+35	+28	° -41	+31	° +90	-13	° -49
914	355	438	9215	2241	1409	946	853
900	360	420	9161	2177	1354	942	848
+14	-5	+18	+54	+64	+55	+4	+5
920	369	438	9534	2221	1345	980	877
902	360	421	9175	2180	1356	943	849
+18	+9	+17	*** +359	+41	-11	+37	+28
938	361	407	9096	2198	1215	950	857
873	348	407	8879	2110	1313	913	822
° +65	+13	0	° +217	° +88	** -98	+37	+35
868	313	389	8542	2057	1268	861	771
838	335	391	8525	2026	1260	876	789
+30	-22	-2	+17	+31	+8	-15	-18
809	305	354	8120	1998	1214	880	758
791	316	369	8050	1913	1190	827	745
+18	-11	-15	+70	° +85	+24	° +53	+13
708	313	381	7837	1867	1196	822	718
771	308	359	7843	1864	1159	806	726
° -63	+5	+22	-6	+3	+37	+16	-8
799	354	401	8626	2018	1336	884	826
867	346	404	8821	2096	1304	907	817
° -68	+8	-3	-195	-78	+32	-23	+9
951	347	412	9162	2157	1318	967	866
938	375	437	9543	2268	1411	981	883
+13	-28	-25	*** -381	° -111	**-93	-14	-17
949	354	434	9488	2217	1386	982	900
956	382	446	9731	2312	1439	1000	901
-7	-28	-12	-243	-95	-53	-18	-1

☐ positive ■ negative   ° noteworthy case ** significant *** highly significant

		Policeman	Lawyer	Journalist	Musicia
Aries	Actual Workers	1344	584	808	409
	Expected Workers	1349	586	839	390
	Significance/Difference	-5	-2	-31	+19
Taurus	Actual Workers	1298	587	824	383
	Expected Workers	1274	553	793	368
	Significance/Difference	+24	+34	+31	+15
Gemini	Actual Workers	1236	603	864	395
	Expected Workers	1296	563	806	375
	Significance/Difference	** -60	+40	° +58	+20
Cancer	Actual Workers	1250	532	795	371
	Expected Workers	1219	529	759	352
	Significance/Difference	+31	+3	+36	+19
Leo	Actual Workers	1266	535	748	353
	Expected Workers	1221	530	760	353
	Significance/Difference	+45	+5	-12	0
Virgo	Actual Workers	1172	517	749	302
	Expected Workers	1182	513	735	341
	Significance/Difference	-10	+4	+14	° -39
Libra	Actual Workers	1053	506	724	317
	Expected Workers	1135	492	706	328
	Significance/Difference	** -82	+14	+18	-11
Scorpio	Actual Workers	1056	472	601	301
	Expected Workers	1071	465	667	310
	Significance/Difference	-15	+7	** -66	-9
Sagittarius	Actual Workers	1073	401	637	280
	Expected Workers	1044	453	649	302
	Significance/Difference	+29	° -52	-12	-22
Capricorn	Actual Workers	1206	506	712	348
	Expected Workers	1174	510	731	339
	Significance/Difference	+32	-4	-19	+9
Aquarius	Actual Workers	1279	525	799	378
	Expected Workers	1270	551	790	367
	Significance/Difference	+9	-26	+9	+11
Pisces	Actual Workers	1297	538	780	362
	Expected Workers	1295	562	806	374
	Significance/Difference	+2	-24	-26	-12

Part 3)

Decora-tor	Interior Designer	Hotel Manager	Hair-dresser	Doctor (Gen.Pract.)	Physio-therapist	Dentist	Paediatric Nurse
427	456	3226	2271	1905	686	398	466
433	470	3234	2344	1951	722	400	443
-6	-14	-8	-73	-46	-36	-2	+23
414	435	2974	2190	1959	669	402	435
409	444	3053	2213	1842	682	377	419
+5	-9	° -79	-23	** +117	-13	+25	+16
404	461	3108	2254	1997	716	387	452
416	452	3107	2252	1875	694	384	426
-12	+9	+1	+2	° +122	+22	+3	+26
402	434	2916	2188	1835	644	389	410
391	425	2923	2118	1763	653	361	401
+11	+9	-7	+70	+72	-9	+28	+9
389	416	2980	2162	1804	629	369	395
392	426	2927	2121	1766	654	362	401
-3	-10	+53	+41	+38	-25	+7	-6
376	443	2885	2094	1649	621	346	366
379	412	2833	2053	1709	632	350	388
-3	+31	+52	+41	-60	-11	-4	-22
403	428	2795	2092	1537	586	305	361
364	396	2720	1971	1641	607	336	373
° +39	° +32	+75	** +121	** -104	-21	° -31	-12
378	371	2622	2044	1569	601	311	337
344	374	2568	1861	1550	573	317	352
° +34	-3	+54	*** +183	+19	+28	-6	-15
345	374	2530	1873	1402	554	312	323
335	364	2502	1813	1510	559	309	343
+10	+10	+28	° +60	** -108	-5	+3	-20
349	416	2780	1939	1657	586	341	392
377	409	2814	2040	1698	628	348	386
-28	+7	-34	° -101	-41	-42	-7	+6
396	390	2956	2055	1786	766	353	419
408	443	3045	2207	1837	680	376	417
-12	** -53	-89	*** -152	-51	*** +86	-23	+2
381	443	3060	2081	1916	719	390	420
416	452	3105	2250	1873	693	384	426
-35	-9	-45	*** -169	+43	+26	+6	-6

☐ positive ■ negative   ° noteworthy case ** significant *** highly significant

		Nurse	Social Worker	Teacher	Vicar
Aries	Actual Worker	5234	599	866	384
	Expected Worker	5172	586	853	426
	Significance/Difference	+62	+13	+13	° -42
Taurus	Actual Worker	4799	524	799	408
	Expected Worker	4883	553	805	402
	Significance/Difference	° -84	-29	-6	+6
Gemini	Actual Worker	5079	556	815	448
	Expected Worker	4969	563	820	409
	Significance/Difference	+110	-7	-5	° +39
Cancer	Actual Worker	4667	611	856	401
	Expected Worker	4674	530	771	385
	Significance/Difference	-7	*** +81	** +85	+16
Leo	Actual Worker	4699	500	791	379
	Expected Worker	4682	530	772	386
	Significance/Difference	+17	-30	+19	-7
Virgo	Actual Worker	4447	525	727	371
	Expected Worker	4530	513	747	373
	Significance/Difference	-83	+12	-20	-2
Libra	Actual Worker	4285	475	659	359
	Expected Worker	4350	493	717	358
	Significance/Difference	-65	-18	° -58	+1
Scorpio	Actual Worker	4004	456	616	323
	Expected Worker	4108	465	678	338
	Significance/Difference	-104	-9	° -62	-15
Sagittarius	Actual Worker	4014	422	660	313
	Expected Worker	4002	453	660	330
	Significance/Difference	+12	-31	0	-17
Capricorn	Actual Worker	4538	491	717	359
	Expected Worker	4501	510	742	371
	Significance/Difference	+37	-19	-25	-12
Aquarius	Actual Worker	4824	598	855	412
	Expected Worker	4870	552	803	401
	Significance/Difference	-46	° +46	° +52	+11
Pisces	Actual Worker	5117	554	827	433
	Expected Worker	4965	563	819	409
	Significance/Difference	** +152	-9	+8	+24

University Teacher	High School Teacher	Further Education Teacher	Primary School Teacher	Kinder-garten-Teacher	Psycho-logist	Chemist
433	726	963	4283	856	332	483
425	728	975	4063	830	329	447
+8	-2	-12	*** +220	+26	+3	° +36
399	703	1020	4023	848	285	432
402	687	921	3836	783	311	422
-3	+16	*** +99	** +187	° +65	-26	+10
459	692	1001	4011	758	348	434
409	699	937	3903	797	316	429
° +50	-7	° +64	+108	° -39	° +32	+5
390	694	929	3734	761	322	414
384	658	881	3671	750	298	404
+6	+36	+48	+63	+11	+24	+10
376	662	874	3650	747	318	421
385	659	883	3677	751	298	404
-9	+3	-9	-27	-4	+20	+17
380	615	790	3409	719	282	390
373	638	854	3558	727	288	391
+7	-23	° -64	° -149	-8	-6	-1
337	635	728	3212	703	264	382
358	612	820	3416	698	277	376
-21	+23	*** -92	*** -204	+5	-13	+6
330	542	656	2866	573	235	384
338	578	775	3226	659	261	355
-8	-36	*** -119	*** -360	*** -86	-26	° +29
329	505	671	2861	623	244	354
329	563	755	3143	642	255	346
0	° -58	** -84	*** -282	-19	-11	+8
371	649	846	3483	685	261	356
370	634	849	3535	722	287	389
+1	+15	-3	-52	-37	-26	-33
417	719	1014	4032	794	347	374
400	685	918	3825	781	310	421
+17	+34	*** +96	*** +207	+13	** +37	° -47
360	699	1013	4190	867	308	387
408	699	936	3900	796	316	429
* -48	0	*** +77	*** +290	** +71	-8	° -42

☐ positive ■ negative   ° noteworthy case ** significant *** highly significant

What was extraordinarily striking was that these signs all occur side by side: on the one hand, Sagittarius through to Aries are farmers, while Taurus through to Libra are non-farmers. The only agriculturally neutral sign, Scorpio, stands between these two groups.

This gives rise to a whole series of fascinating speculations, but we could prove nothing. All we can say here is that we simply found it extremely curious.

We were so captivated by the 'farming mystery' that we would be tempted to pursue it. Nevertheless, we suspected that investigating the phenomenon would take us on a very long detour. Another time, perhaps.

7

WHO DIES OF WHAT?

'How disease may be recognized through astrological calculation and without inspecting urine.'

Title of a manuscript by Gilbertus Anglicus (c. AD 1200)

The 'Father of Medicine', Hippocrates (*c.* 460–350 BC), is credited with the words: 'The doctor who knows nothing of astrology is an ignoramus.'

Swiss physician, astrologer and alchemist Paracelsus (1493–1541) is quoted as saying: 'A doctor who understands nothing of astrology should better be called a fool than a doctor.' Today, however, the doctor who knows a little about astrology is often branded a gullible fool.

The alliance between the art of star-gazing and the art of healing, or the marriage between magic and medicine, dates back thousands of years. It is based on the assumption that the human organism – or microcosm – corresponds with the universal organism – or macrocosm. The traditional theory is that our limbs, and sensory and internal organs are ruled by different signs and planets – as are animals and plants, precious stones, drugs and metals.

The Ancient Egyptians were convinced 'that Man is identical to the natural world'. According to the Ancient Greeks, Mars caused fevers and inflammation, diseases of the reproductive organs were induced by Venus and mental illness by the Moon. The word 'lunatic' is still sometimes used to describe the mentally sick. And, indeed, there is scientific evidence that life on earth is affected by lunar cycles.

In the late Middle Ages, Paracelsus, *see* page 27, conjectured that cosmic forces produced human characteristics. These in turn caused disease: 'Envy disturbs the functioning of the gall bladder . . . jealousy leads to trembling of the muscles and joints . . . selfishness affects the stomach . . . meanness cramps the intestines . . .' Today, many homeopaths and natural healers still adhere to these beliefs. And, like astrology and other esoteric practices, astromedicine has taken on a new lease of life in this century.

In his book on astromedicine, astropharmacy and astrodiatetics (published in 1931) Friedbert Asboga warned people born under Aries to take care when nodding their heads. Capricornians were advised that the lower leg was a weak point and they should watch out for twisted knees. This rather ludicrous advice is based on tradition, for Aries is said to rule the head, while Capricorn rules the knees.

There is not much reliable data round about nodding Arians or weak-kneed Capricornians. What did interest us, though, was whether there was any significant relationship between specific star signs and fatal illnesses.

ANALYSIS

We thought long and hard about whether it made any sense at all to explore the phenomenon of astromedicine and its validity using statistical methods. Our main problem was that we could not get hold of much in the way of reliable data on illnesses and star signs, arranged according to standardized guidelines that could be reproduced at any time.

An American clinic specializing in the treatment of knee injuries supplied us with the star signs of several hundred patients. However, this did not give us enough material from which to derive any useful findings. And even it it had, it would only have told us about one very specific complaint.

This meant that we had to approach the subject from another angle. All civilized countries keep comprehensive mortality statistics, stating causes of death. If we limited ourselves to looking at only those cases where a recognizable disease proved fatal, we would then be on rather firmer ground.

We based our study on data relating to all men and women who died in Switzerland between 1969 and 1994, categorized by star sign, and also divided according to thirty-two different causes of death. Altogether this information covered 1,195,174 deaths.

On the recommendation of the statisticians advising us, we made some additional adjustments to this large amount of data before starting our investigation. Rare causes of death which, because of their sparse numbers, would not provide any useful results were discarded. We also disregarded those which, from the point of view of astromedicine, would have little or no meaning. These included deaths caused by fatal complications in pregnancy or childbirth, or deaths resulting from acts of violence.

In this way the data was reduced to 20 causes of death among 657,492 deceased persons, whose dates of birth and star signs we knew.

Once again, we draw up a two-dimensional table with 12 × 20 fields. We noted how often each combination of star sign and cause of death occurred during the twenty-six-year period under review.

The chi-square test of independence (*see* page 46), produced a probability value of 0.0037. This meant that the probability that the various causes of death were spread throughout the twelve star signs purely by chance was less than 0.37 per cent, or 1 in 127. We can, therefore, confidently reject the hypothesis that there is no correlation between birth sign and cause of death. There is little risk that we might be wrong.

Separate analysis of the deviations between actual values and mathematical expectations over all 240 fields of our table revealed one deviation which was highly significant, four which were significant, and twenty-five noteworthy cases. In other words, 12.5 per cent of all combinations of star sign and cause of death showed significant correlations.

The results are shown in full in the tables on pages 144–147.

Naturally, the raw material was somewhat imprecise.

We have, nevertheless, devoted a separate chapter to the correlation between star signs and illness/cause of death, because as far as we are aware, this is the first wide-ranging study of this topic. After all, it is based on information about nearly 700,000 deaths gathered by an official institution over a twenty-six-year period.

SUMMARY
The subject of the investigation was the correlation between star signs and causes of death. The survey was based on data relating to 657,492 people who died between 1969 and 1994. Among the twenty causes of death there were five significant deviations and twenty-five 'noteworthy' cases. The influence of chance elements on the observed deviations can be excluded with odds of 1:270.

THE ASTROLOGICAL ANGLE

Astrology books are very reticent with their forecasts about illnesses. They prefer to talk about 'physical correspondences' because, traditionally, each sign rules a different part of the body. If we understand this correctly, it means that in Taureans, for example, the throat, neck, mouth and gullet are the strongest, but also most vulnerable parts of the body. Taurus 'rules' this area in medical astrology.

We believe that such statements have a great deal to do with ancient folklore. Diseases and their manifestations changed over thousands of years, or they were differently diagnosed. Before Columbus discovered the New World, there were no smokers in the Old World, and as doctors tell us, throat cancer barely existed. In the nineteenth century no one knew about the damage to health caused by asbestos. When Brigitte Bardot made *And God Created Woman*,

		AIDS	Alcoholic Cirrhosis of the Liver	Asthma	Bronchi
Aries	Actual Deaths	279	1202	477	1823
	Expected Deaths	280	1153	471	1812
	Significance/Difference	-1	° +49	+6	+11
Taurus	Actual Deaths	258	1095	444	1722
	Expected Deaths	266	1096	448	1723
	Significance/Difference	-8	-1	-4	-1
Gemini	Actual Deaths	294	1143	463	1739
	Expected Deaths	274	1126	460	1770
	Significance/Difference	+20	+17	+3	-31
Cancer	Actual Deaths	264	1078	468	1688
	Expected Deaths	263	1081	442	1699
	Significance/Difference	+1	-3	+26	-11
Leo	Actual Deaths	257	1132	466	1690
	Expected Deaths	273	1122	459	1764
	Significance/Difference	-16	+10	+7	-74
Virgo	Actual Deaths	238	1122	418	1692
	Expected Deaths	264	1087	444	1709
	Significance/Difference	-26	+35	-26	-17
Libra	Actual Deaths	265	1014	422	1608
	Expected Deaths	252	1036	423	1629
	Significance/Difference	+13	-22	-1	-21
Scorpio	Actual Deaths	246	946	390	1555
	Expected Deaths	242	998	408	1568
	Significance/Difference	+4	° -52	-18	-13
Sagittarius	Actual Deaths	241	931	381	1499
	Expected Deaths	232	956	391	1502
	Significance/Difference	+9	-25	-10	-3
Capricorn	Actual Deaths	242	1010	415	1674
	Expected Deaths	251	1032	422	1622
	Significance/Difference	-9	-22	-7	+52
Aquarius	Actual Deaths	275	1082	445	1806
	Expected Deaths	265	1091	446	1715
	Significance/Difference	+10	-9	-1	° +91
Pisces	Actual Deaths	271	1124	474	1748
	Expected Deaths	267	1100	450	1729
	Significance/Difference	+4	+24	+24	+19

144

(Part 1)

Breast Cancer	Cancer of the Uterus	Diabetes	Diseased Colon	Influenza	Urinary Infection	Brain Infection
2726	339	2350	2318	688	1064	10955
2693	337	2327	2251	707	1065	11078
+33	+2	+23	° +67	-19	-1	-123
2515	322	2190	2134	671	1035	10341
2561	320	2213	2140	673	1012	10533
-46	+2	-23	-6	-2	+23	° -192
2660	364	2225	2229	669	1054	10817
2630	329	2273	2198	691	1040	10819
+30	° +35	-48	+31	-22	+14	-2
2434	353	2173	2115	626	988	10391
2525	315	2182	2110	663	998	10385
° -91	° +38	-9	+5	-37	-10	+6
2594	296	2278	2181	664	1022	10994
2621	328	2265	2191	689	1036	10783
-27	-32	+13	-10	-25	-14	** +211
2525	292	2196	2137	670	1015	10631
2540	317	2195	2122	667	1004	10446
-15	-25	+1	+15	+3	+11	° +185
2492	277	2097	2024	702	992	10062
2421	302	2092	2023	636	957	9956
+71	-25	+5	+1	** +66	+35	+106
2294	325	1980	1943	607	981	9619
2331	291	2014	1948	612	921	9586
-37	° +34	-34	-5	-5	° +60	+33
2237	258	1996	1865	620	902	9289
2232	279	1929	1866	586	882	9182
+5	-21	+67	-1	+34	+20	+107
2367	317	2049	1954	658	984	9712
2411	301	2083	2015	633	953	9916
-44	+16	-34	° -61	+25	+31	° -204
2596	312	2220	2122	643	967	10466
2549	318	2203	2130	670	1007	10484
+47	-6	+17	-8	-27	-40	-18
2643	304	2243	2119	684	887	10462
2570	321	2221	2148	675	1016	10570
° +73	-17	+22	-29	+9	*** -129	-108

▢ positive ◼ negative ° noteworthy case ** significant *** highly significant

		Heart Attack	Pulmonary Embolism	Lung Cancer
Aries	Actual Deaths	16971	773	4447
	Expected Deaths	16764	760	4615
	Significance/Difference	° +207	+13	° -168
Taurus	Actual Deaths	15872	757	4349
	Expected Deaths	15939	723	4388
	Significance/Difference	-67	+34	-39
Gemini	Actual Deaths	16536	728	4434
	Expected Deaths	16372	743	4507
	Significance/Difference	+164	-15	-73
Cancer	Actual Deaths	15788	694	4319
	Expected Deaths	15714	713	4326
	Significance/Difference	+74	-19	-7
Leo	Actual Deaths	16340	737	4545
	Expected Deaths	16316	740	4492
	Significance/Difference	+24	-3	° +53
Virgo	Actual Deaths	15736	738	4355
	Expected Deaths	15807	717	4351
	Significance/Difference	-71	+21	+4
Libra	Actual Deaths	14878	703	4299
	Expected Deaths	15066	683	4147
	Significance/Difference	-188	+20	° +152
Scorpio	Actual Deaths	14397	637	3995
	Expected Deaths	14506	658	3993
	Significance/Difference	-109	-21	+2
Sagittarius	Actual Deaths	13618	641	3852
	Expected Deaths	13895	630	3825
	Significance/Difference	° -277	+11	+27
Capricorn	Actual Deaths	15148	702	4166
	Expected Deaths	15005	681	4130
	Significance/Difference	+143	+21	+36
Aquarius	Actual Deaths	15943	653	4407
	Expected Deaths	15865	720	4367
	Significance/Difference	+78	** -67	+40
Pisces	Actual Deaths	16017	730	4377
	Expected Deaths	15995	726	4403
	Significance/Difference	+22	+4	-26

(Part 2)

Stomach Cancer	Physical Deformity	Pneumonia	Prostate Cancer	Tuberculosis	Accident
1893	111	2477	2146	223	5595
1905	117	2512	2150	254	5613
-12	-6	-35	-4	° -31	-18
1829	110	2383	2136	257	5431
1811	112	2388	2044	241	5337
+18	-2	-5	° +92	+16	+94
1796	109	2423	2075	253	5401
1860	115	2453	2100	248	5482
° -64	-6	-30	-25	+5	-81
1738	107	2351	2021	244	5251
1785	110	2354	2015	238	5262
-47	-3	-3	+6	+6	-11
1795	105	2425	2110	250	5433
1854	114	2445	2092	247	5463
-59	-9	-20	+18	+3	-30
1817	102	2385	2057	245	5173
1796	111	2368	2027	239	5293
+21	-9	+17	+30	+6	-120
1665	104	2259	1972	238	4985
1712	105	2257	1932	228	5045
-47	-1	+2	+40	+10	-60
1752	100	2265	1838	218	4921
1648	101	2173	1860	220	4857
** +104	-1	° +92	-22	-2	+64
1566	111	2133	1769	196	4766
1579	97	2082	1782	210	4652
-13	+14	+51	-13	-14	+114
1795	108	2289	1902	230	4981
1705	105	2248	1924	227	5024
° +90	+3	+41	-22	+3	-43
1847	128	2313	1992	253	5262
1802	111	2377	2035	240	5312
+45	° +17	-64	-43	+13	-50
1781	115	2352	1995	228	5496
1817	112	2397	2051	242	5356
-36	+3	-45	-56	-14	° +140

⬜ positive ⬛ negative   ° noteworthy case ** significant *** highly significant

147

nobody had been struck down by AIDS. In the electronic age there is little trace of the greatest killer of the Middle Ages, elevated to the embodiment of terror by Edgar Allan Poe and Albert Camus: the plague. Fatal diseases like leukaemia were neither known nor recognized in the era of Louis XIV. According to death certificates, monarchs and underlings alike seem to have succumbed to consumption.

How could astrology ever have been able to keep up with this *carousel des maladies*? For this reason we shall make no comment on our enquiry into the causes of death in Switzerland in the past twenty-five years, but simply present the figures and their distributions among the star signs.

8

WHO CHOOSES TO COMMIT SUICIDE?

'It is not out of weakness that we put an end to an unhappy life, but out of a considered judgement which convinces us that a condition in which no one can harm us and nothing disturb our tranquillity is our greatest happiness.'

Frederick the Great in a letter to the Marquis d'Argens, 1760

Like Cleopatra, Hannibal and the virtuous Lucretia of Roman legend, men and women have been committing suicide for thousands of years. It may have been because they were ordered to do so, out of love or despair, as a matter of honour or simply on impulse. There are so many reasons. By water, cold steel or rope (and numerous other means) determined individuals have hastened their arrival on the Other Side.

High-spirited Russian princes used to play Russian roulette. They would climb onto the balustrades of their palaces and stand blindfold as they drained endless bottles of vodka. Their fateful fall to earth was, perhaps, written in the starry St Petersburg sky.

With involuntary irony, people who are tired of life have lain across abandoned railway lines or, weighed down by chains and other ballast, plunged into two feet of water.

At many points in history suicide was fashionable. After their last chip had been raked from the gambling table, ruined gamblers in Monte Carlo would take themselves off to the cliffs and leap into the blackness of the Côte d'Azur night. Only a handful of cleverer or more faint-hearted types ever returned. Often, a bellboy from the casino would slip a few hundred francs into the lifeless gentleman's pocket. The casino called this final pay-out 'arranger la vérité'.

The death wish can be catching. Around the turn of the century, a lady afflicted with *chagrin d'amour* flung herself from the Eiffel Tower, and the newspapers were strictly forbidden to report the incident.

In Great Britain in 1994, a total of 8,223 people (6,486 men and 1,737 women) committed suicide. The most frequent time of year: March. The most frequent day of the week: Sunday.

Even animals are afflicted with the 'English malady'. Toothache drives elephants to kill themselves. Lemmings appear to do it to stem over-population.

After reading George Minois' *History of Suicide*, we concluded that the subject had to be included in our research.

ANALYSIS

Experience shows that doctors sometimes do not make a great deal of effort to state the exact cause of death on death certificates. This gives rise to a certain scepticism.

Despite the fact that in the movies many murders are branded as suicide, there is one cause of death where the accuracy of the record can be in little doubt: suicide.

The data on causes of death which we discussed in the

previous chapter provided us with the opportunity to carry out a statistical study of the possible influence of star signs on suicidal tendencies. We had the dates of birth of 30,358 Swiss men and women who took their own lives between 1969 and 1994. The following table shows the distribution among the individual star signs.

Star signs	Number of deaths in Switzerland 1969 - 1994	Number of suicides 1969 - 1994
Aries	61.582	2.725
Taurus	58.552	2.701
Gemini	60.143	2.731
Cancer	57.727	2.636
Leo	59.939	2.625
Virgo	58.069	2.525
Libra	55.346	2.288
Scorpio	53.288	2.279
Sagittarius	51.044	2.173
Capricorn	55.120	2.417
Aquarius	58.280	2.548
Pisces	58.760	2.710
	687.850	30.358

This enabled us to carry out a chi-square test of goodness of fit (*see* page 46) on the suicide statistics alone. The resulting probability value was 0.00084, which meant that it was highly probable that the deviations between actual distribution and mathematical expectation were most probably not pure chance.

We then moved in to the separate analyses. The sample was the same as for the previous chapter:

- The population was 687,850 deaths.
- Among the deceased were 61,582 born under the sign of Aries, namely 8.95 per cent of all those who died.

- A total of 30,358 men and women committed suicide.
- It might have been expected that 2,717 of these were born under Aries (8.95 per cent of 30,358 = mathematical expectation).
- In fact, during the period under review 2,725 Arians committed suicide (= actual value).
- The same calculation was carried out for the other eleven star signs.
- We then investigated whether the deviations between actual values and mathematical expectations could be regarded as significant, highly significant or slightly significant.

The results are summarized in the table opposite:

These findings can be summed up in very few words:

- There were significantly more suicides among people born under the signs of Taurus, Cancer and Pisces than might have been expected.
- There were significantly fewer Libran and Sagittarian suicides than expected, the deviation of Libra was even highly significant.

SUMMARY
The subject of the investigation was the correlation between star sign and suicide. The survey was based on data relating to 30,358 men and women who had taken their own lives. There were five significant deviations. The influence of chance elements on the observed deviation can be excluded with odds of 1:1000.

Who chooses to commit suicide?

Star signs	Deaths 1969 - 1994	Percentage of deaths for years 1969 - 1994	Actual suicides	Expected suicides	Deviation from expected figure in percent (see graphic)	Degree of significance
Aries	61.582	8,95 %	2.725	2.718	+0,26 %	neutral
Taurus	58.552	8,51 %	2.701	2.584	+4,52 %	* +
Gemini	60.143	8,74 %	2.731	2.654	+2,89 %	neutral
Cancer	57.727	8,39 %	2.636	2.548	+3,46 %	* +
Leo	59.939	8,71 %	2.625	2.645	-0,77 %	neutral
Virgo	58.069	8,44 %	2.525	2.563	-1,48 %	neutral
Libra	55.346	8,05 %	2.288	2.443	-6,33 %	*** -
Scorpio	53.288	7,75 %	2.279	2.352	-3,10 %	neutral
Sagittarius	51.044	7,42 %	2.173	2.253	-3,54 %	* -
Capricorn	55.120	8,01 %	2.417	2.433	-0,65 %	neutral
Aquarius	58.280	8,47 %	2.548	2.572	-0,94 %	neutral
Pisces	58.760	8,54 %	2.710	2.593	+4,50 %	** +
	687.850	100,00 %	30.358	30.358		

* slightly significant   ** significant   *** highly significant

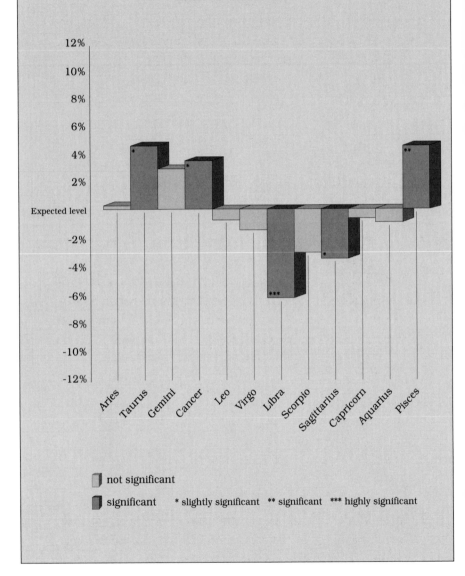

Deviation of actual suicides from expected suicides in percent

Actual suicides: 30.358

not significant

significant   * slightly significant   ** significant   *** highly significant

THE ASTROLOGICAL ANGLE

This study is particularly interesting since suicide as a cause of death is closely bound up with the very nature of the personality – certainly far more than, say, pulmonary embolism.

According to astrology books, Pisceans have a predisposition to melancholy and a 'death wish', and Cancerians a tendency to escape into depression. Taureans are said to possess 'spiritual complexity with depressive tendencies'.

By contrast, optimistic attitudes are attributed to Librans and Sagittarians. They tend to look on the bright side of life and are repelled by any kind of violence.

Our results did not always coincide with the picture painted by astrological literature. Scorpio, for example, often portrayed as the most suicidal of star signs, did not appear to have a significantly high suicide rate, indeed it was negative.

In the course of the investigation we learned something of the methods used by certain star signs to take their own lives. Since the results are based on a relatively small population their significance should not, however, be overestimated:

- Significant numbers of Pisceans resort to sleeping pills to end their lives.
- Taureans are more likely to commit suicide by inhaling exhaust gas or shooting themselves.
- Cancerians, meanwhile, very rarely use firearms to kill themselves.

Famous suicides born under the star signs most at risk include: the German Expressionist painter Ernst Ludwig Kirchner (Taurus), the writer Ernest Hemingway (Cancer),

Marlon Brando's daughter, Tarita Cheyenne (Pisces), the mistress of Crown Prince Rudolph of Austria, Baroness Marie von Vetsera (Pisces), rock musician Kurt Cobain (Pisces) and Swedish safety match magnate Ivar Kreuger (Pisces).

9

WHO COMMITS WHICH CRIMES?

'He who does not punish an evil act bears responsibility for it.'
Leonardo da Vinci (1452–1519)

Crime is as old as history. Cain slew his brother Abel. Lee Harvey Oswald shot Kennedy (or maybe he didn't). Just as ancient is the struggle between cops and robbers. This eternal conflict between good and evil has always exerted a strange fascination. Evil captures our imagination and fills us with fear. Literature and the cinema have turned it into an art form. Neither religion nor law can ever eradicate it. Evil recognizes neither frontiers nor seasons.

There are as many motives for an evil deed as there are human weaknesses: hatred; revenge or jealousy; rage; envy or sex; greed; meanness or hedonism. It seems that every human being carries the seeds of evil. We have all broken the Biblical Ten Commandments, even if only in thought. But not all of us commit crimes. Perhaps because our conscience will not allow it, or because we fear retribution.

And not all those who commit a crime are punished.

When talking about her craft, British crime writer Agatha Christie once said: 'The best murders are those that are not recognised as murder, and the second best are those where the murderer goes undetected.'

The American writer Elbert Hubbard defined the court

sentence as 'the justice which the guilty mete out to those who get caught'.

Different countries show different sympathies towards the detective and the baddy he is hunting down. Sir Arthur Conan Doyle's master detective Sherlock Holmes, for instance, was the darling of English gentlemen and English criminals alike. Le Blanc's master thief Arsène Lupin was the *enfant chéri* of the French underworld and French high society. The archetypal Englishman believes in law and order, the typical Frenchman mistrusts all authority: the establishment versus the forces of anarchy.

America invented Mike Hammer, the hard-bitten sleuth who takes the law into his own hands, and in Germany, which has produced no detective literature worth mentioning, a TV crime series made Derrick a popular hero.

The age-old struggle between cops and robbers has become an increasingly sophisticated affair: one side improves its methods, the other sharpens its weapons – and this is likely to continue until the end of time.

We were unable to ascertain what various star signs feel about the cops, but their attitudes to the robbers proved enlightening. Here too there are significant differences between the star signs.

Fortunately for our study, one aspect of the campaign against crime has changed for the better. In the Bronze Age, nobody kept records of villians and villainy. In the computer age they do – with the accuracy of a shot from a Smith and Wesson.

ANALYSIS

For our investigation we were able to employ data relating to 325,866 convictions by courts in Switzerland for twenty-five different types of offences committed between 1986 and 1994 (*see* table, page 160). The birth dates of the offenders were arranged according to star sign. These twenty-five types of offence are the same used to compile the official crime statistics.

The convictions registered at the Central Criminal Records Office form an objective population which can be validated at any time. If one offender was found guilty of several infringements of the same law, he or she would only be included in the figures once. Moreover, we agreed to exclude particularly sensitive types of crime, such as sexual offences or offences against minors.

First we carried out the chi-square test of independence (*see* page 46) on the entire set of data, consisting of 300 fields (25 offences × 12 star signs). This was to check whether there was any correlation at all between types of offence and star signs. The result was clear. There was a strong probability that we could reject the hypothesis that types of offence and star sign were independent of one another. The probability value was 0.00000001. We could assume that a correlation existed. Then, in the usual way, we did the separate analyses, putting each offence/star sign combination under the microscope.

In the 300 fields there were six highly significant, twelve significant and thirty-seven slightly significant results. So a total of fifty-five fields (i.e. 18 per cent) clearly showed deviations that were unlikely to be explained by chance.

CRIME	NUMBER OF CONVICTIONS
Premeditated Killing/Murder	591 Cases
Grievous Bodily Harm	407 Cases
Brawling/Affray	1.002 Cases
Assault	9.260 Cases
Financial Deception/Embezzlement	640 Cases
Receiving Stolen Goods	12.706 Cases
Blackmail/Extortion	525 Cases
Bankruptcy with Fraudulent Intent	343 Cases
Threat/Extortion	3.602 Cases
Coercion	3.215 Cases
False Accusation	2.165 Cases
False Evidence	871 Cases
Hit-And-Run	27.355 Cases
Car Theft (for joy-riding)	20.090 Cases
Driving Without Licence	40.637 Cases
Theft	97.919 Cases
Fraud	22.565 Cases
Robbery	4.221 Cases
Embezzlement	12.048 Cases
Defamation of Character	864 Cases
Swearing	3.493 Cases
Forgery of Documents	12.971 Cases
Forgery of Identity Cards/Papers	8.640 Cases
Drug Dealing	12.458 Cases
Drug Use	27.198 Cases
Total Crimes/Convictions Analysed	**325.866 Cases**

For more than half of the twenty-five crimes, including murder, grievous bodily harm and blackmail, there were only a few thousand or, in some cases, a few hundred, offenders over the nine years. With so few cases, each star sign field contained relatively low figures. This meant that results produced by statistical evaluation would be barely tenable.

To avoid this problem we confined our calculations to the ten crimes for which there were more than 12,000 convictions during the period under review, namely:

- Theft
- Embezzlement
- Receiving stolen goods
- Fraud
- Forgery: identity cards/papers
- Hit-and-run
- Car theft (temporary theft of a motor vehicle for joy-riding)
- Driving without licence
- Drug dealing
- Drug use

These ten criminal offences account for almost 88 per cent of all convictions and so are thoroughly representative of Swiss crime in general.

So we now had a slimmed-down table with 120 fields (12 star signs × 10 violations), with at least 900 cases in each field. This gave us something to work on.

The chi-square test of independence (*see* page 46) confirmed that, with this new table too, there was a highly significant correlation between the ten most common crimes and the star signs of the offenders. The probability that the different types of offence are evenly distributed over the twelve star signs is less than 0.016 per cent.

The separate analyses of the figures showed one highly significant, six significant and sixteen slightly significant deviations. In other words, one-fifth of the fields relating to the ten most common crimes showed deviations between actual values and mathematical expectations that could be termed at least slightly significant.

The table on pages 162 and 163 summarizes the results.

		Theft	Em-bezzle-ment	Receiving Stolen Goods	Fra
Aries	Actual Convictions	8761	1079	1126	20!
	Expected Convictions	8719	1073	1131	20(
	Significance/Difference	+42	+6	-5	+∠
Taurus	Actual Convictions	8276	1093	1091	19:
	Expected Convictions	8417	1036	1092	194
	Significance/Difference	* -141	* +57	-1	-!
Gemini	Actual Convictions	8555	1090	1119	20!
	Expected Convictions	8562	1053	1111	197
	Significance/Difference	-7	+37	+8	* +:
Cancer	Actual Convictions	8124	1037	1103	18∠
	Expected Convictions	8170	1005	1060	18!
	Significance/Difference	-46	+32	+43	-∠
Leo	Actual Convictions	8123	1012	1112	18!
	Expected Convictions	8214	1011	1066	18!
	Significance/Difference	-91	+1	+46	-:
Virgo	Actual Convictions	8164	968	1060	18(
	Expected Convictions	8129	1000	1055	18:
	Significance/Difference	+35	-32	+5	-!
Libra	Actual Convictions	8035	994	986	18:
	Expected Convictions	7917	974	1027	18:
	Significance/Difference	* +118	+20	-41	
Scorpio	Actual Convictions	7626	902	965	17:
	Expected Convictions	7500	923	973	17:
	Significance/Difference	* +126	-21	-8	
Sagittarius	Actual Convictions	7332	885	931	16:
	Expected Convictions	7333	902	952	16!
	Significance/Difference	-1	-17	-21	-:
Capricorn	Actual Convictions	8207	965	1089	18!
	Expected Convictions	8247	1015	1070	19(
	Significance/Difference	-40	* -50	+19	
Aquarius	Actual Convictions	8567	1058	1088	20(
	Expected Convictions	8527	1049	1106	19(
	Significance/Difference	+40	+9	-18	+∠
Pisces	Actual Convictions	8149	965	1036	18!
	Expected Convictions	8185	1007	1062	18!
	Significance/Difference	-36	-42	-26	-:

Forgery: Documents	Hit-And -Run	Car Theft (for joy-riding)	Driving Without Licence	Drug Dealing	Drug Use
1201	2503	1743	3582	1136	2290
1155	2436	1789	3618	1109	2420
+46	+67	-46	-36	+27	** -130
1159	2417	1743	3520	1072	2292
1115	2351	1727	3493	1071	2336
+44	+66	+16	+27	+1	-44
1190	2431	1702	3510	1023	2352
1134	2392	1757	3553	1089	2377
* +56	+39	-55	-43	* -66	-25
1031	2313	1728	3397	958	2357
1082	2282	1676	3391	1039	2268
* -51	+31	+52	+6	* -81	+89
1082	2312	1716	3432	1060	2279
1088	2295	1685	3409	1045	2280
-6	+17	+31	+23	+15	-1
1109	2213	1658	3388	1034	2265
1077	2271	1668	3373	1034	2256
+32	-58	-10	+15	0	+9
1016	2179	1605	3165	991	2255
1049	2212	1624	3285	1007	2197
-33	-33	-19	* -120	-16	* +58
917	2076	1557	3081	916	2139
994	2095	1539	3113	954	2082
* -77	-19	+18	-32	-38	* +57
937	1981	1587	3041	912	2108
971	2049	1505	3043	933	2036
-34	-68	** +82	-2	-21	* +72
1090	2250	1681	3382	1193	2337
1092	2304	1692	3423	1049	2289
-2	-54	-11	-41	*** +144	+48
1164	2330	1737	3590	1053	2353
1130	2382	1750	3539	1085	2367
+34	-52	-13	+51	-32	-14
1075	2350	1633	3549	1110	2153
1084	2287	1679	3397	1041	2272
-9	* +63	-46	* +152	** +69	** -119

positive negative * slightly significant ** significant *** highly significant

SUMMARY
The subject of the investigation was the correlation between star sign and criminal activity. The survey was based on data relating to 325,866 male and female offenders convicted between 1986 and 1994. Among the ten offences examined, there were twenty-three significant deviations. The influence of chance elements on the observed deviation can be excluded with odds of 1:5,000.

THE ASTROLOGICAL ANGLE

A measure of caution is advised when providing possible explanations for the above-mentioned results. Our analysis was based simply on actual convictions.

If, for example, significantly small numbers of Geminis were shown as convicted of theft, there are – at least – three possible explanations:

- Geminis steal less often than other star signs;
- they are more careful in their lawbreaking activities and are therefore less often caught;
- they are better at defending themselves in court and therefore are less often convicted.

We cannot say which of these is the correct answer. Most probably it is a combination of several factors, and a similar criterion applies to other offences.

But whichever way you look at it and whatever the possible explanation a correlation between people's star signs and the way they behave can be assumed.

10

WHO DRIVES HOW?

'Drivers who stand up for their rights usually
do so by tapping their foreheads.'

Gerhard Uhlenbruck

The invention of the car in the twentieth century created a
new problem for the industrialized nations: traffic.
Darwinism has made an unexpected comeback on the
motorways, where it is certainly a case of the survival of the
fittest. As a grumpy Munich pedestrian once put it, 'Traffic
is managing to stay alive against the odds'.

In Great Britain 70 per cent of all households have at least
one motor vehicle and more than half of the 65 million
British citizens hold a driving licence. The car has gained the
reputation of being one of Britain's favourite children.

Not every country has such an intimate relationship with
the automobile, but everywhere it fires people's imagination.
'Today's troubadours no longer use mandolins but car
horns', mocked the Russian composer Igor Stravinsky. 'The
way a man drives a car is the way he would like to be',
observed Italian actress Anna Magnani.

Tell me how you drive and I will tell you who you are.
Scarcely any other activity appears more capable of betray-
ing people's characters than driving – whether they are
phlegmatic and cautious, polite, or impatient and careless. In

scarcely any other sphere do so many prejudices flourish. Don't men drive more aggressively than women, the English more slowly than the Italians? Aren't young people worse drivers than the elderly?

And how do star signs figure in all this? Does fiery Aries flash the headlights more often? Does luxury-loving Leo lust after a Rolls? Does every intersection present a challenge for the apparently indecisive Libran?

Or are we all the same behind the wheel?

ANALYSIS

It is an interesting question whether there is a correlation between star signs and driving behaviour. It proved something of a problem, however, to get hold of reliable and usable data. This time, we were not lucky enough to be able to fall back on extensive official statistics. Rather, we had to strike out in different directions in order to research this subject.

In fact we thought that insurance companies would be the most likely source of comprehensive data. We wanted to work out which star signs were involved in the most or the fewest traffic accidents. So we approached a number of German and Swiss insurance companies, without much initial success. The firms we wrote to either did not have the technical facilities, or were disinclined to make material available to us. Some had only recorded the year of birth of their insured, but not the exact date of birth. Others took cover behind data protection considerations, although this was ludicrous since we only needed compilations of numbers and no personal data whatsoever. Maybe they were secretly worried that people born under star signs with a significantly lower accident rate might turn around and demand lower premiums.

Data from a British insurance company

We were about to abandon this approach when we learned from an inconspicuous report by the German Press Agency that a British-based accident and insurance management company called VELO had no such misgivings and had produced statistics on this subject. The British insurers had data on around 25,000 claims made in 1996, including the dates of birth of the drivers involved, and they were willing to make the data material available to us.

When it came to traffic accidents we could see immediately there were obvious deviations between actual values and mathematical expectations.

First of all, the data provided did not include the dates of birth and the star signs to which they relate. Rather, the insurance statisticians from VELO had carried out their own percentage calculations and willingly gave us the results of their tests. We had absolutely no reason to doubt the thoroughness and accuracy of the evaluations made by a large British insurance company.

When it came to traffic accidents, we could see immediately that there were obvious deviations between actual values and mathematical expectations.

Could these figures still just be mere coincidence? Or can we conclude with some certainty that Scorpios are the best and Taureans the lousiest drivers?

Who drives how?

Star signs	Number of births in Great Britain for years 1938 - 1979	Percentage of births for years 1938 - 1979	Actual accidents	Expected accidents	Deviation from expected in percent (see graphic)	Degree of significance
Aries	2.696.253	8,90 %	2.135	2.225	-4,04 %	neutral
Taurus	2.600.366	8,58 %	2.440	2.146	+13,72 %	*** +
Gemini	2.738.137	9,04 %	2.258	2.259	-0,06 %	neutral
Cancer	2.595.212	8,56 %	2.120	2.141	-1,00 %	neutral
Leo	2.606.939	8,60 %	1.963	2.151	-8,74 %	*** -
Virgo	2.559.415	8,45 %	2.240	2.112	+6,07 %	*** +
Libra	2.404.725	7,94 %	2.043	1.984	+2,96 %	neutral
Scorpio	2.333.536	7,70 %	1.778	1.926	-7,66 %	*** -
Sagittarius	2.266.066	7,48 %	1.835	1.870	-1,86 %	neutral
Capricorn	2.428.008	8,01 %	2.053	2.003	+2,47 %	neutral
Aquarius	2.520.537	8,32 %	2.030	2.080	-2,39 %	neutral
Pisces	2.552.121	8,42 %	2.108	2.106	+0,10 %	neutral
	30.301.315	100,00 %	25.003	25.003		

* slightly significant   ** significant   *** highly significant

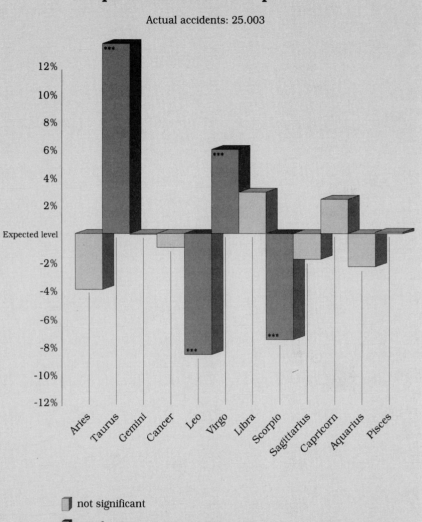

Deviation of actual accidents from expected accidents in per cent

Actual accidents: 25.003

not significant

significant   * slightly significant   ** significant   *** highly significant

The result: the distribution of star signs involved in accidents differed significantly from their distribution within the population of the study. The resulting odds were less than 1 in 1000, indicating that the deviations could scarcely be attributed to pure chance.

Having worked out the mathematical expectations, the separate analyses produced the following conclusions:

People born under the signs of Taurus and Virgo were significantly more often involved in traffic accidents than other star signs.

Conversely, Leos and Scorpios had significantly fewer accidents.

The exact values for the distribution of the individual star signs among those involved in traffic accidents and their distribution in population can be seen in the table on page 168.

VELO also recorded the average cost per claim. Using this data, we were able to break down the claimants by star sign. Since we had neither mathematical expectations nor relative claim figures to hand, we shall do no more than show the actual amounts of the claims. Nevertheless, we can assume that the cost of the claim indicates the seriousness of the damage, which leads us to some interesting conclusions:

- British Taureans and Virgos are not only involved in above-average numbers of traffic accidents, the damage they cause is also unusually serious.
- According to these figures, Leos and Scorpios appear to be the best drivers, the latter putting in significantly lower damage claims.

Who drives how?	
Star signs 25,003 drivers in total	Average cost of damage caused by accidents
Virgo	£786
Taurus	£725
Aquarius	£707
Cancer	£707
Aries	£687
Libra	£687
Leo	£682
Gemini	£680
Capricorn	£665
Scorpio	£647
Sagittarius	£610
Pisces	£606

Data from the Swiss Crime Statistics

In the previous chapter we looked at the correlation between star signs and criminal offences, basing our study on the Swiss Crime Statistics. Included in the investigation were three motoring offences:

Driving without licence
Hit-and-run
Car theft

Car theft refers to an incident where someone steals a car,

takes it for a long or short spin and then abandons it some-where.

Let us take another brief look at the results described in chapter 9, relating to car crime:

We found altogether four significant deviations from the mathematical expectation:

The following star signs were convicted more frequently than average of one of the aforementioned offences:

- Sagittarius – Car theft (significant)
- Pisces – Driving without licence and hit-and-run (each slightly significant)
- Fewer Librans than might have been expected were con-victed of driving without licence (slightly significant)

According to the insurance company's statistics, Sagittarians had a less than average likelihood of being involved in traf-fic accidents and their damage claims were exceptionally low. So it is surprising to find that they are over-represented in the car crime figures. Even so, this is not necessarily a con-tradiction, since driving without a licence or joy-riding in a stolen vehicle does not automatically lead to accidents.

SUMMARY
The subject of the investigation was the correlation between star sign and driving behaviour. The survey was based on data supplied by a British insurance company relating to a total of 25,000 traffic accidents in 1996. The results showed four significant deviations. The influence of chance elements on the observed deviations can be excluded with odds of 1:10,000,000.

Data from the Swiss Central Crime Register relating to 85,598 persons convicted of traffic offences between 1986 and 1994 was also examined. Here there were also four significant deviations.

The influence of chance on the observed deviations can be excluded with odds of 1: 5,000.

THE ASTROLOGICAL ANGLE

To complete our findings on the subject of people and their cars, we include the results of a study by the Institut für Demoskopie, Allensbach, Germany.

Twice a year, the Institute carries out an analysis of advertising media on behalf of the consumer goods industry. The main purpose is to find out as much as possible about the buying habits of those questioned.

During the survey, a total of 13,283 people were interviewed. They were chosen in such a way as to represent the entire population of Germany. The complete Allensbach study can be found in the appendix to this book.

For information about cars interviewees were first asked if they held a driving licence. Those who said they did were then asked a series of further questions:

- what type of motor vehicle (car, lorry, motorcycle, motor scooter, moped, etc) they had personally driven within the previous six months;
- what type of motor vehicle they owned and, if it was a car, what make it was;
- approximately how many kilometres they drove each year;
- whether they had a special interest in cars;
- whether environmental considerations played any part in their choice of car.

All driving licence holders were also asked their date of birth.

Based on the results of the survey, two tables were compiled (*see* pages 176–177 and pages 178–179). Deviations which are significantly higher than expected appear on a white background, those that are significantly lower, on a black one.

In the table relating to driving habits on pages 176–177, the first box in the column headed 'aged 14+' shows that of the 13,283 people interviewed, an average of 64.7 per cent said they had driven a car in the previous six months.

We might have expected that a figure of 64.7 per cent would appear in the same box for all the star signs from Capricorn to Sagittarius.

However, the first significant deviation appeared under Pisces:

Instead of the expected 64.7 per cent of the 937 Pisceans questioned (= 606 people), 69.1 per cent of the 937 Pisceans questioned (= 647 people) had, in fact, driven a car. In other words, the actual value was seven per cent above the mathematical expectation. Statistical analysis shows that this deviation is significant.

Comparison of the tables also reveals that:

- The largest percentage of car drivers are Virgos, but people born under this sign are the least likely to have expert knowledge of cars.
- Scorpios very frequently drive more than 20,000 kilometres per year, while Sagittarians are significantly more likely to drive less than 10,000 kilometres annually.
- Drivers born under Capricorn prefer vehicles with high horse-power engines.

Apart from significant deviations, the tables also show some remarkable and entertaining peculiarities. For example:

- Virgos and Scorpios are the most environmentally conscious, while Aquarians are not too bothered about protecting the environment;
- There are above-average numbers of Sagittarians driving Mercedes, Libras driving BMWs, Scorpios driving Fords, Leos driving Audis and Pisceans behind the wheel of a VW or an Opel;
- After Leo, Taurus is the star sign of the largest number of lorry drivers, but Taureans account for the lowest proportion of car drivers.

	Population aged 14+	Aries	Taurus	Gemini	Cancer
Survey sample	**13.283**	987	928	1021	913
Last 6 months:	Ø %				
Car	64,7 %	68,1 %	60,9 %	64,2 %	65,7 %
H.G.V.	11,0 %	12,6 %	12,8 %	11,8 %	12,3 %
Motorcycle (over 80cc)	4,3 %	3,3 %	4,1 %	5,3 %	6,1 %
Motorcycle (under 80cc)	2,0 %	2,2 %	1,0 %	2,4 %	3,0 %
Scooter	2,1 %	2,0 %	2,8 %	2,4 %	2,6 %
Moped	3,1 %	2,8 %	3,6 %	2,0 %	4,3 %
per year: Frequent driver 20,000 km and above	10,6 %	11,7 %	11,0 %	11,1 %	9,2 %
Moderate driver 10 - 20,000 km	28,9 %	30,5 %	26,8 %	29,3 %	30,3 %
Infrequent driver 10,000 km	20,9 %	21,4 %	19,3 %	21,3 %	21,8 %
Interested car experts	6,6 %	6,2 %	7,1 %	8,1 %	7,7 %
Environmentally committed car drivers	12,2 %	11,2 %	13,2 %	12,7 %	13,1 %

Finally, one fact which cannot be verified statistically: 'When a man opens the car door for a woman, either the woman or the car is new.'

Driving habits and interests

	Leo 925	Virgo 909	Libra 812	Scorpio 820	Sagittarius 760	Capricorn 837	Aquarius 909	Pisces 937
64,2 %	69,8 %	63,1 %	67,9 %	68,3 %	61,7 %	61,6 %	69,1 %
13,2 %	11,3 %	11,2 %	11,2 %	10,5 %	10,8 %	8,9 %	12,2 %
5,0 %	5,3 %	5,4 %	4,5 %	4,0 %	3,5 %	3,5 %	4,6 %
2,5 %	2,3 %	1,6 %	3,0 %	1,9 %	2,4 %	1,7 %	2,4 %
2,2 %	2,4 %	2,4 %	1,9 %	2,8 %	1,9 %	2,4 %	2,2 %
4,4 %	3,8 %	3,3 %	3,3 %	3,1 %	3,1 %	2,5 %	4,1 %
10,3 %	10,0 %	11,6 %	12,7 %	11,4 %	12,4 %	10,1 %	10,7 %
28,2 %	31,8 %	28,1 %	31,7 %	28,8 %	25,7 %	24,5 %	33,0 %
22,0 %	21,5 %	20,6 %	19,0 %	24,8 %	20,9 %	23,8 %	22,0 %
8,4 %	5,4 %	6,6 %	5,7 %	6,6 %	7,3 %	7,8 %	7,8 %
12,5 %	14,8 %	11,7 %	14,8 %	14,1 %	11,0 %	9,5 %	13,4 %

☐ positive significance ■■ negative significance

	Population aged 14+	Aries	Taurus	Gemini	Cance:
Survey sample	**13.283**	987	928	1021	913

(Drive themselves) Car/Household: ∅ %

Car	60,5 %	63,6 %	57,2 %	61,7 %	61,3 %
Second car	7,6 %	8,8 %	8,2 %	7,0 %	7,0 %
Used car	31,4 %	33,9 %	28,4 %	33,7 %	32,2 %
New car	28,8 %	29,3 %	28,1 %	27,8 %	29,1 %
Car over 90 H.P.	16,9 %	17,2 %	14,7 %	16,5 %	16,0 %

Make of Car/Household:
Two or more cars

household	26,1 %	28,9 %	27,0 %	26,8 %	28,3 %
Audi	3,4 %	3,8 %	3,3 %	3,3 %	2,8 %
BMW	3,3 %	2,8 %	2,6 %	3,3 %	3,6 %
Ford	6,6 %	7,2 %	5,5 %	7,1 %	8,0 %
Mercedes	4,2 %	4,5 %	4,4 %	4,5 %	3,5 %
Opel	10,9 %	10,5 %	10,6 %	10,2 %	11,3 %
VW	15,0 %	16,2 %	14,5 %	15,0 %	14,0 %
Italian Make	1,9 %	2,3 %	1,1 %	2,0 %	1,7 %
French Make	4,8 %	4,2 %	6,0 %	5,4 %	4,9 %
Japanese Make	7,0 %	8,2 %	6,4 %	7,0 %	8,9 %

Plans to purchase in 1-2 years:

Used car	9,5 %	11,6 %	10,1 %	9,1 %	11,9 %
New car	6,0 %	6,8 %	4,7 %	6,8 %	4,4 %
Motorcycle over 80 cc	1,6 %	1,4 %	1,6 %	1,2 %	1,8 %

makes and plans to purchase

Leo	Virgo	Libra	Scorpio	Sagittarius	Capricorn	Aquarius	Pisces
925	909	812	820	760	837	909	937
0,7 %	63,3 %	60,3 %	63,7 %	64,9 %	59,0 %	58,4 %	65,9 %
7,1 %	7,7 %	8,4 %	8,8 %	7,7 %	8,4 %	7,4 %	8,3 %
3,6 %	33,5 %	30,5 %	32,7 %	32,3 %	28,5 %	28,8 %	32,6 %
6,8 %	29,6 %	29,5 %	30,7 %	32,3 %	30,5 %	29,3 %	33,1 %
9,0 %	15,5 %	16,8 %	18,0 %	18,2 %	19,5 %	16,7 %	17,6 %
8,0 %	25,5 %	26,6 %	29,2 %	30,7 %	26,6 %	26,7 %	28,8 %
4,5 %	3,4 %	3,0 %	4,3 %	3,5 %	2,9 %	3,4 %	3,3 %
3,3 %	3,2 %	4,6 %	3,4 %	2,5 %	4,4 %	3,2 %	3,1 %
5,4 %	5,7 %	7,3 %	9,3 %	4,8 %	5,9 %	6,3 %	7,4 %
5,1 %	4,6 %	3,4 %	4,2 %	5,1 %	4,4 %	3,1 %	4,6 %
1,3 %	11,6 %	10,0 %	10,8 %	13,0 %	9,3 %	10,7 %	13,7 %
3,8 %	17,1 %	15,2 %	13,6 %	14,9 %	15,2 %	13,3 %	17,6 %
2,0 %	2,4 %	2,2 %	1,9 %	2,4 %	1,6 %	1,9 %	1,9 %
4,4 %	4,9 %	5,5 %	4,7 %	4,8 %	4,2 %	4,8 %	4,8 %
7,3 %	8,0 %	5,8 %	7,2 %	9,2 %	7,0 %	6,4 %	6,3 %
0,3 %	10,1 %	10,9 %	10,4 %	10,6 %	8,5 %	11,1 %	9,8 %
6,4 %	6,6 %	7,0 %	6,8 %	7,1 %	6,3 %	7,6 %	6,2 %
2,6 %	1,0 %	1,5 %	1,3 %	1,4 %	2,5 %	1,5 %	1,7 %

☐ positive significance ■ negative significance

11

WHO PLAYS FOOTBALL?

'Don't tell me anything about the secrets of football. Just get the ball out of our half and into the other's goal.'

Jackie Charlton

Many sports are played with a soft or a hard object that has all the points on its periphery at the same distance from its centre. Whether it is ping-pong in Shanghai, basketball in New York backyards, volley ball at the Copacabana or cricket on a well-groomed British pitch. No matter if it is marbles, tennis or baseball, handball, water polo or fives, hockey, golf – or even roulette.

While still small children, we succumb to the fascination of round objects: balloons, soap bubbles and balls. They are all flying about somewhere in the children's wonderland.

In our youth, the fascination turns into a passion. Flying and intercepted balls, or balls turned into goals are man's favourite drug. Whether as a player or spectator, whether in the stadium or in front of the TV. No result escapes him. And no page of the daily newspaper is read as assiduously as the sports page. Of the enormous number of different ball games, none is more important to those of us living in the western world as football.

Yet in 1519 pupils of Eton public school kicked around a 'ball full of wind' as sport. In the year 1555 the statutes of St

John's College in Oxford mention a gamed called 'pila pedalis' – using your feet to play with a ball.

In the meantime football has become part of our mentality. Romantic feelings are seldom attached to it. Instead barriers are crushed with disastrous consequences, flags are burned and whole neighbourhoods are wrecked by disappointed fans. You hear of rigging when players are transferred for scandalous prices, and of South-American referees who flee to the pampas for fear of death.

'That's part of the game', said John Long, the famous English referee.

But what do the stars say about this game that the masses are so enthusiastic about? Do they have any influence on the birth of a football star? Well, we looked into it.

ANALYSIS

Is there a connection between your star sign and the kind of sport you do? Are there a particularly large number of people born under the sign of Aries, with their reputation for being pugnacious, among boxers? Or does a Virgo, ruled by reason, tend to go in for snooker? Unfortunately there is hardly any statistical material about the star signs of sportsmen and sportswomen, especially as it would have to be a mass sport in order to produce a sufficient population.

But looking through the archives of *Kicker* magazine, we struck lucky. The magazine lists all footballers who have played in the German league from 1963 to the present day (1997/98 season). A total of 4,162 players, and all listed with their date of birth. We evaluated this material in terms of star sign and arrived at a one-dimensional table with the actual figures for the twelve star signs.

For comparison we took the birth statistics of the Federal Office of Statistics for the years 1950–1979, i.e. those years that produced the majority of professional football players. During this 30-year period, 16,874,124 men were born in Germany. The chi-square test conducted with this data produced a value of zero, meaning that the hypothesis that there is no relation with the signs of the zodiac can be refuted with an extremely large measure of certainty. A separate analysis was then attempted using the already familiar approach.

We know, for example, that 7.82 per cent of all men born in the years 1950–1979 were born under the sign of Libra. So you would think that about 7.82 per cent of all footballers would have been born under the sign of Libra. That would amount to 326 players (= mathematical expectation). In fact, according to the *Kicker* archives, 426 football players were born under Libra (= actual value). So the actual value is almost 31 per cent higher than the mathematical expectation! This deviation is highly significant by all statistical criteria.

As the table on pages 184–185 shows, there were highly significant deviations for six star signs:

- Virgo, Libra and Scorpio are disproportionally represented among the footballers.
- Far fewer Aries, Taurus and Gemini have entered a league career than would be expected from their distribution within the population of the study.

Another three deviations are to be rated as significant, and

Who plays football?

Star signs	Number of men born in years 1950 - 1979	Percentage of men born in years 1950 - 1979	Actual number of players in National League	Expected number of players in National League	Deviation from expected figure in in percent (see graphic)	Degree of significance
Aries	1.514.424	8,97 %	296	374	-20,76 %	*** -
Taurus	1.448.208	8,58 %	277	357	-22,45 %	*** -
Gemini	1.512.259	8,96 %	297	373	-20,37 %	*** -
Cancer	1.432.883	8,49 %	309	353	-12,57 %	* -
Leo	1.441.854	8,54 %	400	356	+12,48 %	* +
Virgo	1.432.572	8,49 %	460	353	+30,18 %	*** +
Libra	1.319.924	7,82 %	426	326	+30,85 %	*** +
Scorpio	1.293.785	7,67 %	389	319	+21,90 %	*** +
Sagittarius	1.255.608	7,44 %	341	310	+10,11 %	neutral
Capricorn	1.362.065	8,07 %	345	336	+2,69 %	neutral
Aquarius	1.431.249	8,48 %	321	353	-9,07 %	neutral
Pisces	1.429.293	8,47 %	301	353	-14,62 %	* -
	16.874.124	100,00 %	4.162	4.162		

* slightly significant   ** significant   *** highly significant

Deviation of actual players from expected players in percent

Actual number: 4.162

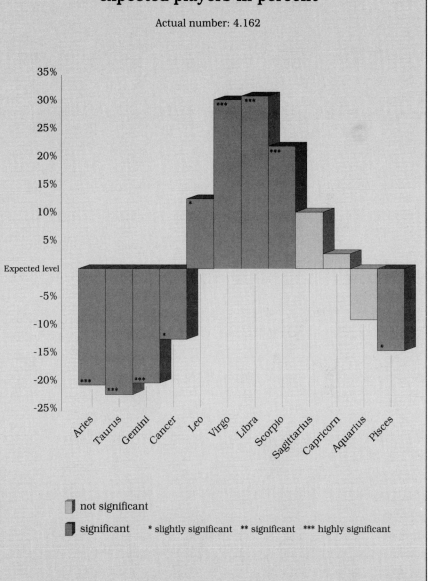

not significant

significant   * slightly significant   ** significant   *** highly significant

for only three star signs the deviations were so slight that they can be put down to pure chance.

There is an obvious objection to this method that critics might raise. Namely, the *Kicker* archives also include foreign footballers who have played in the German league. It is conceivable, although not probable, that the distribution of births throughout the year is different in the Netherlands, France and the other countries where the players come from, to what it is in Germany. But overall the percentage of foreign players in the years 1963 to 1998 has been less than 10 per cent, because in the early years of the German league there were far fewer foreigners than there are today. So any inaccuracy of this order can be tolerated, it has no remarkable effect on the result.

Even though the material from *Kicker* magazine cannot be called official data, and the population (4,162 players) was smaller than in most of our other analyses, one cannot deny the striking relationship between professional footballers and their star sign. In no other subject of investigation were the percentage deviations between actual and expected figures as high as in this case.

SUMMARY
The subject of the investigation was the correlation between star sign and playing football. The survey was based on data relating to 4,162 men who played as professional footballers in the German league. There were nine significant deviations. The influence of chance elements on the observed deviations can be excluded with odds of 1:10,000,000.

THE ASTROLOGICAL ANGLE

The deviations among football players between actual value and the mathematical expectation – as much as 31 per cent upwards and 22.5 per cent downwards – are quite astonishing. For no other subject investigated in our book were the percentage deviations anywhere near as large.

What is striking is the fact that those star signs which are disproportionally represented (Leo through to Capricorn) are all next to one another in one half of the year, while all those which are under-represented (Aquarius through to Cancer) appear in the other half of the year. What is more, the maximum deviations lie in the middle of the halves of the year in each case, +31 per cent for Libra and –22.5 per cent for Taurus.

It is obvious that we have to rack our brains. There are unanswered questions, very cryptic coincidences and statistical nuts of an unknown nature to crack. We will try to get to the bottom of all of them.

STAR SIGNS AT A GLANCE

Aries at a glance

WHO BUYS ASTROLOGY BOOKS?				***
WHO MARRIES WHOM?	Aries Men Marry		Aries Women Marry	
	Aries Women	**	Aries Men	**
	Scorpio Women	*	Cancer Men	*
			Leo Men	**
			Sagittarius Men	**
WHO IS KEEN TO MARRY?				neutral
WHO DIVORCES WHOM?	Aries Men Divorce		Aries Women Divorce	
	Aries Women	**	Aries Men	**
	Leo Women	**		
WHO IS SINGLE?				neutral
WHO IS KEEN TO STUDY?				***
WHO STUDIES WHAT?	Law			*
	Psychology			**
	Dentistry			**
WHO DOES WHICH JOB?	Self-Employed			***
	White Collar/Blue Collar Worker			***
WHO DOES WHAT WORK?	Farmer			***
	Florist			o
	Bricklayer			o
	Carpenter/Furniture Maker			o
	Bank Clerk			o
	Book-Keeper			o
	Vicar			o
	Primary School Teacher			***
	Chemist			o
WHO DIES OF WHAT?	Alcoholic Cirrhosis of the Liver			o
	Disease of the Colon			o
	Heart Attack			o
	Lung Cancer			o
	Tuberculosis			o
WHO CHOOSES TO COMMIT SUICIDE?				neutral
WHO IS CONVICTED OF WHAT?	Drug Use			**
WHO DRIVES HOW?				neutral
WHOSE CAR ACCIDENTS CAUSE SERIOUS DAMAGE? (1-12)				5th Place
WHO PLAYS FOOTBALL?				***

☐ positive ■■ negative ° noteworthy case * slightly significant ** significant *** highly significant

Taurus at a glance

WHO BUYS ASTROLOGY BOOKS?				***
WHO MARRIES WHOM?	**Taurus Men Marry**		**Taurus Women Marry**	
	Taurus Women	*	Taurus Men	*
	Gemini Women	*	Aquarius Men	***
	Leo Women	*		
	Libra Women	**		
WHO IS KEEN TO MARRY?	Taurus Men	neutral	Taurus Women	***
WHO DIVORCES WHOM?	**Taurus Men Divorce**			
	Cancer Women	*		
WHO IS SINGLE?				neutral
WHO IS KEEN TO STUDY?				***
WHO STUDIES WHAT?	Law			*
	Psychology			**
WHO DOES WHICH JOB?	White Collar/Blue Collar Worker			***
WHO DOES WHAT WORK?	Farmer			**
	Baker			**
	Carpenter			°
	Bricklayer			***
	Painter			°
	Mechanical Engineer			°
	Architect			**
	Architectural Draughtsman/Woman			°
	Hotel Manager			°
	Doctor - General practitioner			**
	Nurse			°
	Further Education Teacher			***
	Primary Teacher			**
	Kindergarten Teacher			°
WHO DIES OF WHAT?	Brain Infection			°
	Prostate Cancer			°
WHO CHOOSES TO COMMIT SUICIDE?				*
WHO IS CONVICTED OF WHAT?	Theft			*
	Embezzlement			*
WHO DRIVES HOW?				***
WHOSE CAR ACCIDENTS CAUSE SERIOUS DAMAGE? (1-12)				2nd Place
WHO PLAYS FOOTBALL?				***

positive ■■ negative ° noteworthy case * slightly significant ** significant *** highly significant

Gemini at a glance

WHO BUYS ASTROLOGY BOOKS?			***
WHO MARRIES WHOM?	**Gemini Men Marry**	**Gemini Women Marry**	
	Gemini Women **	Taurus Men	*
		Gemini Men	**
		Scorpio Men	*
WHO IS KEEN TO MARRY?			neutral
WHO DIVORCES WHOM?		**Gemini Women Divorce**	
		Scorpio Men	**
		Sagittarius Men	**
		Aquarius Men	**
WHO IS SINGLE?			neutral
WHO IS KEEN TO STUDY?			***
WHO STUDIES WHAT?	Business Management		*
	Psychology		**
	Pharmaceutics		*
WHO DOES WHICH JOB?	Executive		***
	Middle Management		***
	White Collar/Blue Collar Worker		***
WHO DOES WHAT WORK?	Farmer		***
	Bricklayer		***
	Painter		**
	Fitter/Metalworker		○
	Mechanical Engineer		***
	Company Owner		○
	Computer Scientist		○
	Policeman		**
	Journalist		○
	Doctor - General Practitioner		○
	Vicar		○
	University Teacher		○
	Further Education Teacher		○
	Kindergarten Teacher		○
	Psychologist		○
WHO DIES OF WHAT?	Cancer of the Uterus		○
	Stomach Cancer		○
WHO CHOOSES TO COMMIT SUICIDE?			neutral
WHO IS CONVICTED OF WHAT?	Fraud		*
	Forgery of Documents		*
	Drug Dealing		*
WHO DRIVES HOW?			neutral
WHOSE CAR ACCIDENTS CAUSE SERIOUS DAMAGE? (1-12)			8th Place
WHO PLAYS FOOTBALL?			***

___ positive ■■■ negative ○ noteworthy case * slightly significant ** significant *** highly significant

Cancer at a glance

WHO BUYS ASTROLOGY BOOKS?			***
WHO MARRIES WHOM?	Cancer Men Marry		
	Aries Women	*	
WHO IS KEEN TO MARRY?	Cancer Men neutral	Cancer Women	***
WHO DIVORCES WHOM?		Cancer Women Divorce	
		Taurus Men	*
WHO IS SINGLE?			neutral
WHO IS KEEN TO STUDY?			***
WHO STUDIES WHAT?	Architecture		*
	Biology		*
	Dentistry		*
WHO DOES WHICH JOB?	Executive		***
	White Collar/Blue Collar Worker		***
WHO DOES WHAT WORK?	Farmer		***
	Tailor		o
	Bricklayer		***
	Fitter/Metalworker		o
	Mechanical Engineer		**
	Carpenter/Furniture Maker		o
	Bank Clerk		o
	Social Worker		***
	Teacher		**
WHO DIES OF WHAT?	Breast Cancer		o
	Cancer of the Uterus		o
WHO CHOOSES TO COMMIT SUICIDE?			*
WHO IS CONVICTED OF WHAT?	Forgery of Documents		*
	Drug Dealing		*
WHO DRIVES HOW?			neutral
WHOSE CAR ACCIDENTS CAUSE SERIOUS DAMAGE? (1-12)			4th Place
WHO PLAYS FOOTBALL?			*

☐ positive ■ negative ° noteworthy case * slightly significant ** significant *** highly significant

Leo at a glance

WHO BUYS ASTROLOGY BOOKS?				***
WHO MARRIES WHOM?	Leo Men Marry		Leo Women Marry	
	Aries Women	**	Taurus Men	*
	Aquarius Women	**		
WHO IS KEEN TO MARRY?	Leo Men	neutral	Leo Women	***
WHO DIVORCES WHOM?	Leo Men Divorce		Leo Women Divorce	
	Libra Women	**	Aries Men	**
WHO IS SINGLE?				neutral
WHO IS KEEN TO STUDY?				neutral
WHO STUDIES WHAT?	Business Management			*
	Law			*
	Pharmaceutics			*
WHO DOES WHICH JOB?	Executive			***
	White Collar/Blue Collar Worker			**
WHO DOES WHAT WORK?	Farmer			***
	Tailor			**
	Bricklayer			***
	Painter			**
	Company Owner			***
WHO DIES OF WHAT?	Brain Infection			**
	Lung Cancer			°
WHO CHOOSES TO COMMIT SUICIDE?				neutral
WHO IS CONVICTED OF WHAT?				
WHO DRIVES HOW?				***
WHOSE CAR ACCIDENTS CAUSE SERIOUS DAMAGE? (1-12)				7th Place
WHO PLAYS FOOTBALL?				*

positive ■ negative ° noteworthy case * slightly significant ** significant *** highly significant

Virgo at a glance

WHO BUYS ASTROLOGY BOOKS?				***
WHO MARRIES WHOM?	Virgo Men Marry		Virgo Women Marry	
	Virgo Women	**	Virgo Men	**
			Pisces Men	*
WHO IS KEEN TO MARRY?				neutral
WHO DIVORCES WHOM?				
WHO IS SINGLE?				neutral
WHO IS KEEN TO STUDY?				neutral
WHO STUDIES WHAT?	Biology			*
	Medicine			*
	Psychology			**
	Dentistry			**
WHO DOES WHICH JOB?	Self-Employed			**
WHO DOES WHAT WORK?	Farmer			***
	Bricklayer			***
	Painter			°
	Fitter/Metalworker			°
	Insurance Salesman			°
	Company Owner			°
	Book-Keeper			°
	Computer Scientist			**
	Musician			°
	Further Education Teacher			°
	Primary School Teacher			°
WHO DIES OF WHAT?	Brain Infection			°
WHO CHOOSES TO COMMIT SUICIDE?				neutral
WHO IS CONVICTED OF WHAT?				
WHO DRIVES HOW?				***
WHOSE CAR ACCIDENTS CAUSE SERIOUS DAMAGE? (1-12)				1st Place
WHO PLAYS FOOTBALL?				***

positive ■■ negative ° noteworthy case * slightly significant ** significant *** highly significant

Libra at a glance

WHO BUYS ASTROLOGY BOOKS?			neutral
WHO MARRIES WHOM?	Libra Men Marry	Libra Women Marry	
	Libra Women *	Taurus Men	**
		Libra Men	*
		Pisces Men	*
WHO IS KEEN TO MARRY?	Libra Men neutral	Libra Women	***
WHO DIVORCES WHOM?		Libra Women Divorce	
		Leo Men	**
WHO IS SINGLE?			neutral
WHO IS KEEN TO STUDY?			***
WHO STUDIES WHAT?	Law		***
	Dentistry		***
WHO DOES WHICH JOB?	Self-Employed		**
	White Collar / Blue Collar Worker		***
WHO DOES WHAT WORK?	Farmer		***
	Baker		***
	Tailor		°
	Bricklayer		***
	Painter		***
	Cabinet Maker		**
	Architectural Draughtsman / Woman		°
	Bank Clerk		°
	Policeman		**
	Decorator		°
	Interior Designer		°
	Hairdresser		**
	Doctor - General Practitioner		**
	Dentist		°
	Teacher		°
	Further Education Teacher		***
	Primary School Teacher		***
WHO DIES OF WHAT?	Influenza		**
	Lung Cancer		°
WHO CHOOSES TO COMMIT SUICIDE?			***
WHO IS CONVICTED OF WHAT?	Theft		*
	Driving Without License		*
	Drug Use		*
WHO DRIVES HOW?			neutral
WHOSE CAR ACCIDENTS CAUSE SERIOUS DAMAGE? (1-12)			6th Place
WHO PLAYS FOOTBALL?			***

☐ positive ■ negative ° noteworthy case * slightly significant ** significant *** highly significant

Scorpio at a glance

WHO BUYS ASTROLOGY BOOKS?		***
WHO MARRIES WHOM?	Scorpio Men Marry	Scorpio Women Marry
	Gemini Women *	Aries Men *
	Pisces Women **	Aquarius Men **
		Pisces Men **
WHO IS KEEN TO MARRY?	Scorpio Men neutral	Scorpio Women ***
WHO DIVORCES WHOM?	Scorpio Men Divorce	Scorpio Women Divorce
	Gemini Women **	Pisces Men **
WHO IS SINGLE?	Scorpio Men ***	Scorpio Women neutral
WHO IS KEEN TO STUDY?		neutral
WHO STUDIES WHAT?	Psychology	*
WHO DOES WHICH JOB?	Middle Management	**
	White Collar/Blue Collar Worker	***
WHO DOES WHAT WORK?	Baker	***
	Tailor	**
	Bricklayer	***
	Painter	***
	Carpenter/Furniture Maker	o
	Book-Keeper	o
	Computer Programmer	o
	Journalist	**
	Decorator	o
	Hairdresser	***
	Teacher	o
	Further Education Teacher	***
	Primary School Teacher	***
	Kindergarten Teacher	***
	Chemist	o
WHO DIES OF WHAT?	Alcoholic Cirrhosis of the Liver	o
	Cancer of the Uterus	o
	Urinary Infection	o
	Stomach Cancer	**
	Pneumonia	o
WHO CHOOSES TO COMMIT SUICIDE?		neutral
WHO IS CONVICTED OF WHAT?	Theft	*
	Forgery of Documents	*
	Drug Use	*
WHO DRIVES HOW?		***
WHOSE CAR ACCIDENTS CAUSE SERIOUS DAMAGE? (1-12)		10th Place
WHO PLAYS FOOTBALL?		***

positive ■ negative ° noteworthy case * slightly significant ** significant *** highly significant

Sagittarius at a glance

WHO BUYS ASTROLOGY BOOKS?				***
WHO MARRIES WHOM?	**Sagittarius Men Marry**		**Sagittarius Women Marry**	
	Aries Women	**	Sagittarius Men	**
	Sagittarius Women	**		
	Pisces Women	*		
WHO IS KEEN TO MARRY?				neutral
WHO DIVORCES WHOM?	**Sagittarius Men Divorce**			
	Gemini Women	**		
	Aquarius Women	**		
WHO IS SINGLE?	**Sagittarius Men**	***	**Sagittarius Women**	neutral
WHO IS KEEN TO STUDY?				***
WHO STUDIES WHAT?	Veterinary Medicine			**
WHO DOES WHICH JOB?				
WHO DOES WHAT?	Farmer			***
	Gardener			**
	Bricklayer			**
	Painter			°
	Fitter/Metalworker			°
	Mechanical Engineer			°
	Insurance Salesman			°
	Lawyer			°
	Hairdresser			°
	Doctor - General Practitioner			**
	Secondary High School Teacher			°
	Further Education Teacher			**
	Primary School Teacher			***
WHO DIES OF WHAT?	Heart Attack			°
WHO CHOOSES TO COMMIT SUICIDE?				*
WHO IS CONVICTED OF WHAT?	Car Theft			**
	Drug Use			*
WHO DRIVES HOW?				neutral
WHOSE CAR ACCIDENTS CAUSE SERIOUS DAMAGE? (1-12)				11th Place
WHO PLAYS FOOTBALL?				°

■ positive ■ negative ° noteworthy case * slightly significant ** significant *** highly significant

Capricorn at a glance

WHO BUYS ASTROLOGY BOOKS?			neutral
WHO MARRIES WHOM?	Capricorn Men Marry	Capricorn Women Marry	
	Capricorn Women ***	Capricorn Men ***	
WHO IS KEEN TO MARRY?	Capricorn Men ***	Capricorn Women neutral	
WHO DIVORCES WHOM?	Capricorn Men Divorce		
	Pisces Women **		
WHO IS SINGLE?			***
WHO IS KEEN TO STUDY?			***
WHO STUDIES WHAT?	Business Management		**
WHO DOES WHICH JOB?	White Collar/Blue Collar Worker		***
WHO DOES WHAT WORK?	Farmer		***
	Gardener		***
	Carpenter		**
	Bricklayer		***
	Fitter/Metalworker		°
	Mechanical Engineer		**
	Cabinet Maker		°
	Insurance Salesman		°
	Hairdresser		°
WHO DIES OF WHAT?	Brain Infection		°
	Stomach Cancer		°
WHO CHOOSES TO COMMIT SUICIDE?			neutral
WHO IS CONVICTED OF WHAT?	Embezzlement		*
	Drug Dealing		***
WHO DRIVES HOW?			neutral
WHOSE CAR ACCIDENTS CAUSE SERIOUS DAMAGE? (1-12)			9th Place
WHO PLAYS FOOTBALL?			neutral

positive ▭ ■ negative ° noteworthy case * slightly significant ** significant *** highly significant

Aquarius at a glance

WHO BUYS ASTROLOGY BOOKS?				***

WHO MARRIES WHOM?	Aquarius Men Marry		Aquarius Women Marry	
	Taurus Women	***	Leo Men	**
	Scorpio Women	**	Aquarius Men	***
	Aquarius Women	***		

WHO IS KEEN TO MARRY?				neutral

WHO DIVORCES WHOM?	Aquarius Men Divorce		Aquarius Women Divorce	
	Gemini Women	**	Sagittarius Men	**

WHO IS SINGLE?	Aquarius Men	**	Aquarius Women	***

WHO IS KEEN TO STUDY?		neutral

WHO STUDIES WHAT?	Law	*
	Psychology	**

WHO DOES WHICH JOB?	Self-Employed	***
	Executive	***

WHO DOES WHAT WORK?	Farmer	***
	Baker	**
	Painter	**
	Cabinet Maker	○
	Carpenter/Furniture Maker	○
	Architectural Draughtsman/woman	○
	Bank Clerk	○
	Company Owner	***
	Book-Keeper	○
	Computer Scientist	**
	Interior Designer	**
	Hairdresser	***
	Physiotherapist	***
	Social Worker	○
	Teacher	○
	Further Education Teacher	***
	Primary School Teacher	***
	Psychology	**
	Chemist	○

WHO DIES OF WHAT?	Bronchitis	○
	Pulmonary Embolism	**
	Physical Deformity	○

WHO CHOOSES TO COMMIT SUICIDE?		neutral

WHO IS CONVICTED OF WHAT?		

WHO DRIVES HOW?		neutral

WHOSE CAR ACCIDENTS CAUSE SERIOUS DAMAGE? (1-12)		3rd Place

WHO PLAYS FOOTBALL?		○

☐ positive ■ negative ○ noteworthy case * slightly significant ** significant *** highly significant

200

Pisces at a glance

WHO BUYS ASTROLOGY BOOKS?				***
WHO MARRIES WHOM?	Pisces Men Marry		Pisces Women Marry	
	Virgo Women	*	Scorpio Men	**
	Libra Women	*	Sagittarius Men	*
	Scorpio Women	**		
WHO IS KEEN TO MARRY?	Pisces Men	***	Pisces Women	neutral
WHO DIVORCES WHOM?	Pisces Men Divorce		Pisces Women Divorce	
	Scorpio Women	**	Capricorn Men	**
WHO IS SINGLE?	Pisces Men	***	Pisces Women	neutral
WHO IS KEEN TO STUDY?				neutral
WHO STUDIES WHAT?	Psychology			**
	Veterinary Medicine			*
WHO DOES WHICH JOB?	Executive			***
WHO DOES WHAT WORK?	Farmer			***
	Baker			**
	Carpenter			o
	Painter			**
	Mechanical Engineer			**
	Carpenter/Furniture Maker			o
	Bank Clerk			o
	Hairdresser			***
	Nurse			**
	Further Education Teacher			***
	Primary School Teacher			***
	Kindergarten Teacher			**
	Chemist			o
WHO DIES OF WHAT?	Breast Cancer			o
	Urinary Infection			***
	Accident			o
WHO CHOOSES TO COMMIT SUICIDE?				**
WHO IS CONVICTED OF WHAT?	Hit-And-Run			*
	Driving Without License			*
	Drug Dealing			**
	Drug Use			**
WHO DRIVES HOW?				neutral
WHOSE CAR ACCIDENTS CAUSE SERIOUS DAMAGE? (1-12)				12th Place
WHO PLAYS FOOTBALL?				*

☐ positive ■ negative ° noteworthy case * slightly significant ** significant *** highly significant

201

THE AMAZINGLY CONCLUSIVE
NATURE OF AN
EXCEPTIONAL EXPERIMENT

Artificial star signs

At this point we would like to present another calculation which provides some of the most impressive evidence for our hypothesis about the effect of star signs.

Thanks to the meticulous work of the statisticians in Switzerland, we were in the happy position of having at our disposal data not only for the respective star signs, but also for each day of the year. For example we could tell how many couples with the birthday combination 3 March/30 October had married, or how many people, born on 28 July, had committed suicide.

Thus the statisticians were able to mix the data at random and create artificial star signs. To do so they left the traditional star signs in the same order within the year, but provided these with artificial, i.e. false birth dates. In this way an artificial year resulted, beginning with 6 April, for example, followed by 11 November etc.

If the astrologers' statements about the effects of star signs were invalid, there would be significant findings here too. However, if there were no significant correlation between the artificial signs, this would be almost indisputable evidence that star signs do indeed have an effect.

The chi-square test showed no significant correlation for marriages and suicides of artificial star signs. In addition, the results of the individual follow-up analyses were in both cases statistically entirely unremarkable. There was no single significant deviation.

To elucidate this we illustrate the effect of this experiment among suicide candidates in the diagram below.

The upper diagram shows the evaluation with the known deviations. For purposes of comparison, the lower diagram illustrates the evaluation curve for artificial signs. This is far flatter.

The amazingly conclusive nature of this thought-provoking experiment has become a cornerstone of our research.

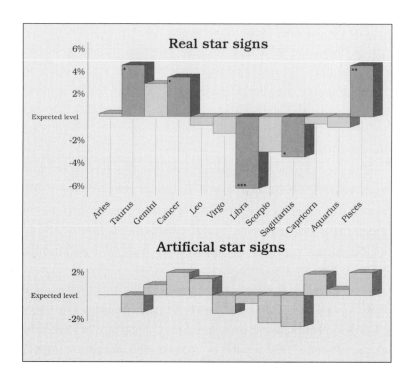

CONCLUSION

We are now at the end of the eleven chapters in which we investigated whether people born under different star signs behave in different ways.

Ten enquiries revealed highly significant results while even the eleventh showed clearly significant correlations.

The main purpose of our study was not to produce interesting individual results – these were, in fact, no more than entertaining by-products of our project. Rather, the declared aim of our research was to establish whether there was a correlation between star signs and human behaviour and predispositions.

We have proved it – there is a correlation.

ASTROLOGY AND STATISTICS
DR RITA KÜNSTLER

(Graduate statistician and
Doctor of Political Science at the
Ludwig-Maximilian University, Munich)

In April 1995, I received a request for statistical advice from the IMWA Institute.

Up to that point, my experience of astrology was limited to taking a surreptitious look at the horoscopes in the daily newspapers or women's magazines in moments of crisis – and then promptly forgetting their predictions.

As a scientist, I was initially sceptical about the undertaking: what could be the relationship between astrology and statistics?

Then I was told about the aim of this project: to use sets of data to test whether people born under different star signs behaved differently from one another.

Not bad as objectives go. But then came my first professional misgivings:

The more wide-ranging the sample, the more exact the statistical evaluations, and the tests based upon them. Where – as in this case – there were twelve distinguishing features (namely the twelve star signs), a suitably large sample would be necessary if we were to reach a reliable conclusion. And where were we going to get hold of this material, bearing in mind that different spheres of activity were involved, not to mention the well-known problem of data protection?

The IMWA Institute succeeded in achieving what I had thought impossible: public servants and official bodies, publishing houses, insurance companies and universities provided large, in some cases extremely large, sets of data.

The data was so extensive that we were able to apply stricter statistical procedures to all the IMWA studies.

The rest was 'detailed statistical work': consideration of birth-rates, determining the right population, chi-square tests of goodness of fit and chi-square tests of independence, sensitivity analyses, separate studies and evaluations, all in accordance with the laws of statistics.

Many of the separate analyses carried out for the book required a very large number of tests, so presenting the probability of a 'multiple test problem'. This is because the more separate studies carried out in the course of a statistical study, the greater the probability of discovering deviations, which might not necessarily be significant.

In other words: if one investigated 252 combinations of illness and star signs at a level of significance of five per cent, some of the significant results could be a matter of chance. For this reason, we thought about adjusting the level of significance in the multiple tests and not pointing out slight levels of significance. My colleague Dr Klinger and I discussed the problem in detail.

We decided not to make any adjustments, since the global chi-square test would always determine whether or not a correlation existed. In nine studies, however, the test revealed a clearly significant correlation and in only one study was the correlation shown to be slightly significant.

Nevertheless, we decided that, when it came to multiple tests of illnesses and occupations where the number of separate investigations was particularly large, we would not show slight significances but merely classify them as 'noteworthy'. All told, it becomes apparent that the chi-square test is of primary importance in determining the effect of star signs on human behaviour. The individual analyses which examine whether the deviation observed is significant in either direction are, from a statistical point of view, of a rather exploratory nature, in other words, they should be seen as simply pointing out irregularities. So the correlation between star signs and human behaviour has a statistical proof, while the particular findings should only be interpreted carefully.

The longer and more closely we observed astrology through the magnifying glass of science, the more fascinating our task became. Some of the clearly significant results surprised me.

Of course, it can never be the responsibility of statisticians to determine causality by means of an observational study. Even so, in all our studies, a link between star signs and human behaviour was proved in accordance with the laws of statistics.

After my two year involvement as statistician with the IMWA Institute investigation, even I now look at the night sky through different eyes.

ADIEU, ASTROLOGY

My idea was quite simple – to find out, as accurately as possible, how different people behave. And now we have mathematical and statistical proof of a correlation between star signs and human behaviour in all the fields of activity we researched. For the first time, astrology has scientific support.

Since the very beginning of our enterprise I have been plagued by one question: How is it possible that neither scientists, nor the powers that be, have attempted previously to get to the bottom of the age-old phenomenon of astrology?

On the one hand millions are squandered around the world every day on trivialities. On the other, no bright spark from government, institution or university has ever put up the money for basic astrological research, despite the fact that for thousands of years more people have believed in astrology than in most world religions. And yet our investigation cost less than the factory price of a 1998 Jaguar XK8.

As our work progressed, shafts of light began to penetrate the darkness of people's traditional qualms about astrology.

Ministers, university deans, editors-in-chief of influential newspapers and people commissioning expensive research projects were all interested. Some of them genuinely wanted to know more about astrology and the messages it has for us. But none of them would openly admit it.

Astrology is like a mistress whom you desire and make love to – but you keep hidden from your friends and the world at large because you are ashamed of her. As Heine put it:

Oh, don't disgrace me, love, my own,
Don't greet me under the lindens, please.
But when we are at home alone,
Then all will be sorted out with ease.

Playboys have an easier time. For two years, astrology has been an enigmatic companion whose mystery I had to penetrate. I was fascinated by the notion of lifting her veil to discover whether myth or reality lay hidden beneath.

Now our work is done. So ends our fleeting foray into the age-old world of the stars, and the ideas surrounding them.

I must disappoint friends and journalists who have bombarded me with hypotheses, suggestions and questions. No, I have not founded a *nouvelle astrologie*, neither am I about to set up a fund for astrological research, nor will I embark on a long exploration of astronomy.

Instead I will return to the other kind of stars, the ones in my photographs and their far more fascinating 'statistics'.

Astrology – *mes respects* –
Astrology – *merci* –
Astrology – *adieu* –

ACKNOWLEDGEMENTS

My thanks go to

- My friend Claus Jacobi, who encouraged me to write this book, and who wrote the introduction.

- Ms Bumbacher and Mr Wuest and all the other splendid helpers at the Federal Office of Statistics in Berne, and Mr Bosse at the Federal Office of Statistics in Wiesbaden, who gave us access to the first large series of data. Likewise to all authorities and companies who supported us by providing usable data.

- Professor Noelle-Neumann of the Institut für Demoskopie, Allensbach for her help and advice.

- Dr Künstler and Professor Küchenhof of the Faculty of Statistics at Ludwig-Maximilian University, Munich, for their splendid technical work and their endless patience with our concerns.

- Our master mathematician, Hanswerner Schwenk.

- Our tireless comrade-in-arms and diplomat Markus Gohr.

- Our computer designer Lei Ren from Shanghai, who produced titles, tables and graphs with innumerable changes.

- My secretary 'Keiserli' Kundert, who was always ready with astrological terminology.

My special thanks to my wife Mirja and my sons, who much of the time had rather a raw deal while I was working on this book.

GUNTER SACHS
AUTUMN 1997

THE ALLENSBACH STUDY

To complement the IMWA analyses, the second part of this book shows the results of a representative survey carried out by the Institut für Demoskopie, Allensbach, with over 13,000 participants.

The survey is primarily interested in the political, ethical and philosophical attitudes of the German population, together with their patterns of consumption. Some of the Allensbach findings are derived from relatively small populations in comparison with the very extensive data of our study. This results from the need to divide the surveyed population into twelve groups (the star signs) in order to carry out significance testing.

Results were recognized as significant where, in the opinion of the Allensbach researchers, there was an adequate population available.

Many of the figures from the study provide interesting, sometimes downright amusing, information. Although this is not its stated aim, the study supports our findings.

INSTITUT FÜR DEMOSKOPIE, ALLENSBACH EMPIRICAL SOCIAL RESEARCH AND ASTROLOGY

A secondary statistical analysis of data obtained by the *Allensbach Media Market Analysis* (Allensbacher Werbeträgeranalyse or AWA) to identify significant deviations in personal characteristics according to the Sun's position in the zodiac at the time of respondents' birth.

SOURCE

Allensbach Archives, IfD Surveys 6020 and 6026.
AWA 1996, waves 1, 2 and 3, winter 1995/1996 and spring 1996

CONTENTS

CONTENTS

FOREWORD

'No reasonable person puts the slightest faith in astrology. "*Nos sumus domini stellarum*! – We are the masters of the stars", said Luther, with the freedom of a Christian. But perhaps this is not entirely true. There are still unexplained connections between human destiny and the planets. The fact that Taureans were at the top of the latest list of the wealthiest Britons, and Sagittarians were at the bottom may simply fuel a common prejudice, but what about the research by the late Michel Gauquelin? As the impeccable rationalist, H.J. Eysenck, pointed out, even Gauquelin's critics had been unable to disprove his Mars effect. According to this, the most outstanding athletes are born when Mars has just passed its zenith. Gauquelin found similar connections between actors and Jupiter, and Saturn and scientists.'

Johannes Gross, Tacheles gesprochen. Notizbuch 1990–1995

Stuttgart 1996, pp. 206–207

'*Ecrasez l'infâme!*' cried Voltaire, by which he also meant, 'Stamp out superstition!' His call takes on a new meaning today. Superstition is now stamped out not only by the power of rational thought but also by the tools of social research. We question reality, and statisticians bring the findings to light in numerical form.

This is the highest task of empirical social research, which must not be daunted by accusations of encouraging superstition or by complaints of lacking political correctness. As

Paul L. Lazarsfeld (1901–1976), the great Austrian-American pioneer of social research, once put it, there are no lofty or lowly subjects of research.

In the summer of 1995, when Gunter Sachs asked the Allensbach Institute whether any of his curious statistical observations concerning the star signs could be investigated using the methods of survey research, the idea did not startle us. Preliminary studies on the subject can be found in the Allensbach Archives dating as far back as the early 1950s.

The Institute's largest survey, which has been conducted for almost forty years, is the *Allensbach Media Market Analysis*, which is currently completed annually based on a sample of 20,000 interviews representative of the German population age 14 and over. We included three questions concerning respondents' birthdays in the study: i.e. the date of birth, whether respondents were born during the day or at night, and the exact time of birth.

We obtained a sufficiently broad statistical base to assign respondents to the twelve star signs. We subsequently examined whether the several hundred attributes ascertained in the *Allensbach Media Market Analysis* showed any statistically significant deviations between respondents of the different star signs. A second survey followed to establish systematically whether statistically significant deviations from the average appeared for those born under particular signs.

The following report describes the procedure employed and the findings obtained. It consists of a collection of uninterpreted statistical facts. Further research can be conducted at any time to broaden the statistical base and to eliminate any suspicion that the findings are the result of chance. Going back to the remarks by Johannes Gross at the start of this foreword, the findings of the French researcher, Michel

Gauquelin, have never been refuted. If we continue along the path upon which the present study sets out, we shall discover which statistically significant correlations between particular attributes and birth under a particular star sign are irrefutable.

Allensbach, Germany
1 July 1997

Prof. Elisabeth Noelle-Neumann

INTRODUCTION

The following collection of data should be viewed as a pilot project.

Over the past fifty years, representative surveys have become so widespread throughout the world that we now have a wealth of data which can be employed for secondary statistical analyses. In other words, the data can be used to look for answers to questions which were not on the agenda of the original surveys.

One such compilation of data is the *Allensbach Media Market Analysis* (AWA), which has been conducted annually since 1959. Its primary aim is to provide advertisers and advertising agents with information about various advertising media – principally the print media but also television and radio. It comprises two elements: firstly, identifying the audience of the advertising media – currently 231 magazines, daily and weekly newspapers and 55 units of television- and radio-advertising time and secondly, ascertaining 348 characteristics of the respondents interviewed.

Subsequently, it is possible to establish connections between the individuals who belong to the broader or narrower audience of the various advertising media and their demographic and psychological characteristics, their consumption habits, what they own or plan to purchase, their political orientation and general attitudes towards life, society and their lifestyle, their interests, the influence they exert and their state of health. These data are combined and processed by computer so as to arrive at the best possible strategies for advertising campaigns.

The annual edition of the *Allensbach Media Market Analysis* is based on a sample of approximately 20,000 interviews representative of the population age 14 and over. The surveys are completed by about 900 of the Allensbach Institute's regular interviewers. Interviewing begins each year in September and continues until May of the following year. The findings are processed in two waves – the autumn wave and the winter/spring wave. The annual publication combines the winter/spring wave of the previous year with the two subsequent waves, thus arriving at a total base of about 20,000 interviews.

For some time now brand name manufacturers and retailers have been interested in the question of whether statistically significant connections can be demonstrated between individuals born under a particular astrological constellation – e.g. the position of the Sun in the zodiac, the ascendant, and the meridian – and other characteristics, such as occupations.

In his book, *Astrologie ohne Aberglauben** (Astrology without Superstition), published in 1978, Thomas Ring reports that two German doctors, F. Schwab and von Klöckler, began applying statistical methods to astrological problems in the 1920s and 1950s, thus initiating the movement to establish astrology for the first time as an empirical science.**

As an additional example, he cites Michel Gauquelin's

*Düsseldorf: Econ-Verlag, p. 146 ff.

** F., Schwab, *Sternenmächte und Mensch* (Berlin-Lichterfelde: Bermühler Verlag, 1923); H. Frh. v. Klöckler, *Kursus der Astrologie* (Berlin: Astra-Verlag, 1956); *Astrologie als Erfahrungswissenschaft* (Leipzig: F. Reinke, 1927).

studies, *L'influence des astres* (The Influence of the Stars, Paris 1955) and *Die Uhren des Kosmos gehen anders* (Cosmic Clocks Keep Different Time, Munich 1973).

This is where the present pilot study comes in. In autumn 1995 and winter/spring 1996, the following three questions were included in the *Allensbach Media Market Analysis* in order to determine the position of the Sun in the zodiac at the time of the respondent's birth:

* When is your birthday?
* Were you born during the day or at night?
* What was your exact time of birth?

For the present pilot project, we had to forego ascertaining any further information such as the place of birth (or the nearest large town), which is needed to determine the ascendant. Our primary aim was to test the fundamental concept of whether persons born under a particular sign of the zodiac do in fact display any significant deviations in terms of the numerous attributes ascertained in the *Allensbach Media Market Analysis*.

The following report, with its numerous graphs and tables, requires the reader to make a major adjustment. The hundreds of characteristics tested for significance at the 1 per cent and 5 per cent levels* may appear strange in this 'secondhand' analysis. Readers must always keep in mind that these characteristics were not selected from an astrological perspective but were originally intended to define target groups and media for advertising campaigns.

* *See*: 'Information on the accuracy of representative surveys (tolerance limits of the results)', p. 333.

At the same time, however, we should also be aware of the advantages of this secondary analysis of the AWA data. Applying the laws of probability to astrological questions requires a very large statistical base, which would normally be unobtainable for financial reasons. Here we have it. The list below shows the sample size included in the AWA for each of the twelve signs of the zodiac.

Moreover, the long duration of the study (around seven months) and the fact that it was completed in two separate waves also enables us to consider only those significant deviations which appeared in both waves, thus corroborating the existence of these differences more firmly. At the same time, the statistical base is broad enough to allow us to analyse the findings obtained in the autumn 1995 or winter/spring 1996 waves separately, without any excessive tolerances.

Star sign	Sample size in the AWA
Capricorn	837
Aquarius	909
Pisces	937
Aries	987
Taurus	928
Gemini	1021
Cancer	913
Leo	925
Virgo	909
Libra	812
Scorpio	820
Sagittarius	760
Total	10,758*

* A breakdown of total respondents by gender and by wave is given on page 331.

A second advantage of completing a secondary analysis of this kind based on the findings of the AWA is that nothing in the survey invites respondents, in describing their personality, to attribute characteristics to themselves in light of their prior knowledge of astrology.* There are no references to astrology which might direct respondents' thoughts in this direction in the entire questionnaire, apart from the date and time of birth at the end of the interview in the statistics section.

Of course, the fact that the characteristics under investigation are not drawn from astrological personality profiles does pose difficulties. The study thus depends heavily on the intuition of its users and interpreters in recognizing the significantly deviating characteristics as indicators of astrologically important traits. In this sense, even the wealth of marketing data contained in the AWA can be useful, shedding light for example on respondents' relationships to cars, buildings, savings, etc.

The material presented in the ensuing sections is organized as follows:

1. As the first step, the 923 characteristics and attributes included in the AWA are examined to determine the extent to which respondents belonging to the various star signs show deviations from the average for all respondents at the 1 per cent and 5 per cent levels.
2. The next step is to see whether these characteristic deviations appear in both the autumn 1995 and the win-

---

* Kurt Pawlik and Lothar Buse, 'Selbst-Attribuierung als differentiell-psychologische Moderatorvariable: Nachprüfung und Erklärung von Eysencks Astrologie-Persönlichkeits-Korrelationen', Zeitschrift für Sozialpsychologie, 10 (1979): 54–69.

ter/spring 1996 waves. There were 84 confirmed significant deviations which reached the 1 per cent level in at least one wave and the 5 per cent level in the other wave.

Selected characteristics where significant deviations appeared have been presented in graphic form, showing the extent to which respondents born under the various star signs either fell below or exceeded the average (*see* figures 1–30, pages 230–259).

3. The number of characteristics which show confirmed significant deviations varies greatly for the different star signs, ranging from only one confirmed significant deviation for those born under Capricorn to 12 and 13 for Gemini and Pisces.

Tables 1–12 show the significantly deviating characteristics for each star sign, forming a kind of portrait (*see* pages 262–273).

4. The appendix contains the entire AWA sample data from the autumn 1995 and winter/spring 1996 waves, broken down according to star signs (*see* pages 278–330). All significant deviations have been designated as such. In addition, there is also a page which establishes the statistical tolerance limits, the so-called confidence interval.

We have refrained from offering any professional commentary on the results of this pilot study. The authors are not trained astrologers. It can, however, be observed that the significant deviations found in this study, while small in absolute terms, do nevertheless demand an explanation.

Institut für Demoskopie, Allensbach
2 September 1996

PRESENTATION OF STRIKINGLY
SIGNIFICANT FINDINGS

The following graphs present those characteristics for which individual star signs show significant deviations from the average for all respondents. Only those deviations which occur in both waves of the AWA study are taken into account here. Deviations must have attained the 1 per cent significance level in at least one wave and the 5 per cent level in the same direction in the other.

The significance calculations assume a random sample in which every element in the universe investigated has an equal chance of appearing in the sample.

The graphs show the percentage to which the values obtained for the various star signs deviate from the average for the entire sample, which is entered on the y-axis on the left hand side.

Since the 2,525 respondents who did not indicate their date of birth are also included in the calculation of the average value for all 13,283 respondents, there may in certain cases be a difference from the average value, which can be derived from the values for the individual star signs.

Graph 1

Deviations from the mean in interest in motor racing and motorcycle racing

Question: It often happens that one would like to find out more about one subject, while another one interests one less. Could you look at these cards and arrange the subjects on this list according to how much they interest you.

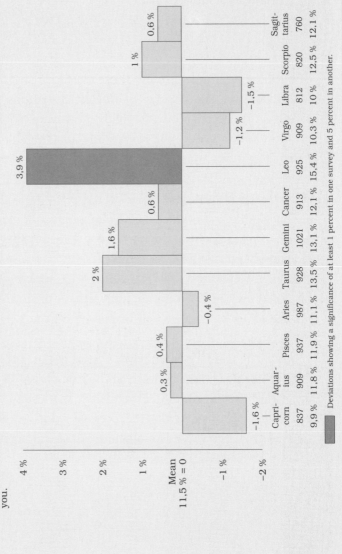

	Capri-corn	Aquar-ius	Pisces	Aries	Taurus	Gemini	Cancer	Leo	Virgo	Libra	Scorpio	Sagit-tarius
	837	909	937	987	928	1021	913	925	909	812	820	760
	9,9 %	11,8 %	11,9 %	11,1 %	13,5 %	13,1 %	12,1 %	15,4 %	10,3 %	10 %	12,5 %	12,1 %
	−1,6 %	0,3 %	0,4 %	−0,4 %	2 %	1,6 %	0,6 %	3,9 %	−1,2 %	−1,5 %	1 %	0,6 %

Deviations showing a significance of at least 1 percent in one survey and 5 percent in another.

Graph 2

Deviation from the mean in special interests in building, modernisation and renovation

Question: It often happens that one would like to find out more about one subject, while another one interests one less. Could you look at these cards and arrange the subjects on this list according to how much they interest you.

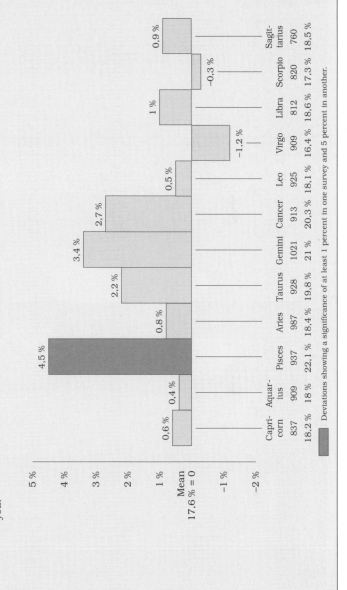

Deviations showing a significance of at least 1 percent in one survey and 5 percent in another.

Graph 3

Deviations from the mean in special interest in nature conservancy and environmental protection

Question: It often happens that one would like to find out more about one subject, while another one interests one less. Could you look at these cards and arrange the subjects on this list according to how much they interest you.

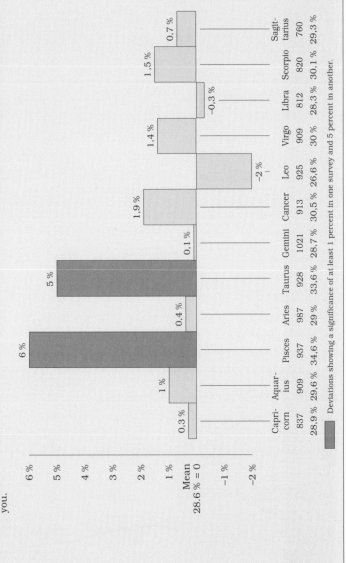

	Capri-corn	Aquar-ius	Pisces	Aries	Taurus	Gemini	Cancer	Leo	Virgo	Libra	Scorpio	Sagit-tarius
	837	909	937	987	928	1021	913	925	909	812	820	760
	28.9 %	29.6 %	34.6 %	29 %	33.6 %	28.7 %	30.5 %	26.6 %	30 %	28.3 %	30.1 %	29.3 %
	0.3 %	1 %	6 %	0.4 %	5 %	0.1 %	1.9 %	-2 %	1.4 %	-0.3 %	1.5 %	0.7 %

Deviations showing a significance of at least 1 percent in one survey and 5 percent in another.

Graph 4

Deviations from the mean in advice-givers and experts in further professional training

Questions: It often happens that one would like to find out more about one subject while another one interests you less. Could you look at these cards and arrange the subjects on this list according to how much they interest you. Look through the list again and indicate every subject about which you often give acquaintances or relatives advice or are often asked for advice on: those subjects in which you are regarded as an expert.

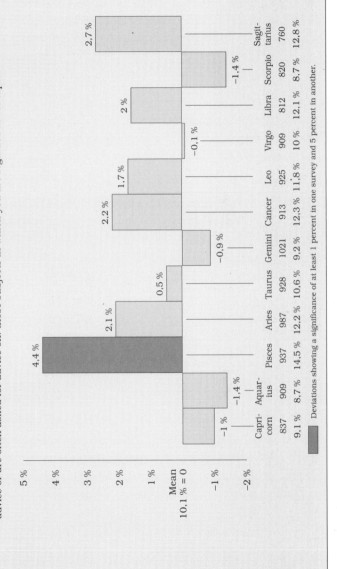

Deviations showing a significance of at least 1 percent in one survey and 5 percent in another.

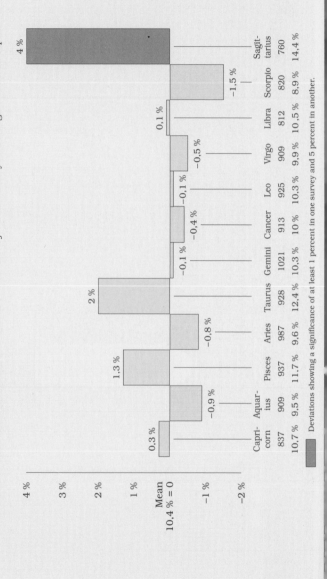

Deviations from the mean in advice-givers and experts in alternative medicine

Questions: It often happens that one would like to find out more about one subject while another one interests one less. Could you have a look at these cards and arrange the subjects on this list according to how much they interest you? Look through the list again and indicate every subject about which you often give acquaintances or relatives advice or are often asked for advice on: those subjects in which you are regarded as an expert.

	Capri-corn	Aquar-ius	Pisces	Aries	Taurus	Gemini	Cancer	Leo	Virgo	Libra	Scorpio	Sagit-tarius
	837	909	937	987	928	1021	913	925	909	812	820	760
	10,7 %	9,5 %	11,7 %	9,6 %	12,4 %	10,3 %	10 %	10,3 %	9,9 %	10,5 %	8,9 %	14,4 %
Deviation	0,3 %	-0,9 %	1,3 %	-0,8 %	2 %	-0,1 %	-0,4 %	-0,1 %	-0,5 %	0,1 %	-1,5 %	4 %

Mean 10,4 % = 0

■ Deviations showing a significance of at least 1 percent in one survey and 5 percent in another.

Graph 6

Deviations from the mean in advice-givers and experts in politics

Questions: It often happens that one would like to find out more about one subject while another one interests one less. Could you have a look at these cards and arrange the subjects on this list according to how much they interest you? Look through the list again and indicate every subject about which you often give acquaintances or relatives advice or are often asked for advice on: those subjects in which you are regarded as an expert.

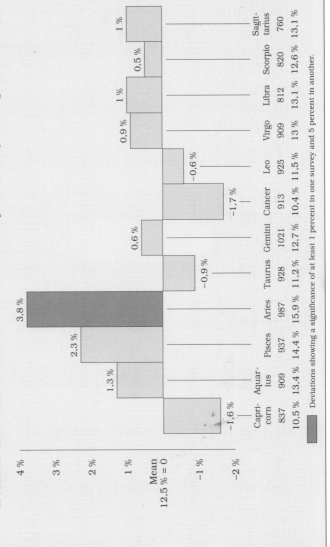

	Capricorn	Aquarius	Pisces	Aries	Taurus	Gemini	Cancer	Leo	Virgo	Libra	Scorpio	Sagittarius
	837	909	937	987	928	1021	913	925	909	812	820	760
	10.5 %	13.4 %	14.4 %	15.9 %	11.2 %	12.7 %	10.4 %	11.5 %	13 %	13.1 %	12.6 %	13.1 %

Deviations showing a significance of at least 1 percent in one survey and 5 percent in another.

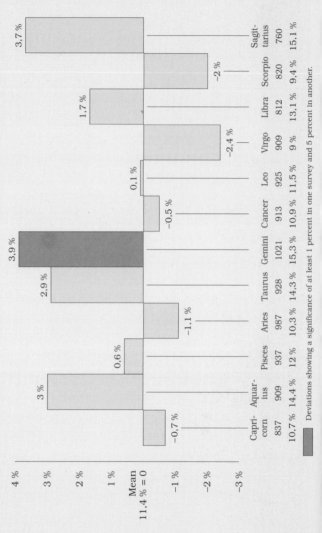

Graph 7

Deviations from the mean in advice-givers and experts in sewing and knitting

Questions: It often happens that one would like to find out more about one subject while another one interests one less. Could you have a look at these cards and arrange the subjects on this list according to how much they interest you? Look through the list again and indicate every subject about which you often give acquaintances or relatives advice or are often asked for advice on: those subjects in which you are regarded as an expert.

	Capri-corn	Aquar-ius	Pisces	Aries	Taurus	Gemini	Cancer	Leo	Virgo	Libra	Scorpio	Sagit-tarius
	837	909	937	987	928	1021	913	925	909	812	820	760
	10.7 %	14.4 %	12 %	10.3 %	14.3 %	15.3 %	10.9 %	11.5 %	9 %	13.1 %	9.4 %	15.1 %

Deviation values: Capricorn −0.7 %, Aquarius 3 %, Pisces 0.6 %, Aries −1.1 %, Taurus 2.9 %, Gemini 3.9 %, Cancer −0.5 %, Leo 0.1 %, Virgo −2.4 %, Libra 1.7 %, Scorpio −2 %, Sagittarius 3.7 %

Y-axis: 4 %, 3 %, 2 %, 1 %, Mean 11.4 % = 0, −1 %, −2 %, −3 %

Deviations showing a significance of at least 1 percent in one survey and 5 percent in another.

236

Graph 8

Deviations from the mean in decision-making about buying insurance

Question: When something has to be bought in your household, who decides what it is, what brand, for example, it should be or what it should cost? Do you make the decision alone or with other people or do you play no part at all in the decision?

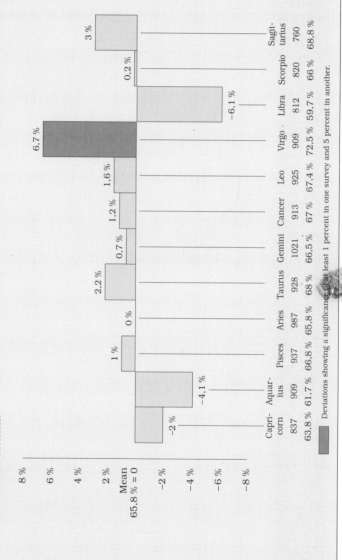

Deviations showing a significance of at least 1 percent in one survey and 5 percent in another.

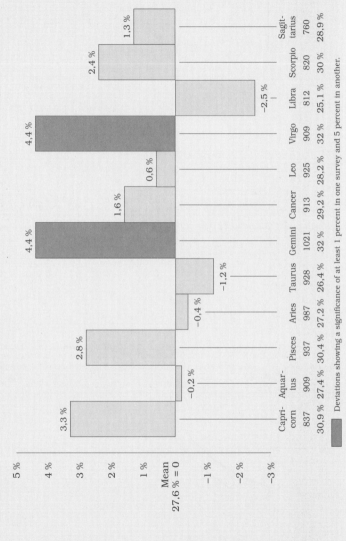

Graph 9

Deviations from the mean in the core group concerning insurance

Survey of those households in which at least five of the ten selected types of insurance are used.

Deviations showing a significance of at least 1 percent in one survey and 5 percent in another.

	Capri-corn	Aquar-ius	Pisces	Aries	Taurus	Gemini	Cancer	Leo	Virgo	Libra	Scorpio	Sagit-tarius
	837	909	937	987	928	1021	913	925	909	812	820	760
	30,9 %	27,4 %	30,4 %	27,2 %	26,4 %	32 %	29,2 %	28,2 %	32 %	25,1 %	30 %	28,9 %
	3,3 %	-0,2 %	2,8 %	-0,4 %	-1,2 %	4,4 %	1,6 %	0,6 %	4,4 %	-2,5 %	2,4 %	1,3 %

Graph 10

Deviations from the mean in ownership of multiple dwellings

Question: Do you or someone in your household own a house or a flat?

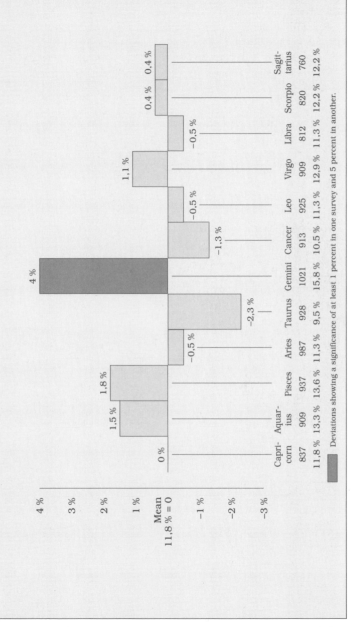

Deviations showing a significance of at least 1 percent in one survey and 5 percent in another.

Graph 11

Deviations from the mean in household ownership of video recorders

Question: We've written on this list things people don't buy for themselves every day. Which of them do you personally own or have at your disposal in your household?

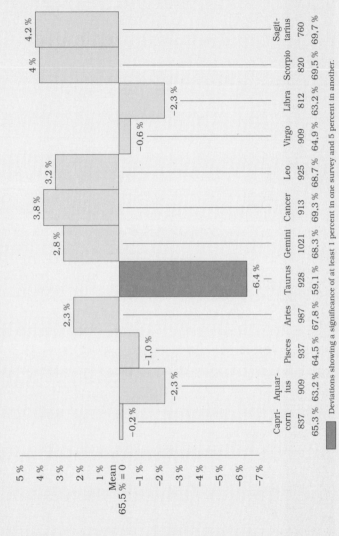

Deviations showing a significance of at least 1 percent in one survey and 5 percent in another.

Graph 12

Deviations from the mean in household ownership of prints, sculptures and paintings

Question: We've written on this list things people don't buy for themselves every day. Which of them do you personally own or have at your disposal in your household?

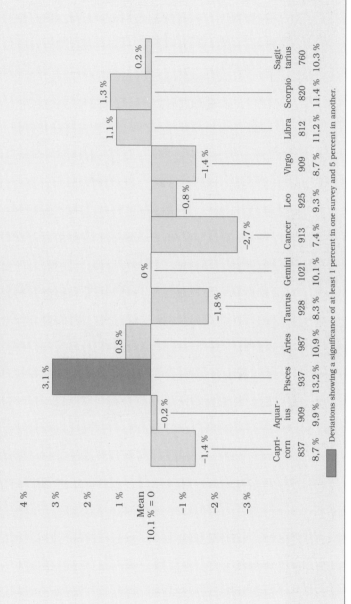

Deviations showing a significance of at least 1 percent in one survey and 5 percent in another.

Graph 13

Deviations from the mean in purchase and drinking of spirits

Question: Which of you have personally drunk or bought spirits in the last fortnight?

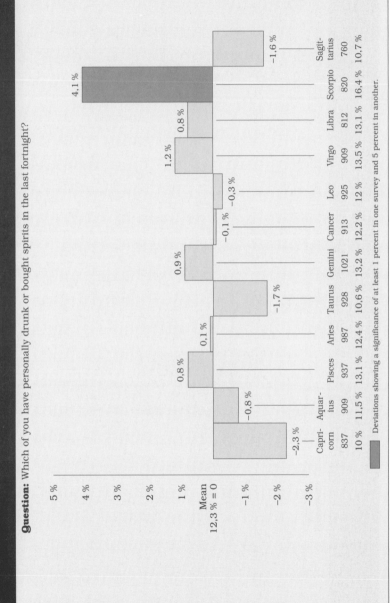

	Capri-corn	Aquar-ius	Pisces	Aries	Taurus	Gemini	Cancer	Leo	Virgo	Libra	Scorpio	Sagit-tarius
	837	909	937	987	928	1021	913	925	909	812	820	760
	10 %	11,5 %	13,1 %	12,4 %	10,6 %	13,2 %	12,2 %	12 %	13,5 %	13,1 %	16,4 %	10,7 %
deviation	−2,3 %	−0,8 %	0,8 %	0,1 %	−1,7 %	0,9 %	−0,1 %	−0,3 %	1,2 %	0,8 %	4,1 %	−1,6 %

Deviations showing a significance of at least 1 percent in one survey and 5 percent in another.

Graph 14

Deviations from the mean in (private) car driving

Question: Is there one or more cars in your household? If yours is a car-owning household, do you drive this car/one of these cars yourself?

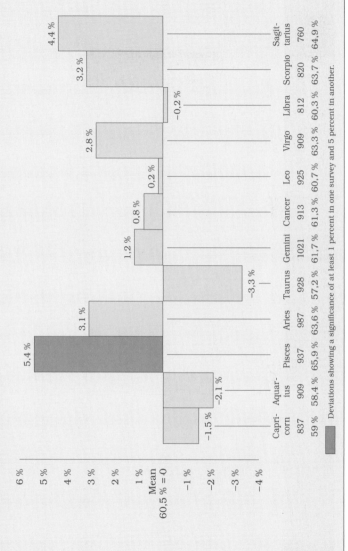

Deviations showing a significance of at least 1 percent in one survey and 5 percent in another.

	Capri-corn	Aquar-ius	Pisces	Aries	Taurus	Gemini	Cancer	Leo	Virgo	Libra	Scorpio	Sagit-tarius
	837	909	937	987	928	1021	913	925	909	812	820	760
	59 %	58,4 %	65,9 %	63,6 %	57,2 %	61,7 %	61,3 %	60,7 %	63,3 %	60,3 %	63,7 %	64,9 %
Deviation	−1,5 %	−2,1 %	5,4 %	3,1 %	−3,3 %	1,2 %	0,8 %	0,2 %	2,8 %	−0,2 %	3,2 %	4,4 %

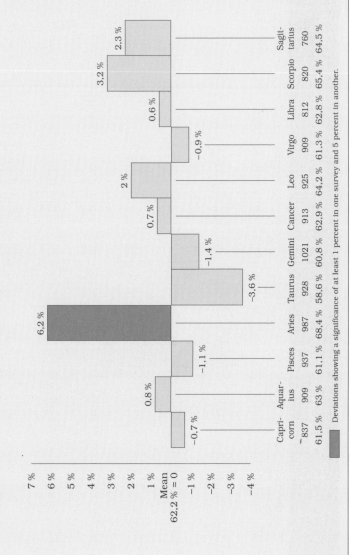

Graph 15

Deviations from the mean in use of spray deodorant

Question: Which of you have used a spray deodorant in the last seven days?

Deviations showing a significance of at least 1 percent in one survey and 5 percent in another.

Graph 16

Deviations from the mean in leisure activities: painting, woodwork, interior decoration

Question: What leisure activities have you personally done in the last twelve months?

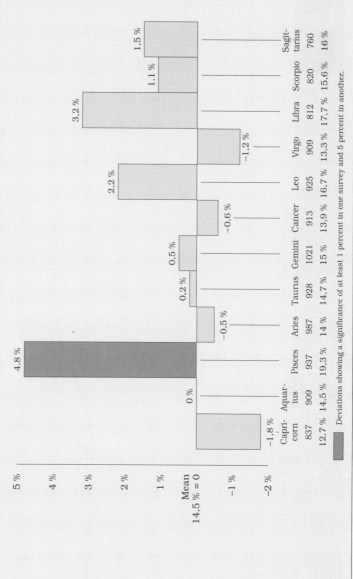

	Capri-corn	Aquar-ius	Pisces	Aries	Taurus	Gemini	Cancer	Leo	Virgo	Libra	Scorpio	Sagit-tarius
	837	909	937	987	928	1021	913	925	909	812	820	760
	12,7 %	14,5 %	19,3 %	14 %	14,7 %	15 %	13,9 %	16,7 %	13,3 %	17,7 %	15,6 %	16 %

Deviations showing a significance of at least 1 percent in one survey and 5 percent in another.

Graph 17

Deviations from the mean in leisure activities: minor car repairs

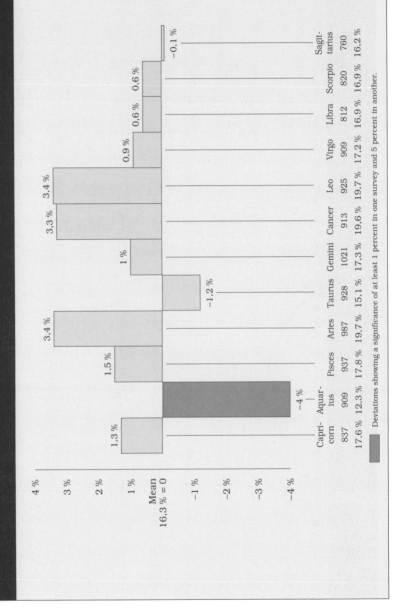

	Capricorn	Aquarius	Pisces	Aries	Taurus	Gemini	Cancer	Leo	Virgo	Libra	Scorpio	Sagittarius
	837	909	937	987	928	1021	913	925	909	812	820	760
	17,6 %	12,3 %	17,8 %	19,7 %	15,1 %	17,3 %	19,6 %	19,7 %	17,2 %	16,9 %	16,9 %	16,2 %

Deviations showing a significance of at least 1 percent in one survey and 5 percent in another.

246

Graph 18

Deviations from the mean in leisure activities: gardening

Question: What do you do in your leisure time, at the appropriate time of year? Indicate by each activity whether you do this frequently, occasionally or never.

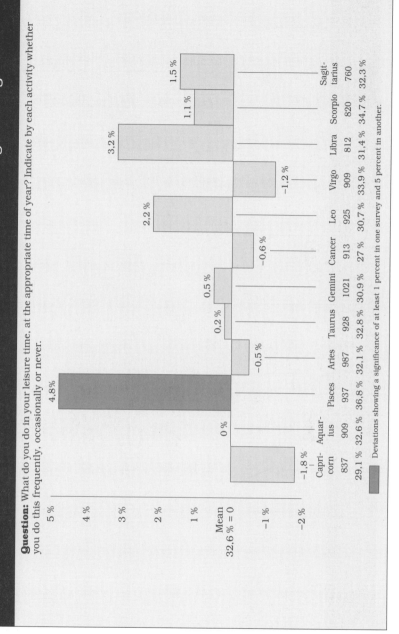

	Capri-corn	Aquar-ius	Pisces	Aries	Taurus	Gemini	Cancer	Leo	Virgo	Libra	Scorpio	Sagit-tarius
	837	909	937	987	928	1021	913	925	909	812	820	760
	29.1 %	32.6 %	36.8 %	32.1 %	32.8 %	30.9 %	27 %	30.7 %	33.9 %	31.4 %	34.7 %	32.3 %

Deviations showing a significance of at least 1 percent in one survey and 5 percent in another.

5 %
4 %
3 %
2 %
1 %
Mean 32.6 % = 0
-1 %
-2 %

-1.8 % · 0 % · 4.8 % · -0.5 % · 0.2 % · 0.5 % · -0.6 % · 2.2 % · -1.2 % · 3.2 % · 1.1 % · 1.5 %

Graph 19

Deviations from the mean in leisure activities: listening to folk music

Question: What do you do in your leisure time, at the appropriate time of year? Indicate by each activity whether you do this frequently, occasionally or never.

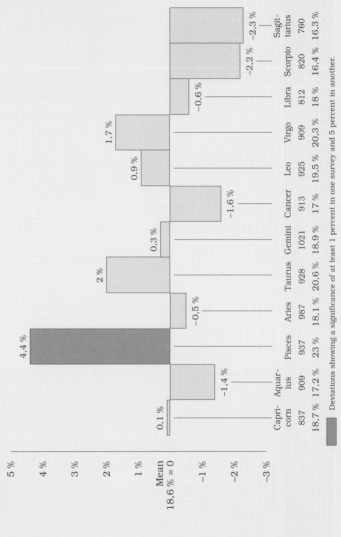

	Capri-corn 837	Aquar-ius 909	Pisces 937	Aries 987	Taurus 928	Gemini 1021	Cancer 913	Leo 925	Virgo 909	Libra 812	Scorpio 820	Sagit-tarius 760
	18.7 %	17.2 %	23 %	18.1 %	20.6 %	18.9 %	17 %	19.5 %	20.3 %	18 %	16.4 %	16.3 %

Deviations showing a significance of at least 1 percent in one survey and 5 percent in another.

Graph 20

Deviations from the mean in leisure activities: watching sport on TV

Question: What do you do in your leisure time, at the appropriate time of year? Indicate by each activity whether you do this frequently, occasionally or never.

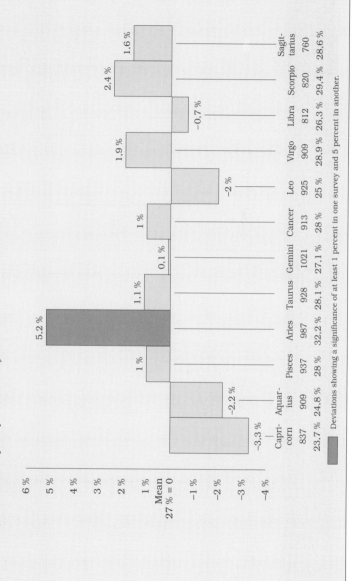

Deviations showing a significance of at least 1 percent in one survey and 5 percent in another.

Graph 21

Deviations from the mean in satellite and cable TV access

Question: How do you receive television programmes in your household?

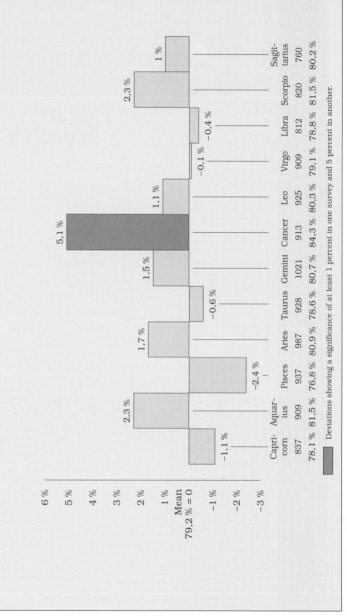

Deviations showing a significance of at least 1 percent in one survey and 5 percent in another.

	Capri-corn	Aquar-ius	Pisces	Aries	Taurus	Gemini	Cancer	Leo	Virgo	Libra	Scorpio	Sagit-tarius
	837	909	937	987	928	1021	913	925	909	812	820	760
	78.1%	81.5%	76.8%	80.9%	78.6%	80.7%	84.3%	80.3%	79.1%	78.8%	81.5%	80.2%

Deviations: -1.1%, 2.3%, -2.4%, 1.7%, -0.6%, 1.5%, 5.1%, 1.1%, -0.1%, -0.4%, 2.3%, 1%

Mean 79.2% = 0

Graph 22

Deviations from the mean in preference for moral and emotional arguments

Question: At a panel discussion on the greenhouse effect and climate change, two experts were talking about what the latest statistics and measurements indicated about the current state of the climate and the amount of pollutants actually in the atmosphere. Suddenly one of the audience jumps up and shouts, 'Why should I be interested in these figures and statistics? How can you talk so coldly about a subject which is going to decide our whole future?' Would you say that he was absolutely right?

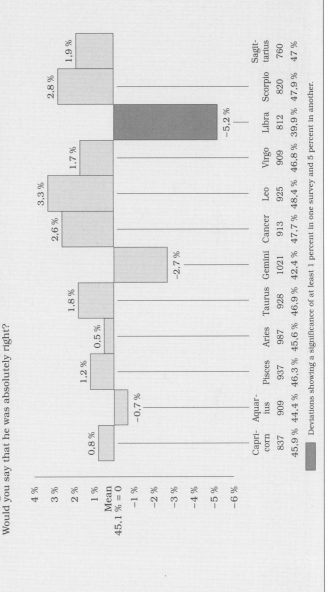

Deviations showing a significance of at least 1 percent in one survey and 5 percent in another.

Graph 23

Deviations from the mean in approval for factual arguments

Question: At a panel discussion on the greenhouse effect and climate change, two experts were talking about what the latest statistics and measurements indicated about the current state of the climate and the amount of pollutants actually in the atmosphere. Suddenly one of the audience jumps up and shouts, 'Why should I be interested in these figures and statistics? How can you talk so coldly about a subject which is going to decide our whole future? Would you say that he's wrong?

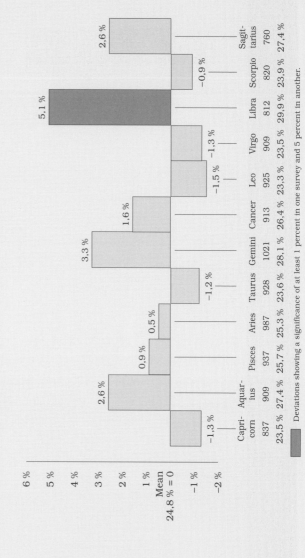

	Capri-corn	Aquar-ius	Pisces	Aries	Taurus	Gemini	Cancer	Leo	Virgo	Libra	Scorpio	Sagit-tarius
	837	909	937	987	928	1021	913	925	909	812	820	760
	23,5 %	27,4 %	25,7 %	25,3 %	23,6 %	28,1 %	26,4 %	23,3 %	23,5 %	29,9 %	23,9 %	27,4 %

Deviations showing a significance of at least 1 percent in one survey and 5 percent in another.

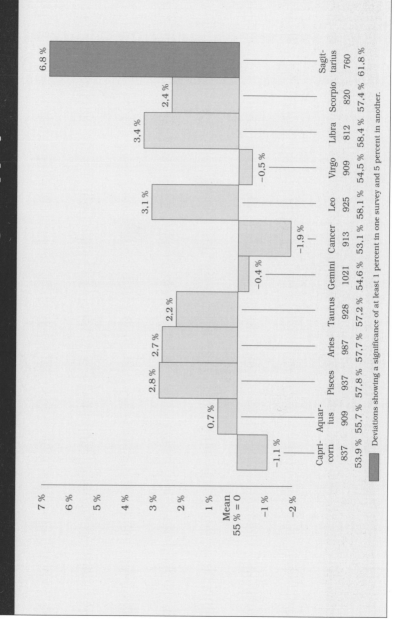

Graph 24

Deviations from the mean in striving to help people in need

	Capri-corn	Aquar-ius	Pisces	Aries	Taurus	Gemini	Cancer	Leo	Virgo	Libra	Scorpio	Sagit-tarius
	837	909	937	987	928	1021	913	925	909	812	820	760
	53,9 %	55,7 %	57,8 %	57,7 %	57,2 %	54,6 %	53,1 %	58,1 %	54,5 %	58,4 %	57,4 %	61,8 %

Deviations: −1,1 %, 0,7 %, 2,8 %, 2,7 %, 2,2 %, −0,4 %, −1,9 %, 3,1 %, −0,5 %, 3,4 %, 2,4 %, 6,8 %

Deviations showing a significance of at least 1 percent in one survey and 5 percent in another.

253

Graph 25

Deviations from the mean in striving for tolerance towards foreigners and those of other faiths

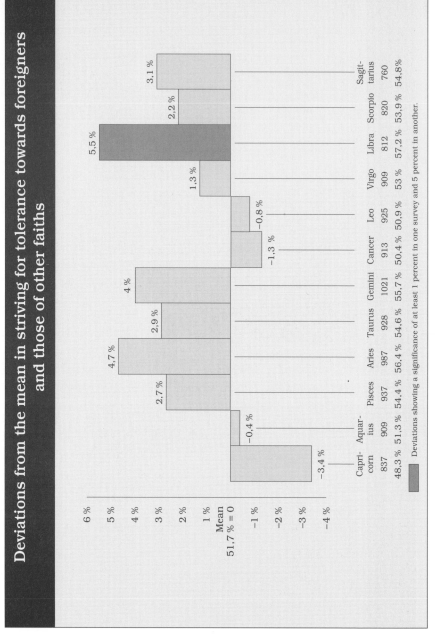

	Capri-corn	Aquar-ius	Pisces	Aries	Taurus	Gemini	Cancer	Leo	Virgo	Libra	Scorpio	Sagit-tarius
	837	909	937	987	928	1021	913	925	909	812	820	760
	48,3	51,3 %	54,4 %	56,4 %	54,6 %	55,7 %	50,4 %	50,9%	53 %	57,2 %	53,9 %	54,8%

Deviations showing a significance of at least 1 percent in one survey and 5 percent in another.

Graph 26

Deviations from the mean in reading TV guides/supplements

Question: People who read at least one title of the media group regularly or comparatively often.

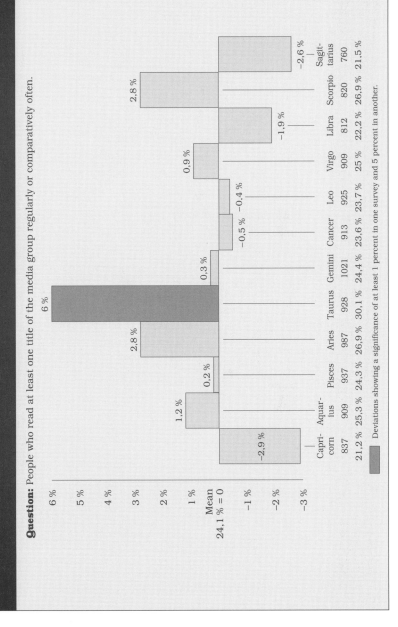

	Capri-corn	Aquar-ius	Pisces	Aries	Taurus	Gemini	Cancer	Leo	Virgo	Libra	Scorpio	Sagit-tarius
	837	909	937	987	928	1021	913	925	909	812	820	760
	21.2 %	25.3 %	24.3 %	26.9 %	30.1 %	24.4 %	23.6 %	23.7 %	25 %	22.2 %	26.9 %	21.5 %

Deviations showing a significance of at least 1 percent in one survey and 5 percent in another.

255

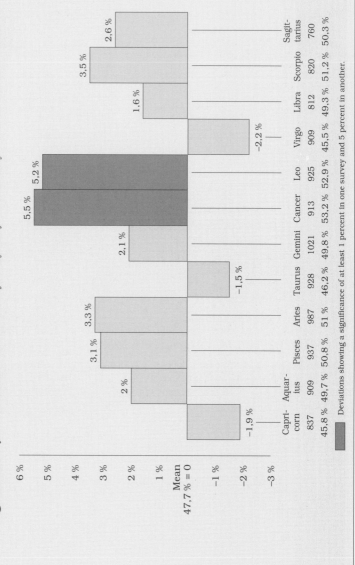

Deviations from the mean in wearing denim daily or almost daily

Question: Do you wear denim clothes? Would you say: daily – almost daily – from time to time – never?

	Capri-corn	Aquar-ius	Pisces	Aries	Taurus	Gemini	Cancer	Leo	Virgo	Libra	Scorpio	Sagit-tarius
	837	909	937	987	928	1021	913	925	909	812	820	760
	45,8 %	49,7 %	50,8 %	51 %	46,2 %	49,8 %	53,2 %	52,9 %	45,5 %	49,3 %	51,2 %	50,3 %
	−1,9 %	2 %	3,1 %	3,3 %	−1,5 %	2,1 %	5,5 %	5,2 %	−2,2 %	1,6 %	3,5 %	2,6 %

Mean 47,7 % = 0

Deviations showing a significance of at least 1 percent in one survey and 5 percent in another.

Graph 28

Deviations from the mean in reading nature or animal magazines

The 231 selected newspaper and magazine titles are combined in 40 media groups. People are users of a media group when they read at least one title of a media group regularly or comparatively often.

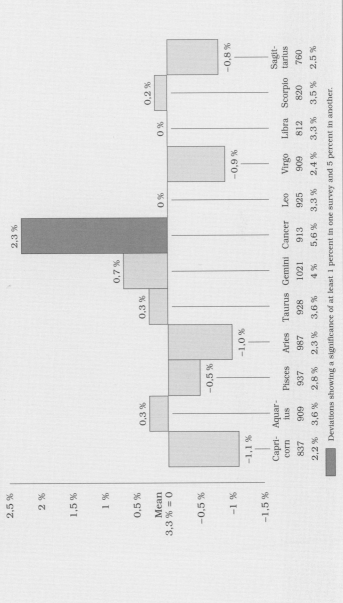

	Capri-corn	Aquar-ius	Pisces	Aries	Taurus	Gemini	Cancer	Leo	Virgo	Libra	Scorpio	Sagit-tarius
	837	909	937	987	928	1021	913	925	909	812	820	760
	2,2 %	3,6 %	2,8 %	2,3 %	3,6 %	4 %	5,6 %	3,3 %	2,4 %	3,3 %	3,5 %	2,5 %

Deviations: -1,1 %, 0,3 %, -0,5 %, -1,0 %, 0,3 %, 0,7 %, 2,3 %, 0 %, -0,9 %, 0 %, 0,2 %, -0,8 %

Deviations showing a significance of at least 1 percent in one survey and 5 percent in another.

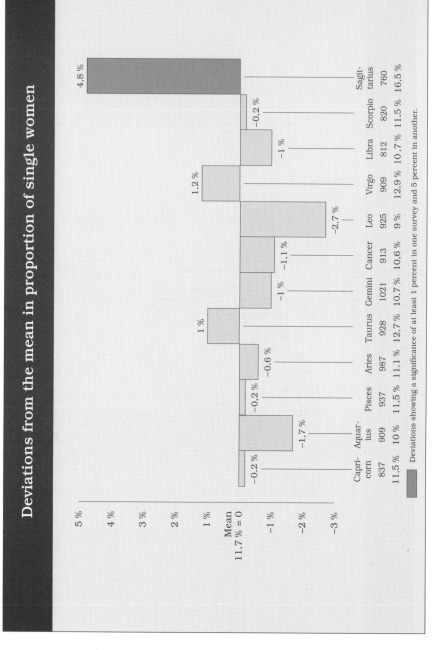

Deviations from the mean in proportion of single women

	Capri-corn	Aquar-ius	Pisces	Aries	Taurus	Gemini	Cancer	Leo	Virgo	Libra	Scorpio	Sagit-tarius
	837	909	937	987	928	1021	913	925	909	812	820	760
	11,5 %	10 %	11,5 %	11,1 %	12,7 %	10,7 %	10,6 %	9 %	12,9 %	10,7 %	11,5 %	16,5 %
deviation	–0,2 %	–1,7 %	–0,2 %	–0,6 %	1 %	–1 %	–1,1 %	–2,7 %	1,2 %	–1 %	–0,2 %	4,8 %

Deviations showing a significance of at least 1 percent in one survey and 5 percent in another.

Graph 29

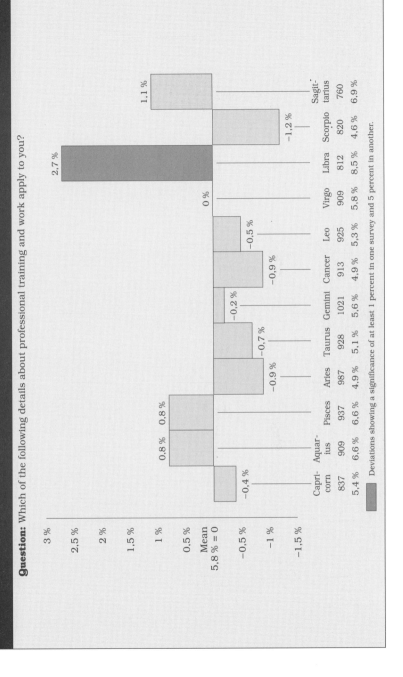

Graph 30

Deviations from the mean in university education and studies

Question: Which of the following details about professional training and work apply to you?

3 %

2,5 %

2 %

1,5 %

1 %

0,5 %

Mean
5,8 % = 0

−0,5 %

−1 %

−1,5 %

	Capri-corn	Aquar-ius	Pisces	Aries	Taurus	Gemini	Cancer	Leo	Virgo	Libra	Scorpio	Sagit-tarius
	837	909	937	987	928	1021	913	925	909	812	820	760
	5,4 %	6,6 %	6,6 %	4,9 %	5,1 %	5,6 %	4,9 %	5,3 %	5,8 %	8,5 %	4,6 %	6,9 %

−0,4 % 0,8 % 0,8 % −0,9 % −0,7 % −0,2 % −0,9 % −0,5 % 0 % 2,7 % −1,2 % 1,1 %

Deviations showing a significance of at least 1 percent in one survey and 5 percent in another.

SIGNIFICANT DEVIATIONS SHOWN BY THE VARIOUS STAR SIGNS

The following section lists, in order of star sign, those values which deviate significantly from the average for each particular star sign. Once again, only deviations which appear in both AWA waves are considered, and these must have reached a significance level of at least 1 per cent in one wave and 5 per cent in the other in the same direction.

The significance calculations assume a random sample in which every element in the universe investigated has an equal chance of appearing in the sample. This assumption is supported by the agreement between numerous indicator values and other statistical data.

Significant deviations appearing under the star sign Aries

Survey sample	Total population 13 283	Aries 987	Deviation
Politics: Advice-Givers, Experts	13.1 %	15.9 %	+ 2.8 %
Kölsch Beer: Bought/Drunk, 14 days	3.3 %	5.3 %	+ 2.0 %
Bath Essence, Bath Gel: Use, 7 days	39.2 %	32.4 %	− 6.8 %
Spray Deodorant: Use, 7 days	62.2 %	68.4 %	+ 6.2 %
Always or Mainly the Same Holiday Destination	15.1 %	18.7 %	+ 3.6 %
Frequently Watch Sport on TV in Leisure Time	27.0 %	33.2 %	+ 6.2 %
More Conservative Women	30.8 %	25.6 %	− 5.2 %
Connection to Church	24.5 %	19.1 %	− 5.4 %

Significant deviations appearing under the star sign Taurus

Survey sample	Total population 13 283	Taurus 928	Deviation
Special Interest in Nature Conservancy/Environment	28.6 %	33.6 %	+ 5.0 %
Video Recorder: Households Own	65.1 %	59.1 %	– 6.0 %
Use of Hygiene Products for Dentures, 7 days	25.6 %	31.2 %	+ 5.6 %
Pipe Smoker: Consumer Typology	1.1 %	2.6 %	+ 1.5 %
TV Programme Supplements, Media Group	24.1 %	30.1 %	+ 6.0 %
Work: Working or Helping	49.2 %	42.8 %	– 6.4 %
Work: Retired, Pensioner	25.0 %	30.7 %	+ 5.7 %
Size of Place of Residence: 500,000 Inhabitants or More	14.0 %	9.8 %	– 4.2 %

Significant deviations appearing under the star sign Gemini

Survey sample	Total population 13 283	Gemini 1021	Deviation
Films, Videos: Advice-Givers, Experts	5,6 %	8,2 %	+ 2,6 %
Catering for Guests, Hospitality: Advice-Givers, Experts	18,6 %	22,8 %	+ 4,2 %
Sewing, Knitting: Advice-Givers, Experts	11,4 %	15,3 %	+ 3,9 %
House, Multiple Dwelling: Households Own	11,8 %	15,8 %	+ 4,0 %
Mortgage/Savings Contract with Building Society: Plans to Purchase in 1-2 years	6,1 %	8,9 %	+ 2,8 %
Video Equipment: Households Own	6,5 %	9,5 %	+ 3,0 %
Cocoa, Cocoa Drinks: Purchase, 14 days	14,0 %	17,9 %	+ 3,9 %
I'm Keen to Try Out New Things: Consumer Typology	46,2 %	52,5 %	+ 6,3 %
TV, Video Recorders: Decision-Makers with Specialist Knowledge	2,8 %	5,1 %	+ 2,3 %
Insurance: Core Group	27,6 %	32,0 %	+ 4,4 %
Large Household: 4 People or More	25,8 %	31,2 %	+ 5,4 %

Significant deviations appearing under the star sign Cancer

Survey sample	Total population	Cancer	Deviation
	13 283	913	
Cable, Satellite TV: Special Interest	17,1 %	21,2 %	+ 4,1 %
Video Camera, Camcorder: Households Own	16,6 %	20,9 %	+ 4,3 %
Chewing Gum: Purchase, 14 days	22,5 %	27,2 %	+ 4,7 %
Regularly Make Own Videos in Leisure Time	2,0 %	3,5 %	+ 1,5 %
Cable, Satellite TV Reception in Household	79,2 %	84,3 %	+ 5,1 %
Wearing Denim (almost) Daily: Consumer Typology	47,7 %	53,2 %	+ 5,5 %
Nature, Animal Magazines: Media Group	3,3 %	5,6 %	+ 2,3 %
Size of Place of Residence: Under 20,000 Inhabitants	43,3 %	49,3 %	+ 6,0 %

Significant deviations appearing under the star sign Leo

Survey sample	Total population 13 283	Leo 925	Deviation
Motor Racing, Motorcycle Racing: Special Interest	11,5 %	15,1 %	+ 3,6 %
Answering Machine: Households Own	26,1 %	31,3 %	+ 5,2 %
Use of Aftershave, Shaving Cream, Gel, Lotion	7,8 %	11,0 %	+ 3,2 %
Similar Attitude to Religion as Parents	39,2 %	45,3 %	+ 6,1 %
Above Average TV Viewing	30,1 %	35,4 %	+ 5,3 %
Wearing Denim (Almost) Daily: Consumer Typology	47,7 %	52,9 %	+ 5,2 %
Marriage, Personal Change: 12 months	2,3 %	4,2 %	+ 1,9 %
Cameras, Equipment: Decision Makers, Without Specialist Knowledge	46,0 %	51,3 %	+ 5,3 %
Magazines Plus and TV Plus: Media Type	26,9 %	32,1 %	+ 5,2 %

Significant deviations appearing under the star sign Virgo

Survey sample	Total population 13 283	Virgo 909	Deviation
Insurance: Decision-Maker in Purchasing	67,8 %	72,5 %	+ 4,7 %
Fish, Animals in Household	5,6 %	7,9 %	+ 2,3 %

Significant deviations appearing under the star sign Libra

Survey sample	Total population 13 283	Libra 812	Deviation
Computer, Desktop or Portable: Plan to Purchase in 1-2 years	7,7 %	11,2 %	+ 3,5 %
Women's Accessories: Plan to Purchase in 1-2 years	2,9 %	5,0 %	+ 2,1 %
Preference for Moral or Emotional Arguments	45,1 %	39,9 %	− 5,2 %
Approval of Factual Arguments: Attitude	24,8 %	29,9 %	+ 5,1 %
Tolerance Towards Foreigners, People of Other Faiths: Important	51,7 %	57,2 %	+ 5,5 %
Professional Training: University Studies, Not Engineer	5,8 %	8,5 %	+ 2,7 %

Significant deviations appearing under the star sign Scorpio

Survey sample	Total population 13 283	Scorpio 820	Deviation
Spirits: Bought/Drunk, 14 days	12,3 %	16,4 %	+ 4,1 %
Regularly Play Golf in Leisure Time	0,5 %	1,5 %	+ 1,0 %
Similar Attitude to Other People as Parents	50,1 %	57,4 %	+ 7,3 %
Large Generation Gap	29,4 %	23,6 %	− 5,8 %
Cigar, Cigarillo, Cheroot Smoker: Consumer Typology	1,4 %	2,6 %	+ 1,2 %
Like Buying What Others Already Have: Consumer Typology	7,0 %	9,5 %	+ 2,5 %

Significant deviations appearing under the star sign Sagittarius

Survey sample	Total population 13 283	Sagittarius 760	Deviation
Films, Videos: Special Interest	7,5 %	10,9 %	+ 3,4 %
Hair Care, Hair Styles: Advice-Givers, Experts	11,3 %	15,9 %	+ 4,6 %
Alternative Medicine: Advice-Givers, Experts	10,4 %	14,4 %	+ 4,0 %
Video Camera, Camcorder: Households Own	16,6 %	12,6 %	– 4,0 %
Family Pack of Ice, Deep Frozen: Purchase, 14 days	17,9 %	23,6 %	+ 5,7 %
Sports Injury, Prevention: Self-Medication, Treatment, 2 months	9,1 %	13,7 %	+ 4,6 %
Helping People in Need: Important	55,0 %	61,8 %	+ 6,8 %
Own Finances, (Very) Good: Consumer Typology	49,3 %	55,4 %	+ 6,1 %
Very Active: Activity Index	29,5 %	35,1 %	+ 5,6 %
Parents Magazine: Media Group	2,4 %	4,2 %	+ 1,8 %
Single Women	11,7 %	16,5 %	+ 4,8 %

Significant deviations appearing under the star sign Capricorn

Survey sample	Total population 13 283	Capricorn 837	Deviation
Bottled Condiments/Sauces: Purchase, 14 days	24,7 %	29,3 %	+ 4,6 %

Significant deviations appearing under the star sign Aquarius

Survey sample	Total population 13 283	Aquarius 909	Deviation
Family Pack of Ice, Deep Frozen: Purchase, 14 days	17,9 %	16,6 %	– 1,3 %
Minor Car Repairs: Leisure Activities, 12 months	16,3 %	12,3 %	– 4,0 %
TV's, Video Recorders	62,8 %	57,1 %	– 5,7 %

Significant deviations appearing under the star sign Pisces

Survey sample	Total population 13 283	Pisces 937	Deviation
Building, Modernisation, Renovation: Special Interest	17.4 %	22.1 %	+ 4.7 %
Catering for Guests, Hospitality: Special Interest	36.0 %	43.0 %	+ 7.0 %
Nature Conservancy, Environmental Protection: Special Int.	28.6 %	34.6 %	+ 6.0 %
Building, Modernisation, Renovation: Advice-Givers, Experts	16.1 %	20.7 %	+ 4.6 %
Further Professional Training: Advice-Givers, Experts	10.1 %	14.5 %	+ 4.4 %
House, Flat to Rent: Households Own	13.0 %	17.5 %	+ 4.5 %
Prints, Sculptures, Paintings: Households Own	10.1 %	13.2 %	+ 3.1 %
Lawn-Mower – Diesel, Battery, Electric: Households Own	33.3 %	39.0 %	+ 5.7 %
(Private) Car Driver, Drive Themselves: Car/Household	60.5 %	65.9 %	+ 5.4 %
Painting, Woodworking, Interior Decoration: Leisure Activities, 12 months	14.5 %	19.3 %	+ 4.8 %
Garden, Gardening: Frequently in Leisure Time	31.0 %	36.8 %	+ 5.8 %
Music, Folk Music: Frequently in Leisure Time	18.6 %	23.0 %	+ 4.4 %
Comfortable Clothing Style	82.9 %	87.5 %	+ 4.6 %

CUMULATIVE DATA
FROM THE AUTUMN
AND SPRING WAVES

The following tables present an analysis of the combined data from the second and third waves of the 1996 AWA survey.

In the case of characteristics which differ for men and for women, the figures shown refer to the totals for the specific group shown in the column heading. For example in the table concerning circles, social strata, groups:

	Aged 14+	Capricorn	Aquarius	
Survey sample	13,283	837	909	...
	%	%	%	...
Liberated	17.8	17.3	17.6	...

This means, for instance, that out of all 13,283 respondents, including both men and women, 17.8 per cent are women who describe themselves as liberated, etc.

Results which were found to be significant at the 1 per cent level in the analysis of the combined data from both studies are set off with a bold-lined box. Significant results repeated in both studies are indicated in a double-lined box.

The significance calculations are based on the null hypothesis, which posits that a certain characteristic, for instance, 'playing golf as a leisure-time activity', occurs with the same frequency in the general population and among persons born under a particular star sign.

This hypothesis is rejected if the deviation between the observed 'actual value' and the expected value is 'too strong'. In order to assess the degree of deviation, a test statistic known as the t-statistic is derived from the actual values. According to the null hypothesis, and given a sufficiently large sample n, the t-statistic will follow a normal distribution.

The hypothesis then states:
mean actual value = mean expected value

The initial hypothesis is rejected at the 1 per cent level if the probability of the observed value of t is less than 1 per cent.

The following may serve as a rule of thumb for determining the required number of respondents, n:

$$n > \frac{9}{p\,(1-p)}$$

If we apply this rule of thumb to the smallest finding in the report, i.e. 'playing golf as a leisure-time activity' among Scorpios (820 respondents in all = 1.5 per cent), we obtain the following:

$$\frac{9}{0.015\,(0.985)} = 609.13 < 820 \ (n: \text{Scorpios surveyed})$$

Thus the procedure used is valid in this case.

The lowest limits derived from this rule of thumb have been applied not only in analysing those results which appeared in both waves, but also to the other significant deviations which are marked in the tabular section of this report.

For added confidence in the latter case, only those results are highlighted which show a proportion (p) of more than 5 per cent both in the total universe of respondents and in the separate groups.

What do you consider especially important and worthwhile in your life?

Survey sample	Aged 14+ 13 283	Capricorn 837	Aquarius 909	Pisces 937	Aries 987	Taurus 928	Gemini 1021	Cancer 913	Leo 925	Virgo 909	Libra 812	Scorpio 820	Sagittarius 760
	Ø%	%	%	%	%	%	%	%	%	%	%	%	%
Neatness, cleanliness	63.3	61.6	58.7	64.9	64.3	67.8	62.9	62.2	64.3	60.1	61.5	66.6	67.2
Rise in social status	36.1	35.6	32.9	37.1	37.7	34.1	35.3	36.5	34.1	37.1	31.3	36.2	30.8
Law and order	70.7	70.3	71.8	73.8	72.0	72.7	68.7	70.4	68.7	68.9	70.6	72.3	70.6
Drive to achieve/work hard	51.6	49.3	51.8	53.0	51.9	49.3	47.9	51.1	51.5	53.2	52.4	50.8	50.4
Technological, scientific progress	25.0	22.7	24.6	25.9	26.2	25.9	24.5	23.7	23.8	24.2	27.3	26.0	21.9
Social justice	70.1	71.0	70.8	71.3	71.1	71.9	71.8	70.8	67.1	71.0	71.0	68.1	68.8
High income, standard of living	32.1	34.3	29.7	29.3	32.3	31.3	31.2	30.4	36.9	29.5	29.2	32.8	30.9
Safety, security	73.9	73.6	76.0	76.1	74.7	75.2	75.3	74.6	73.5	76.5	76.5	73.3	75.4
To help people in need	55.0	53.9	55.7	57.8	57.7	57.2	54.6	53.1	58.1	54.5	58.4	57.4	61.8
To be absolutely there for one's family	53.2	53.8	54.0	54.0	53.9	57.1	53.0	51.4	53.1	51.4	53.2	55.7	55.7
Well-groomed appearance	50.4	50.9	49.9	51.3	53.3	51.9	47.8	50.2	53.9	49.2	47.3	49.5	55.5
Christian life, belief	22.0	21.5	21.8	25.0	20.2	24.4	22.0	19.2	20.3	20.1	27.0	20.5	20.8
Active participation in political life	12.8	10.6	11.4	13.6	12.2	12.9	13.7	11.8	13.2	12.1	14.7	14.6	12.3
Make sacrifices for the environment	29.2	25.8	26.0	30.7	32.0	31.2	29.3	31.1	30.7	27.0	29.7	32.8	29.2
Tolerance towards foreigners/faiths	51.7	48.3	51.3	54.4	56.4	54.6	55.7	50.4	50.9	53.0	57.2	53.9	54.8
Thrift *	44.7	44.0	50.4	51.3	43.1	46.6	42.8	41.0	46.1	46.0	40.1	41.4	44.1
To support peace *	52.1	50.1	54.2	53.2	53.4	54.9	54.0	48.6	53.5	53.1	53.0	54.6	54.5
Freedom and independence *	56.5	56.8	58.0	58.0	63.4	59.7	56.9	56.3	56.9	58.3	53.6	56.4	56.1

Significances which reached 1% in the analysis of the accumulated data of both surveys.
Significances which repeated themselves in both surveys.
□ positive   □ negative

* Only included in 1995 Spring Survey: Survey sample – Population over 14 years: 6,696
Capricorn 390, Aquarius 435, Pisces 459, Aries 513, Taurus 485, Gemini 433, Cancer 460, Leo 490, Virgo 500, Libra 433, Scorpio 433, Sagittarius 357.

Opinions and attitudes

Survey sample	Aged 14+ 13 283	Capricorn 837	Aquarius 909	Pisces 937	Aries 987	Taurus 928	Gemini 1021	Cancer 913	Leo 925	Virgo 909	Libra 812	Scorpio 820	Sagittarius 760
	⊘%	%	%	%	%	%	%	%	%	%	%	%	%
Prefer moral/emotional arguments	45.1	45.9	44.4	46.3	45.6	46.9	42.4	47.7	48.4	46.8	39.9	47.9	47.0
Approve of factual arguments	24.8	23.5	27.4	25.7	25.3	23.6	28.1	26.4	23.3	23.5	29.9	23.9	27.4
Technology makes life simpler	41.4	42.8	44.6	41.6	44.0	38.9	42.8	44.6	42.3	41.3	41.5	39.8	42.5
Technological progress is beneficial	40.5	42.3	40.5	43.3	42.9	42.5	43.0	42.7	45.2	42.4	40.7	43.6	39.7
Would like to know how tech. works	43.2	40.9	42.1	45.8	46.3	46.4	43.7	44.5	48.2	45.3	44.1	44.7	41.9
The main thing about tech. is it works	47.6	50.9	48.6	46.2	45.2	46.5	49.1	46.9	44.7	46.0	47.0	47.0	49.4
Organic food ⊕	68.2	69.3	68.7	71.3	65.7	71.8	70.0	69.0	65.3	69.3	70.3	72.2	70.0
Organic food ⊙	5.7	4.8	4.4	6.1	4.5	2.9	5.5	7.1	6.3	7.4	4.4	5.4	6.4
Speed limits ⊕	39.9	45.3	42.7	47.1	35.7	47.7	34.7	36.2	40.1	38.7	40.4	42.4	38.5
Speed limits ⊙	40.3	37.9	34.9	35.0	45.8	33.8	47.4	41.5	43.2	39.8	42.4	37.4	39.0
Ban on smoking in workplace ⊕	52.1	56.2	53.7	57.2	51.4	53.7	48.1	50.5	55.3	51.5	55.7	53.4	48.3
Ban on smoking in workplace ⊙	27.1	25.9	25.3	22.4	28.7	25.6	31.1	28.6	24.9	29.7	22.5	26.0	29.3
Participation – unauthorised demon. ⊕	10.2	11.7	9.2	7.3	7.8	8.8	10.1	9.3	9.8	13.5	10.3	10.0	8.3
Participation – unauthorised demon. ⊕	67.9	62.8	67.3	70.6	70.8	70.1	68.8	70.1	66.9	66.2	72.8	69.2	73.2

⊕ = more for ⊙ = more against

Significances which reached 1 % in the analysis of the accumulated data of both surveys.
Significances which repeated themselves in both surveys.
  positive   negative

In which areas do you/did you and your parents have similar views?

Survey sample	Aged 14+ 13 283	Capricorn 837	Aquarius 909	Pisces 937	Aries 987	Taurus 928	Gemini 1021	Cancer 913	Leo 925	Virgo 909	Libra 812	Scorpio 820	Sagittarius 760
	⊘%	%	%	%	%	%	%	%	%	%	%	%	%
Attitude to religion	39.2	40.6	41.4	41.4	39.1	41.5	40.1	41.9	45.3	42.1	40.1	40.2	41.1
Moral concepts	43.2	46.3	42.1	45.7	44.2	45.2	44.5	46.4	44.6	42.2	46.7	46.3	44.0
Attitude to other people	50.1	49.6	51.0	51.5	49.5	50.7	52.7	53.5	49.5	54.9	53.4	57.4	50.7
Political views	25.1	25.5	24.1	25.7	26.0	28.5	27.0	27.4	26.5	26.8	27.0	28.3	26.1
Attitude to sexuality	11.3	11.0	12.1	12.9	10.1	11.9	12.4	12.7	13.2	10.5	12.5	10.6	10.6
Small generation gap	12.0	11.9	13.0	13.4	12.3	12.7	12.7	12.8	13.4	13.5	12.9	11.7	12.9
Large generation gap	29.4	27.8	30.0	27.5	29.1	26.7	26.4	24.2	27.1	26.6	24.2	23.6	29.8

Significances which reached 1% in the analysis of the accumulated data of both surveys.
Significances which repeated themselves in both surveys.
☐ positive ☐ negative

Political interests, where people say they stand on the spectrum of left and right

Survey sample	Aged 14+ 13 283	Capri-corn 837	Aquarius 909	Pisces 937	Aries 987	Taurus 928	Gemini 1021	Cancer 913	Leo 925	Virgo 909	Libra 812	Scorpio 820	Sagit-tarius 760
	⌀%	%	%	%	%	%	%	%	%	%	%	%	%
Interest in politics	**43,9**	44,6	48,1	45,9	46,8	43,9	43,3	40,6	44,4	48,3	48,3	43,6	44,3
Political position: (more to the) Right	**14,2**	12,5	15,5	16,8	12,7	11,8	11,5	15,1	12,1	15,1	15,5	14,0	14,8
Political position: Centre	**68,8**	66,8	67,3	64,7	70,6	73,0	71,1	68,1	69,6	68,7	68,3	70,3	68,6
Political position: (more to the) Left	**14,2**	17,3	14,0	15,6	14,6	12,8	13,9	14,3	15,8	13,7	14,3	13,6	13,9

Significances which reached 1% in the analysis of the accumulated data of both surveys.
Significances which repeated themselves in both surveys.

positive   negative

Attitudes, views, inclinations

Survey sample	Aged 14+ 13 283	Capricorn 837	Aquarius 909	Pisces 937	Aries 987	Taurus 928	Gemini 1021	Cancer 913	Leo 925	Virgo 909	Libra 812	Scorpio 820	Sagittarius 760
	Ø%	%	%	%	%	%	%	%	%	%	%	%	%
Interested car experts	6,6	7,3	7,8	7,8	6,2	7,1	8,1	7,7	8,4	5,4	6,6	5,7	6,6
Environmentally committed car drivers	12,2	11,0	9,5	13,4	11,2	13,2	12,7	13,1	12,5	14,8	11,7	14,8	14,1
Active environmentalists	12,8	11,1	12,1	15,1	10,7	16,0	13,4	14,7	12,0	14,7	12,6	15,0	14,2
Interested in environmental protection	15,7	17,8	17,6	19,5	18,3	17,6	15,3	15,9	14,6	15,4	15,8	15,1	15,1
Socially minded/alternative	54,5	54,5	58,5	52,9	54,7	53,8	56,0	55,2	55,0	53,4	51,3	55,0	51,8
Bourgeois/conservative	45,5	45,5	41,5	47,1	45,3	46,2	44,0	44,8	45,0	46,6	48,7	45,0	48,2
Politically committed	9,8	8,1	9,8	9,8	9,7	9,9	10,2	9,1	11,0	9,7	12,8	10,8	9,0
Pol. interested, without commitment	34,1	36,4	38,3	36,1	37,1	34,0	33,1	31,5	33,4	38,6	35,5	32,9	35,3
Politically uninterested	56,1	55,4	51,9	54,1	53,2	56,1	56,7	59,4	55,6	51,7	51,7	56,4	55,7
More of a democratic attitude	43,4	42,5	44,5	46,9	45,9	45,1	43,6	43,9	42,5	43,2	43,3	46,1	45,2
More of an authoritarian attitude	27,4	27,8	27,3	27,0	26,1	27,6	25,1	26,5	26,2	25,7	27,3	26,2	25,4
More for unlimited freedom	16,2	16,4	15,3	13,6	15,9	16,1	18,1	17,9	18,2	19,0	16,0	15,2	15,9
No direction	13,1	13,3	12,9	12,5	12,1	11,2	13,3	11,7	13,1	12,2	13,3	12,5	13,5
Progressive men	17,1	16,7	15,6	17,2	17,6	16,6	17,7	19,1	19,3	19,2	18,2	17,4	15,1
More conservative men	30,4	29,3	29,5	29,5	33,8	29,3	29,0	30,0	30,6	30,5	28,4	30,8	29,0
Progressive women	21,8	20,3	23,2	22,4	23,0	20,6	22,9	20,1	21,5	21,6	22,7	20,7	22,6
More conservative women	30,8	33,7	31,8	30,9	25,6	33,4	30,4	30,8	28,5	28,7	30,7	31,1	33,3

Significances which reached 1% in the analysis of the accumulated data of both surveys.
Significances which repeated themselves in both surveys.
☐ positive ☐ negative

Attitudes, views, inclinations

Survey sample	Aged 14+ 13 283	Capricorn 837	Aquarius 909	Pisces 937	Aries 987	Taurus 928	Gemini 1021	Cancer 913	Leo 925	Virgo 909	Libra 812	Scorpio 820	Sagittarius 760
	∅%	%	%	%	%	%	%	%	%	%	%	%	%
Hedonists	**9,3**	11,4	8,1	9,8	10,8	9,0	10,7	8,3	9,4	8,3	9,6	8,9	10,0
Work-orientated and professionally committed	**11,9**	12,2	10,4	12,7	12,7	9,5	10,1	13,1	12,5	12,2	11,7	11,6	11,7
Androgynous men	**21,1**	19,2	18,5	23,1	24,0	24,5	22,2	22,5	21,9	20,6	19,6	24,0	20,7
Androgynous women	**17,9**	16,7	21,6	18,2	18,5	18,9	18,2	18,6	16,6	17,2	18,7	17,1	17,6
Protestants, with intense commitment and belief	**6,9**	7,0	5,8	9,0	5,7	6,1	6,6	8,2	6,5	7,0	8,6	6,0	7,2
Catholics, with intense commitment and belief	**8,3**	9,5	8,9	10,1	6,3	9,0	7,9	7,2	7,7	6,8	10,7	8,2	7,8
Very active	**29,5**	29,7	29,2	31,6	33,0	31,2	31,1	33,6	31,2	30,5	30,2	30,9	35,1

Significances which reached 1 % in the analysis of the accumulated data of both surveys.
Significances which repeated themselves in both surveys.
positive   negative

Self-description

Survey sample	Aged 14+ 13 283	Capricorn 837	Aquarius 909	Pisces 937	Aries 987	Taurus 928	Gemini 1021	Cancer 913	Leo 925	Virgo 909	Libra 812	Scorpio 820	Sagittarius 760
	Ø%	%	%	%	%	%	%	%	%	%	%	%	%
Older mother/father with young child	3.1	3.0	3.3	2.8	3.9	3.0	2.7	2.4	4.0	3.0	4.3	3.1	3.9
I like, and work hard at, my job	20.7	22.6	19.0	21.9	21.7	18.8	19.5	23.4	22.7	21.5	19.3	20.9	22.2
Driving a car gives me great pleasure	37.6	36.7	36.1	41.2	38.0	37.6	40.2	39.0	39.5	39.8	39.6	42.3	41.4
Double burden: job and household	15.3	15.5	15.0	15.9	15.6	15.4	17.3	15.1	13.4	15.6	15.9	13.0	16.6
Double burden: several generations	3.0	3.0	3.0	3.4	2.7	2.6	4.0	2.9	2.9	4.9	2.6	4.2	2.9
Connoisseur/gourmet	13.3	13.9	14.4	13.5	12.9	13.1	14.1	12.2	14.3	13.7	16.3	11.8	15.0
Home-loving type	50.9	54.3	51.8	52.3	50.3	55.7	52.1	55.7	52.3	52.2	48.6	48.9	53.7
Preferably build a career slowly	14.0	14.6	15.1	14.7	14.9	14.8	16.9	17.4	12.8	15.4	14.1	15.3	15.6
Oppose nuclear power	15.8	15.5	16.1	15.2	15.1	15.7	14.8	15.4	18.3	16.8	14.7	15.5	14.9
Multidimensional behaviour	33.6	33.9	31.1	34.7	36.3	33.1	35.9	36.9	36.2	36.0	39.0	31.0	36.2
Environmentalist	19.1	18.5	17.4	20.3	17.8	22.2	19.0	21.3	19.3	20.9	19.3	21.5	20.6
Religious	19.8	20.5	20.7	22.9	16.1	20.3	17.6	19.0	18.3	18.8	23.5	16.9	20.4
Socially-minded, helpful	45.0	46.7	47.0	48.7	45.9	45.5	46.6	46.7	43.9	49.7	45.5	43.2	43.0

Significances which reached 1 % in the analysis of the accumulated data of both surveys.
Significances which repeated themselves in both surveys.
positive   negative

Self-description

Survey sample	Aged 14+ 13 283	Capricorn 837	Aquarius 909	Pisces 937	Aries 987	Taurus 928	Gemini 1021	Cancer 913	Leo 925	Virgo 909	Libra 812	Scorpio 820	Sagittarius 760
	Ø%	%	%	%	%	%	%	%	%	%	%	%	%
Own mood: excellent	17,1	17,9	16,4	16,3	18,8	15,6	15,5	18,5	18,3	16,7	16,4	17,0	16,1
Own mood: good	32,8	33,1	32,7	32,4	35,5	32,1	35,5	34,0	29,7	31,1	31,5	31,5	36,2
Own mood: rather bad	32,0	32,0	34,5	33,8	29,8	33,7	33,5	28,7	31,4	34,5	32,0	33,5	32,3
Own mood: very bad	18,1	17,0	16,4	17,4	15,9	18,6	15,5	18,8	20,6	17,8	20,0	18,0	15,4
Frequent stress, pressure	25,0	26,0	23,9	26,0	25,1	22,2	25,2	23,5	25,3	26,9	22,8	29,4	28,3
Weight problems	16,4	16,0	17,0	18,4	17,1	19,7	17,2	16,1	16,9	15,6	17,5	15,8	15,4

Significances which reached 1 % in the analysis of the accumulated data of both surveys.
Significances which repeated themselves in both surveys.
positive   negative

Strength of personality scale

Survey sample	Aged 14+ 13283 Ø%	Capricorn 837 %	Aquarius 909 %	Pisces 937 %	Aries 987 %	Taurus 928 %	Gemini 1021 %	Cancer 913 %	Leo 925 %	Virgo 909 %	Libra 812 %	Scorpio 820 %	Sagittarius 760 %
Others envy me a lot	17.0	15.6	17.5	15.9	15.7	15.9	16.3	16.7	20.1	19.1	17.4	17.2	19.7
Others adapt to me	24.6	26.8	26.3	22.3	25.9	26.2	25.4	24.2	28.6	25.1	23.5	24.2	30.2
I'm often one step ahead of other people	12.2	10.9	12.2	13.0	12.9	12.0	12.6	11.8	13.4	13.5	12.2	11.3	14.0
I'm seldom uncertain	45.5	42.7	45.9	45.7	47.5	46.8	45.1	44.7	46.6	49.0	46.6	45.1	45.7
I often give others advice	43.0	46.4	44.5	44.3	44.1	44.6	43.1	41.5	42.2	45.8	46.6	41.4	46.6
I enjoy convincing others	34.5	30.5	34.0	36.4	36.0	33.2	35.4	35.7	38.4	36.4	36.7	37.1	37.4
I can get my way/assert myself*	45.5	42.2	42.0	45.8	49.6	49.3	48.0	43.9	50.1	47.2	43.6	45.8	49.7
I think I'm going to be successful	57.2	56.0	58.5	56.7	58.3	53.6	56.7	56.5	58.7	62.5	56.7	56.6	61.2
I like taking a leadership role	24.3	22.5	23.6	26.6	25.1	23.2	25.9	25.0	27.4	27.4	24.4	22.1	24.8
I like taking on responsibility	48.3	49.8	47.9	52.8	48.5	50.1	48.2	51.0	52.6	51.6	49.3	46.7	48.3
Strength of personality: strong	25.0	23.3	25.0	25.0	27.2	26.5	26.3	25.2	28.1	29.0	23.2	23.3	28.1
Strength of personality: above average	27.8	26.7	28.0	30.4	27.4	29.2	27.2	27.5	30.4	27.0	31.6	28.2	29.3
Strength of personality: moderate	24.8	28.3	24.9	22.6	25.3	22.9	25.0	25.5	22.4	23.4	27.5	25.9	25.0
Strength of personality: weak	22.4	21.7	22.2	22.0	20.2	21.5	21.5	21.9	19.1	20.6	17.6	22.6	17.6

Significances which reached 1% in the analysis of the accumulated data of both surveys.
Significances which repeated themselves in both surveys.
positive   negative

* Only included in 1995 Spring Survey: Survey sample – Population over 14 years: 6,696
Capricorn 390, Aquarius 435, Pisces 459, Aries 513, Taurus 485, Gemini 525, Cancer 460, Leo 490, Virgo 500, Libra 433, Scorpio 433, Sagittarius 357.

Circles, social strata, groups

Survey sample	Aged 14+ 13 283	Capricorn 837	Aquarius 909	Pisces 937	Aries 987	Taurus 928	Gemini 1021	Cancer 913	Leo 925	Virgo 909	Libra 812	Scorpio 820	Sagittarius 760
	⊘%	%	%	%	%	%	%	%	%	%	%	%	%
Working class	19.8	19.0	19.6	18.4	17.8	21.5	18.3	20.7	21.5	18.2	19.4	20.8	17.9
Upwardly mobile	5.0	5.5	3.7	4.1	4.8	5.5	4.4	4.8	6.3	6.6	5.3	4.5	5.5
Liberated	17.8	17.3	17.6	17.9	18.8	17.5	18.0	15.6	17.8	16.9	19.0	16.6	19.3
Company buyer	4.1	4.2	3.5	4.0	3.7	4.0	4.1	4.6	5.6	5.2	5.7	3.6	3.9
Progressive	9.2	9.1	9.6	7.8	8.8	10.3	9.9	9.5	9.4	10.4	9.7	8.5	7.6
Executive in profession	6.7	6.9	5.6	7.6	7.5	5.9	7.6	6.5	7.4	8.3	7.1	5.3	8.6
Manual worker	21.2	19.9	20.6	22.8	22.6	23.5	23.1	20.7	21.6	22.0	22.1	23.1	18.3
Householdhusband	7.8	7.5	6.8	8.3	7.3	9.2	7.8	8.3	8.8	9.0	8.4	10.0	6.3
Liberal	8.9	8.0	8.6	9.1	9.7	8.0	11.2	8.1	9.7	9.1	10.3	8.0	8.5
Middle class	41.2	42.2	38.3	41.2	39.9	37.7	41.4	42.3	40.8	41.2	42.3	40.4	43.0
Increasing use of technology in profession	13.9	13.2	12.9	14.9	14.0	13.1	15.6	13.4	16.3	15.8	12.8	15.3	13.7
Technological intelligentsia	8.1	8.9	8.8	8.5	8.7	7.6	7.8	8.4	8.7	9.0	9.8	7.5	8.5

Significances which reached 1 % in the analysis of the accumulated data of both surveys.
Significances which repeated themselves in both surveys.
☐☐ positive ☐ negative

Special interests

Survey sample	Aged 14+ 13 283	Capricorn 837	Aquarius 909	Pisces 937	Aries 987	Taurus 928	Gemini 1021	Cancer 913	Leo 925	Virgo 909	Libra 812	Scorpio 820	Sagittarius 760
	Ø%	%	%	%	%	%	%	%	%	%	%	%	%
Alcoholic drinks	6,1	7,4	6,9	6,2	6,7	5,8	5,6	6,1	5,6	5,2	7,2	5,6	5,3
Antiques	8,2	6,7	8,2	8,9	8,7	9,7	7,7	9,3	8,6	9,1	7,0	8,0	10,5
Cars, car tests	16,8	17,3	16,2	17,2	17,2	19,5	19,6	18,5	18,6	15,7	16,5	16,4	17,6
Motor racing, motorcycle racing	11,5	9,9	11,8	11,9	11,1	13,5	13,1	12,1	15,4	10,3	10,0	12,5	12,1
Building, modernisation, renovation	17,6	18,2	18,0	22,1	18,4	19,8	21,0	20,3	18,1	16,4	18,6	17,3	18,5
Further professional training	24,5	23,7	24,6	24,9	26,7	24,7	25,4	29,1	25,7	27,6	25,7	24,5	25,9
Books	30,0	28,5	31,5	31,0	29,5	30,0	32,7	32,0	29,2	29,3	34,1	30,7	34,9
Office equipment	3,6	2,9	3,6	3,4	3,9	4,6	3,8	2,2	3,7	3,9	2,4	4,0	4,5
Computer use	14,6	16,3	15,0	13,5	15,0	14,8	17,7	15,9	16,7	17,0	14,2	15,0	17,2
Electrical appliances, large	9,6	10,9	10,0	9,0	8,7	12,0	12,0	9,5	10,4	8,7	9,8	10,0	9,1
Films, videos	7,5	9,4	7,2	6,4	7,7	7,8	10,6	9,3	6,1	7,4	7,5	6,7	10,9
Photography	10,8	11,8	9,7	12,0	11,6	12,4	11,7	12,5	8,6	9,6	13,4	11,9	13,9
Gardening, garden lay-out	25,8	23,6	27,9	31,4	25,4	26,6	25,6	24,0	25,3	27,4	27,8	26,7	28,3
Catering for guests, hospitality	36,0	37,2	36,7	43,0	36,0	38,8	39,1	37,1	32,6	37,2	37,2	36,5	38,2
Financial investments	23,7	25,2	22,7	25,9	26,7	24,5	25,9	28,0	23,2	25,1	23,1	25,7	25,1
Healthy diet, way of life	37,3	37,7	38,3	38,1	38,3	40,8	40,4	37,5	35,0	40,0	37,0	40,0	40,2
Haircare, hairstyles	26,5	25,3	24,1	27,2	27,3	28,9	30,9	25,8	25,6	26,5	29,1	25,7	29,4
Looking after house	25,8	25,1	22,7	27,7	25,9	28,4	27,8	27,4	27,6	25,2	25,5	27,6	28,2

Significances which reached 1 % in the analysis of the accumulated data of both surveys.
Significances which repeated themselves in both surveys.
  positive   negative

Special interests

Survey sample	Aged 14+ 13283	Capricorn 837	Aquarius 909	Pisces 937	Aries 987	Taurus 928	Gemini 1021	Cancer 913	Leo 925	Virgo 909	Libra 812	Scorpio 820	Sagittarius 760
	⊘%	%	%	%	%	%	%	%	%	%	%	%	%
Skin care, personal hygiene	33,2	33,2	33,5	35,2	35,2	36,0	35,2	34,9	32,2	32,9	35,4	35,4	37,8
Handiwork, D.I.Y.	19,6	18,4	19,9	21,6	21,4	21,4	22,6	21,2	19,9	21,0	20,2	20,2	16,2
Hi-fi equipment, technology	12,5	12,2	13,5	10,6	14,4	13,9	13,9	13,5	13,4	11,5	12,0	14,2	13,7
Hotels, restaurants, upmarket	7,6	9,3	5,6	7,2	7,0	8,7	8,6	6,6	8,9	6,4	7,8	6,9	9,7
Cable, satellite TV	17,1	17,6	18,5	17,6	18,6	18,3	17,6	21,2	18,1	16,3	18,1	18,2	18,3
Films at the cinema	15,0	15,3	15,6	14,2	15,5	16,7	16,0	17,6	17,3	13,7	16,2	16,4	16,6
Cooking, recipes	31,8	32,0	31,7	30,9	29,9	35,3	35,9	31,7	31,1	29,1	32,0	33,8	30,9
Local events	43,5	43,0	44,0	47,4	44,5	44,7	42,1	43,2	42,7	44,7	46,7	40,0	42,1
Medical questions	25,0	25,8	26,7	27,2	25,9	29,4	27,3	24,9	22,2	23,1	25,6	26,1	27,3
Fashion, fashion trends	16,7	16,6	14,7	17,4	18,4	18,6	17,5	16,1	17,1	15,8	17,3	17,4	16,5
Model building, modelling shops	4,4	5,0	4,2	4,4	5,1	4,5	4,8	5,8	5,3	4,2	4,0	5,4	4,0
Modern telecommunications	11,0	12,6	9,2	10,2	12,0	10,6	13,2	11,7	11,6	11,8	11,1	11,3	10,9
Motorcycles	7,6	6,4	7,6	8,0	8,8	8,2	9,2	9,2	10,2	6,0	7,5	7,3	8,2
Nature conservancy, environmental protection	28,6	28,9	29,6	34,6	29,0	33,6	28,7	30,5	26,6	30,0	28,3	30,1	29,3
Alternative medicine	18,2	18,7	19,5	19,1	17,8	20,0	18,7	17,1	18,1	18,5	16,5	20,1	20,7
Vintage cars, motorcycles	5,9	6,6	5,5	5,9	6,5	6,9	7,6	7,2	7,3	5,7	5,4	4,9	7,8
Perfume, eau de toilette	17,7	16,3	18,5	18,6	19,3	20,5	18,5	18,5	18,9	17,2	18,2	15,1	20,0
Politics	20,7	18,1	22,9	23,3	20,6	20,7	23,4	19,9	20,2	20,5	24,4	20,7	19,9

Significances which reached 1 % in the analysis of the accumulated data of both surveys.
Significances which repeated themselves in both surveys.
positive   negative

Special interests

Survey sample	Aged 14+ 13 283	Capricorn 837	Aquarius 909	Pisces 937	Aries 987	Taurus 928	Gemini 1021	Cancer 913	Leo 925	Virgo 909	Libra 812	Scorpio 820	Sagittarius 760
	∅%	%	%	%	%	%	%	%	%	%	%	%	%
Cycling, racing	10,0	9,7	10,7	10,1	10,8	12,0	12,0	10,0	9,1	10,8	9,1	12,9	12,1
Records, CD's, cassettes	23,3	24,7	26,1	22,6	25,1	23,6	25,4	26,6	25,1	22,2	23,8	25,6	26,2
Sewing, knitting	11,2	10,9	14,2	11,1	10,6	12,1	13,3	10,8	11,5	8,8	12,3	11,4	12,6
Beauty treatment, make-up	15,9	17,0	14,6	15,0	17,1	16,1	15,7	15,1	15,6	14,6	18,0	15,0	17,4
Holiday & travel	39,2	40,1	39,8	37,6	42,9	43,3	40,5	41,4	39,4	38,8	44,2	38,0	42,9
Insurance	23,2	26,2	22,3	25,1	23,5	26,0	24,9	24,6	25,0	26,6	23,8	22,7	22,7
Video recorders, technology	9,1	10,4	9,9	6,6	9,8	8,1	11,8	11,5	10,3	7,1	8,8	11,4	10,1
Product testing	20,0	19,9	19,6	21,9	21,9	19,0	22,5	19,2	20,9	20,0	22,0	20,4	23,0
Business subjects	14,3	14,4	17,6	15,7	16,1	12,7	16,3	15,0	15,2	15,7	14,6	11,9	13,0
Property/furnishings	32,9	32,9	32,9	36,6	34,1	33,8	35,4	33,8	32,4	32,3	39,1	31,4	36,0

Significances which reached 1% in the analysis of the accumulated data of both surveys.
Significances which repeated themselves in both surveys.
positive   negative

290

Giving advice and tips

Survey sample	Aged 14+ 13 283 ∅%	Capricorn 837 %	Aquarius 909 %	Pisces 937 %	Aries 987 %	Taurus 928 %	Gemini 1021 %	Cancer 913 %	Leo 925 %	Virgo 909 %	Libra 812 %	Scorpio 820 %	Sagittarius 760 %
Alcoholic drinks	6.9	8.4	9.4	7.6	8.3	8.7	8.0	8.3	6.8	6.7	6.5	6.7	6.2
Antiques	4.5	4.4	5.6	4.7	5.3	5.2	4.7	5.2	4.7	3.5	4.2	4.0	4.7
Cars, car tests	11.3	12.5	13.6	11.3	11.1	12.2	13.5	13.0	14.0	11.1	10.9	11.3	10.1
Motor racing, motorcycle racing	5.4	5.7	7.1	5.8	5.1	7.2	5.8	5.3	7.1	6.1	4.9	4.5	5.7
Building, modernisation, renovation	16.1	16.2	16.5	20.7	16.5	18.1	19.4	16.5	15.0	16.3	18.0	18.0	18.6
Further professional training	10.1	9.1	8.7	14.5	12.2	10.6	9.2	12.3	11.8	10.0	12.1	8.7	12.8
Books	19.7	20.0	20.6	20.8	20.3	21.5	23.6	20.9	18.6	20.7	21.1	18.6	23.0
Office equipment	2.7	2.4	3.1	3.4	2.6	3.6	2.7	3.3	2.7	4.4	1.5	1.4	2.6
Computer use	10.8	12.7	10.0	10.5	10.4	10.9	13.0	12.3	12.6	12.8	11.3	10.3	12.8
Electrical appliances, large	6.9	9.1	7.5	8.0	7.8	9.0	8.7	6.8	5.4	4.9	9.4	7.5	7.3
Films, videos	5.6	5.9	6.0	5.0	5.8	6.1	8.2	7.6	5.0	4.7	6.0	4.9	8.1
Photography	8.1	8.4	6.7	8.2	9.3	9.8	9.0	10.7	7.9	9.5	10.8	8.4	9.3
Gardening, garden lay-out	22.5	20.9	23.7	26.6	23.3	24.8	24.4	19.5	22.5	23.9	26.1	24.8	23.0
Catering for guests, hospitality	18.6	19.8	19.7	22.3	18.0	21.1	22.8	21.4	18.5	17.4	19.7	18.7	22.1
Financial investments	13.0	13.9	14.4	15.0	13.2	15.1	14.0	14.9	12.3	13.3	14.6	13.6	14.0
Healthy diet, way of life	20.5	23.0	22.6	22.1	20.3	24.1	21.6	21.7	18.0	21.6	22.3	21.7	22.5
Haircare, hairstyles	11.3	11.0	10.2	10.2	12.4	11.8	14.3	11.7	10.3	12.2	12.4	11.2	15.9
Looking after house	14.7	14.4	14.3	15.9	14.4	18.2	14.2	16.2	15.1	13.8	15.4	15.8	18.5

Significances which reached 1% in the analysis of the accumulated data of both surveys.
Significances which repeated themselves in both surveys.
positive   negative

Giving advice and tips

A 2.6 b

Survey sample	Aged 14+ 13 283	Capricorn 837	Aquarius 909	Pisces 937	Aries 987	Taurus 928	Gemini 1021	Cancer 913	Leo 925	Virgo 909	Libra 812	Scorpio 820	Sagittarius 760
	⊘%	%	%	%	%	%	%	%	%	%	%	%	%
Skin care, personal hygiene	12,3	13,9	14,7	11,9	13,4	15,6	12,5	11,6	12,4	12,8	12,5	11,2	14,9
Handwork, D.I.Y.	18,1	17,2	17,5	20,0	21,4	19,8	20,3	18,1	19,6	18,4	19,9	20,6	15,2
Hi-fi equipment, technology	8,1	9,9	9,4	7,6	9,3	8,1	8,7	9,8	9,2	8,2	6,5	8,1	8,3
Hotels, restaurants, upmarket	7,1	8,4	8,2	7,3	8,1	8,2	7,3	6,7	6,7	7,4	7,7	6,5	9,2
Cable, satellite TV	7,3	9,0	7,7	7,6	8,5	9,6	7,9	9,3	7,0	6,9	7,7	6,5	8,2
Films at the cinema	10,4	11,0	11,1	10,0	11,9	9,8	11,9	12,7	12,4	10,6	12,3	11,1	10,6
Cooking, recipes	29,0	30,0	31,9	30,1	26,7	32,4	34,8	30,3	30,3	25,6	29,5	27,8	33,2
Local events	18,0	19,4	20,1	20,8	19,7	20,6	18,3	20,5	17,7	16,4	22,1	16,1	17,3
Medical questions	14,5	16,3	14,5	16,2	16,6	17,2	16,7	14,5	13,1	15,4	15,1	13,9	17,5
Fashion, fashion trends	11,6	11,4	13,8	11,6	12,6	11,1	13,6	9,7	12,2	12,8	13,4	10,8	13,8
Model building, modelling shops	3,8	4,2	3,7	2,7	3,7	4,9	5,3	5,1	4,3	3,1	4,2	3,3	5,3
Modern telecommunications	6,7	7,9	7,3	6,8	7,3	7,3	8,4	7,2	7,0	7,1	6,5	5,6	7,3
Motorcycles	4,6	4,0	4,5	4,9	4,7	4,3	5,9	5,8	6,4	4,5	4,9	4,0	4,2
Nature conservancy, environmental protection	11,2	10,2	9,8	12,6	13,0	13,6	10,9	12,0	11,7	12,2	12,8	11,2	12,1
Alternative medicine	10,4	10,7	9,5	11,7	9,6	12,4	10,3	10,0	10,3	9,9	10,5	8,9	14,4
Vintage cars, motorcycles	2,9	2,5	3,3	3,4	3,1	2,8	4,0	4,4	3,5	3,8	2,2	2,7	3,3
Perfume, eau de toilette	10,6	9,3	12,2	9,6	12,4	11,6	13,5	11,0	11,7	10,5	11,1	9,4	13,7
Politics	12,1	10,5	13,4	14,4	15,9	11,2	12,7	10,4	11,5	13,0	13,1	12,6	13,1

Significances which reached 1% in the analysis of the accumulated data of both surveys.
Significances which repeated themselves in both surveys.
positive ☐ negative

Giving advice and tips

Survey sample	Aged 14+ 13 283	Capricorn 837	Aquarius 909	Pisces 937	Aries 987	Taurus 928	Gemini 1021	Cancer 913	Leo 925	Virgo 909	Libra 812	Scorpio 820	Sagittarius 760
	∅%	%	%	%	%	%	%	%	%	%	%	%	%
Cycling, racing	4.9	4.3	5.4	5.1	6.4	5.9	5.4	4.5	5.1	6.2	4.0	5.0	5.8
Records, CDs, cassettes	14.9	15.0	16.0	14.1	17.7	15.2	17.4	18.7	16.7	14.4	14.9	17.1	17.1
Sewing, knitting	11.4	10.7	14.4	12.0	10.3	14.3	15.3	10.9	11.5	9.0	13.1	9.4	15.1
Beauty treatment, make-up	8.5	7.8	9.6	7.9	10.4	9.5	9.0	8.4	8.0	5.8	10.0	7.4	11.0
Holiday & travel	24.5	25.2	23.5	26.3	28.7	27.0	27.4	27.6	24.3	27.4	26.5	23.9	25.3
Insurance	10.8	9.7	12.6	12.6	11.6	11.8	11.2	13.1	10.5	13.5	11.7	11.6	11.3
Video recorders, technology	5.9	7.5	8.3	4.4	6.4	5.9	8.2	7.3	5.8	4.8	6.1	6.1	6.9
Product testing	10.4	10.8	10.3	11.7	11.9	10.4	13.3	11.0	11.0	12.4	13.6	11.3	8.7
Business subjects	7.4	7.1	9.7	6.5	9.4	6.6	9.1	6.8	7.6	8.1	8.0	7.9	8.4
Property/furnishings	19.0	18.0	20.9	21.2	20.2	22.8	21.3	18.9	18.5	18.9	21.7	21.1	21.3

Significances which reached 1 % in the analysis of the accumulated data of both surveys.
Significances which repeated themselves in both surveys.
positive   negative

293

Linguistic proficiency

Survey sample	Aged 14+ 13 283	Capricorn 837	Aquarius 909	Pisces 937	Aries 987	Taurus 928	Gemini 1021	Cancer 913	Leo 925	Virgo 909	Libra 812	Scorpio 820	Sagittarius 760
	∅%	%	%	%	%	%	%	%	%	%	%	%	%
Good English	30,6	30,1	30,8	29,6	29,9	29,2	30,9	32,0	32,2	31,1	34,4	27,4	31,6
Good French	7,4	8,2	7,2	9,4	6,5	6,9	6,8	6,6	7,1	7,5	6,6	6,5	7,1
Knowledge of foreign languages	45,6	45,4	45,0	45,7	45,6	43,6	43,6	48,1	48,9	45,0	49,7	45,4	47,8
Use foreign languages professionally	7,2	8,6	5,8	5,8	6,5	7,7	8,8	7,4	8,2	7,9	9,0	6,2	8,2
Use foreign languages privately	23,9	24,1	24,1	24,6	24,5	23,3	22,5	26,1	26,2	22,0	25,5	24,3	24,7
Attend language courses	2,5	2,0	2,9	2,9	1,7	3,0	2,4	3,9	1,5	2,3	3,0	3,1	2,2

Significances which reached 1% in the analysis of the accumulated data of both surveys.
Significances which repeated themselves in both surveys.
positive   negative

294

Travel, holiday destinations, holiday choices

Survey sample	Aged 14+ 13 283	Capri-corn 837	Aquarius 909	Pisces 937	Aries 987	Taurus 928	Gemini 1021	Cancer 913	Leo 925	Virgo 909	Libra 812	Scorpio 820	Sagit-tarius 760
	⊘%	%	%	%	%	%	%	%	%	%	%	%	%
Train travel in general	23,9	24,0	26,6	26,6	26,5	25,5	22,6	26,0	25,0	24,4	27,3	23,4	24,7
Train travel: 1-4 long trips, 12 months	18,0	17,9	20,3	20,7	16,6	18,8	16,7	19,0	16,8	17,5	19,9	18,0	18,6
Train travel: 5 or more long trips, 12 mo.	4,5	5,1	5,1	4,0	6,8	4,4	3,4	5,7	5,5	4,6	5,5	3,2	5,2
Train travel: InterCity, 12 months	8,6	9,3	10,8	9,8	9,6	9,9	7,4	7,9	7,3	8,6	9,1	7,5	8,8
Tt.: I-City, European I-City, Regional, 12 mo.	13,8	14,4	15,0	14,2	15,6	14,6	12,5	16,1	13,1	11,9	15,4	13,9	15,2
Air travel, 12 months	21,3	21,4	19,0	20,8	23,8	21,2	18,9	21,7	23,7	23,8	21,6	19,9	24,8
Private air travel, 12 months	19,8	19,8	17,9	18,8	22,0	20,1	17,7	20,9	22,7	21,7	18,7	18,4	23,5
Business air travel, 12 months	2,4	2,4	1,5	2,1	2,7	2,7	1,7	1,2	2,0	3,2	3,8	2,7	2,9
Air travel: 1-4 trips, 12 months	19,1	19,1	17,2	19,0	21,5	19,3	17,0	19,2	22,1	20,6	18,6	18,0	22,5
Air travel: 5 or more trips, 12 months	2,1	2,1	1,8	1,7	2,2	1,8	1,8	2,5	1,6	3,0	2,9	1,9	2,2
Short holiday trips, 12 months	46,9	46,2	44,4	51,2	50,2	48,5	48,7	50,0	48,4	46,1	48,0	46,4	45,7
City travel (short), 12 months	17,6	20,0	16,2	18,4	17,9	18,8	16,5	18,3	19,4	18,2	19,1	16,4	19,3
Holiday trips (longer), 12 months	60,2	58,2	61,6	61,6	63,9	61,4	59,4	61,0	63,1	61,9	60,5	60,2	64,8

Significances which reached 1% in the analysis of the accumulated data of both surveys.
Significances which repeated themselves in both surveys.
positive ☐ negative

Travel, holiday destinations, holiday choices

Survey sample	Aged 14+ 13 283	Capricorn 837	Aquarius 909	Pisces 937	Aries 987	Taurus 928	Gemini 1021	Cancer 913	Leo 925	Virgo 909	Libra 812	Scorpio 820	Sagittarius 760
	∅%	%	%	%	%	%	%	%	%	%	%	%	%
European countries	**39.5**	40.2	38.4	42.1	41.6	41.1	39.0	41.7	40.5	41.7	41.3	37.5	39.8
Countries outside Europe	**8.5**	8.0	7.8	8.3	8.7	8.9	6.2	10.3	10.3	9.8	9.2	7.5	10.7
Always or mainly the same	**15.1**	15.0	16.6	15.8	18.7	15.1	14.4	15.1	16.5	15.7	14.4	15.1	17.1
Always or mainly new	**38.0**	37.4	39.2	38.0	39.2	38.8	38.8	39.0	39.5	39.0	39.8	36.2	41.2

Significances which reached 1 % in the analysis of the accumulated data of both surveys.
Significances which repeated themselves in both surveys.
positive   negative

296

Household pets

Survey sample	Aged 14+ 13 283	Capricorn 837	Aquarius 909	Pisces 937	Aries 987	Taurus 928	Gemini 1021	Cancer 913	Leo 925	Virgo 909	Libra 812	Scorpio 820	Sagittarius 760
	Ø%	%	%	%	%	%	%	%	%	%	%	%	%
Dog	15,3	14,3	14,7	15,1	16,1	15,3	15,7	16,2	17,5	15,2	12,7	15,7	15,4
Cat	16,2	18,1	16,5	18,0	15,2	14,9	18,9	17,3	15,5	15,0	19,3	15,7	18,4
Bird	8,8	7,1	7,8	9,3	7,9	10,2	11,2	10,6	7,7	11,0	7,8	8,1	9,5
Fish	5,6	5,4	4,0	5,8	5,7	5,8	7,3	5,4	5,3	7,9	6,6	6,6	6,1

Significances which reached 1% in the analysis of the accumulated data of both surveys.
Significances which repeated themselves in both surveys.

positive ▢ negative

What do you do in your leisure time, at the appropriate time of year?

Survey sample	Aged 14+ 13 283 ∅%	Capricorn 837 %	Aquarius 909 %	Pisces 937 %	Aries 987 %	Taurus 928 %	Gemini 1021 %	Cancer 913 %	Leo 925 %	Virgo 909 %	Libra 812 %	Scorpio 820 %	Sagittarius 760 %
Angling, fishing	1.8	1.9	1.5	2.2	2.9	1.2	1.5	1.6	2.7	1.8	1.2	2.4	2.2
Basketball	0.9	0.6	1.1	0.5	1.9	1.0	0.5	0.8	0.6	1.5	0.9	0.7	1.3
Mountain climbing	1.2	0.7	1.5	1.6	1.3	1.3	1.0	1.5	1.0	1.3	0.9	1.0	1.0
Camping, caravanning	3.4	3.2	3.5	4.2	4.0	3.1	3.3	4.1	3.2	3.3	4.6	3.1	3.3
Computer	6.3	8.7	4.5	4.8	8.0	4.4	7.2	7.1	8.6	7.4	5.6	6.3	6.5
Go to discotheques	7.0	5.6	5.7	6.5	7.6	7.0	6.6	9.4	8.1	6.6	7.3	7.0	7.2
Hang gliding	0.2	0.1	0.0	0.2	0.3	0.0	0.2	0.4	0.0	0.1	0.3	0.0	0.4
Eating out	14.5	12.3	14.3	15.8	13.6	15.3	13.1	14.4	15.1	13.5	16.0	15.3	16.0
Playing football	4.1	4.0	3.5	4.3	5.9	3.7	3.9	4.2	4.0	4.6	5.1	3.9	4.7
Gardening	31.0	29.1	32.6	36.8	32.1	32.8	30.9	27.0	30.7	33.9	31.4	34.7	32.3
Golf	0.5	0.4	0.3	0.3	0.5	0.3	0.2	0.5	0.4	0.2	0.2	1.5	1.1
Hunting	0.5	0.9	0.2	0.6	0.8	0.6	0.4	0.7	0.6	0.5	0.2	0.2	1.0
Jogging	3.6	3.1	4.4	3.8	4.2	3.5	3.7	4.3	4.1	4.2	4.0	2.6	3.8
Playing cards	12.8	16.0	11.3	11.0	12.8	12.8	14.0	11.3	13.9	11.1	12.5	14.0	14.1
Skittles, bowling	5.3	4.7	4.2	6.5	6.0	5.5	4.0	6.7	6.4	4.6	4.4	5.2	5.0
Light athletics	1.3	1.1	0.7	1.5	1.6	1.1	1.2	1.7	0.7	1.5	1.0	1.0	1.5
Painting, drawing	4.2	4.8	4.3	4.0	5.2	4.4	3.8	4.2	4.6	4.5	5.1	3.2	5.0
Minigolf	0.6	1.0	0.5	0.3	1.0	0.6	0.6	0.8	0.4	0.3	0.6	0.3	0.8

Significances which reached 1 % in the analysis of the accumulated data of both surveys.
Significances which repeated themselves in both surveys.
☐ positive ☐ negative

What do you do in your leisure time, at the appropriate time of year?

Survey sample	Aged 14+ 13 283 %	Capricorn 837 %	Aquarius 909 %	Pisces 937 %	Aries 987 %	Taurus 928 %	Gemini 1021 %	Cancer 913 %	Leo 925 %	Virgo 909 %	Libra 812 %	Scorpio 820 %	Sagittarius 760 %
Model-building as a hobby	2,4	1,9	1,8	2,8	3,6	2,4	2,3	2,8	3,3	2,2	2,0	1,6	1,3
Modelling, handicrafts, pottery	2,1	1,5	2,9	1,0	2,7	2,0	1,3	2,3	2,0	1,6	3,0	2,2	3,1
Driving motor boat	0,5	0,4	0,6	0,4	0,9	0,2	0,8	0,5	0,4	0,0	0,2	0,3	1,3
Riding mountain bike	3,8	3,7	4,7	4,0	4,4	3,6	3,7	5,5	4,6	3,1	3,0	3,5	4,6
Listening to classical music	11,9	12,6	11,8	13,2	13,5	11,1	11,9	12,2	11,3	14,0	11,5	11,0	11,2
Listening to pop music	26,4	25,5	25,3	25,1	28,1	26,8	27,5	30,9	26,7	25,8	29,4	27,7	27,6
Listening to folk music	18,6	18,7	17,2	23,0	18,1	20,6	18,9	17,0	19,5	20,3	18,0	16,4	16,3
Solving crossword puzzles	17,7	19,8	18,9	16,9	17,5	20,8	17,6	17,8	19,4	19,1	18,1	18,9	18,3
Riding	1,0	1,0	0,9	1,1	1,2	1,4	1,2	1,3	0,5	1,0	0,8	1,6	1,7
Riding/racing, sports bicycle	5,1	4,7	6,2	4,6	6,2	4,6	5,2	7,3	4,9	5,1	5,8	5,1	5,9
Swimming	13,2	11,0	14,4	14,3	12,9	14,5	11,9	13,0	12,5	13,9	11,4	13,6	14,5
Skiing	0,6	0,3	0,2	0,6	0,4	0,0	0,3	0,9	0,8	0,5	0,4	0,6	0,8
Gliding, flying	0,2	0,1	0,2	0,0	0,3	0,2	0,3	0,2	0,2	0,4	0,3	0,0	0,3
Downhill skiing	2,2	3,1	3,4	2,5	2,7	1,9	2,3	2,2	1,2	3,0	1,4	2,4	2,8
Cross-country skiing	1,3	0,4	0,7	2,1	1,9	0,9	1,1	2,1	1,2	2,0	0,5	1,3	1,2
Snowboarding	0,3	0,5	0,5	0,3	0,4	0,2	0,2	0,7	0,5	0,1	0,3	0,4	0,5
Watching sport on TV	27,0	23,7	24,8	28,0	32,2	28,1	27,1	28,0	25,0	28,9	26,3	29,4	28,6
Squash	1,0	1,3	0,7	1,3	1,3	1,0	0,7	0,9	0,7	1,1	0,9	0,8	1,3

Significances which reached 1% in the analysis of the accumulated data of both surveys.
Significances which repeated themselves in both surveys.
positive ◻ negative

What do you do in your leisure time, at the appropriate time of year?

Survey sample	Aged 14+ 13 283	Capri- corn 837	Aquarius 909	Pisces 937	Aries 987	Taurus 928	Gemini 1021	Cancer 913	Leo 925	Virgo 909	Libra 812	Scorpio 820	Sagit- tarius 760
	⌀%	%	%	%	%	%	%	%	%	%	%	%	%
Surfing	0.3	0.2	0.7	0.2	0.2	0.3	0.1	0.2	0.7	0.2	0.2	0.2	0.3
Diving	0.4	0.1	0.5	0.6	0.2	1.0	0.1	0.5	0.5	0.5	0.4	0.3	0.5
Tennis	2.9	4.2	3.5	2.0	3.9	1.8	2.4	3.2	2.4	3.1	2.5	3.6	2.9
Table tennis	2.0	2.0	2.5	1.0	2.4	1.3	2.3	2.1	2.3	2.3	1.7	2.3	3.1
Gymnastics	7.8	8.1	8.1	8.5	8.5	10.0	6.4	7.8	7.1	8.7	7.1	9.3	8.0
Renting videos	3.9	5.0	3.0	4.2	4.1	2.9	3.2	4.8	4.7	3.4	4.6	4.6	2.9
Making your own videos	2.0	2.6	1.7	1.1	2.0	1.7	3.4	3.5	1.5	2.1	1.6	1.5	2.3
Volleyball	1.9	1.7	2.2	1.6	2.1	2.0	2.3	3.0	2.0	2.3	1.7	1.8	2.8
Walking	9.2	8.6	10.6	8.7	11.3	9.7	10.0	9.2	9.5	9.1	8.4	9.5	7.1

Significances which reached 1% in the analysis of the accumulated data of both surveys.
Significances which repeated themselves in both surveys.
positive negative

Which of the following things do you do regularly?

Survey sample	Aged 14+ 13 283	Capricorn 837	Aquarius 909	Pisces 937	Aries 987	Taurus 928	Gemini 1021	Cancer 913	Leo 925	Virgo 909	Libra 812	Scorpio 820	Sagittarius 760
	⌀%	%	%	%	%	%	%	%	%	%	%	%	%
Visit specialist fairs, exhibitions	**4,4**	4,2	3,9	3,9	4,3	4,1	3,8	3,8	5,3	4,4	4,8	4,0	5,2
Reading foreign languages	**4,7**	6,6	5,4	5,4	4,5	4,9	4,4	5,7	3,7	4,4	4,5	5,0	5,5
Cook, bake	**42,8**	42,4	47,3	43,3	40,7	47,2	41,6	40,6	42,4	40,4	43,2	42,6	42,6
Take health cures	**2,5**	3,3	3,1	2,3	2,5	3,1	2,6	1,5	2,0	2,0	3,7	3,1	2,1
Regular medical check-ups	**34,9**	36,1	37,4	36,1	37,0	39,4	33,7	32,7	31,8	35,0	36,7	38,2	39,1
Attend political functions/events	**2,4**	2,3	2,6	2,3	2,1	2,2	1,6	2,3	3,3	2,8	3,3	3,5	2,2
Attend language courses	**2,5**	2,0	2,9	2,9	1,7	3,0	2,4	3,9	1,5	2,3	3,0	3,1	2,2
Visit theatre, opera	**4,9**	4,9	5,7	5,9	4,8	4,0	4,6	4,6	3,7	4,3	5,5	5,1	5,3
Do Football Pools or Lottery	**17,3**	16,6	16,4	18,2	17,6	17,0	17,1	15,6	17,9	18,0	14,9	18,5	18,1
Attend charity functions/events	**12,0**	12,7	12,7	14,7	13,9	9,7	12,1	12,6	11,9	12,8	14,5	11,9	14,7

Significances which reached 1 % in the analysis of the accumulated data of both surveys.
Significances which repeated themselves in both surveys.
positive ☐ negative

Television, radio, video

Survey sample	Aged 14+ 13 283	Capricorn 837	Aquarius 909	Pisces 937	Aries 987	Taurus 928	Gemini 1021	Cancer 913	Leo 925	Virgo 909	Libra 812	Scorpio 820	Sagittarius 760
	⌀%	%	%	%	%	%	%	%	%	%	%	%	%
4 or more hours	21.4	22.3	21.6	18.6	21.6	21.8	19.8	23.8	24.3	19.0	24.9	21.4	19.3
1 to 3 hours	67.6	66.7	66.2	71.7	68.9	69.1	69.3	65.0	66.5	70.4	62.9	70.1	70.1
Less than 1 hour	11.0	11.0	12.2	9.8	9.4	9.1	10.9	11.3	9.2	10.6	12.2	8.5	10.6
Satellite/cable reception	79.2	78.1	81.5	76.8	80.9	78.6	80.7	84.3	80.3	79.1	78.8	81.5	80.2
Only terrestrial TV	19.0	20.6	16.9	21.5	17.0	20.0	18.1	14.3	18.5	19.7	19.7	17.6	17.9
4 or more hours	18.1	19.3	17.7	19.6	19.5	20.8	18.0	18.7	20.0	17.4	20.7	18.7	20.6
1 to 3 hours	48.4	44.8	48.6	49.8	50.6	49.8	46.4	49.8	47.0	47.0	45.8	50.3	43.1
Less than 1 hour	33.5	35.9	33.7	30.6	29.9	29.4	35.7	31.5	33.0	35.6	33.4	31.0	36.2
Video camera, camcorder	16.6	15.7	15.5	15.3	15.0	16.0	19.1	20.9	16.3	17.0	15.7	17.1	22.6
Video recorder	65.5	65.3	63.2	64.5	67.8	59.1	68.3	69.3	68.7	64.9	63.2	69.5	69.7
Video equipment	6.5	6.4	6.0	6.2	5.4	5.8	9.5	9.0	5.4	6.9	6.8	6.4	8.0
Renting videos	3.9	5.0	3.0	4.2	4.1	2.9	3.2	4.8	4.7	3.4	4.6	4.6	2.9
Making your own videos	2.0	2.6	1.7	1.1	2.0	1.7	3.4	3.5	1.5	2.1	1.6	1.5	2.3

Significances which reached 1% in the analysis of the accumulated data of both surveys.
Significances which repeated themselves in both surveys.
positive ☐ negative

Use of the media

Survey sample	Aged 14+ 13283	Capricorn 837	Aquarius 909	Pisces 937	Aries 987	Taurus 928	Gemini 1021	Cancer 913	Leo 925	Virgo 909	Libra 812	Scorpio 820	Sagittarius 760
	⊘%	%	%	%	%	%	%	%	%	%	%	%	%
Topical and popular magazines	26,6	27,5	23,4	26,9	29,2	25,6	27,6	27,9	26,8	25,6	26,6	24,8	25,0
Current affairs magazines	19,6	15,3	18,7	20,9	22,6	16,7	17,7	20,8	19,4	23,0	21,3	18,7	19,2
Magazine supplements	4,8	4,7	4,5	5,9	5,8	5,3	4,1	4,2	4,9	3,9	5,1	3,6	5,0
Expensive TV/radio guides	25,4	25,1	23,1	24,9	26,2	26,1	25,6	25,0	26,7	26,2	24,0	23,6	28,4
Mid-priced, inexpensive TV/radio guides	25,2	25,0	22,8	25,1	24,9	24,6	26,6	23,4	27,7	22,1	24,3	28,1	25,7
Fortnightly TV/radio guides	15,3	16,7	14,8	15,6	14,3	15,9	14,9	17,2	15,0	15,8	15,6	17,3	14,7
TV/radio supplements	24,1	21,2	25,3	24,3	26,9	30,1	24,4	23,6	23,7	25,0	22,2	26,9	21,5
Weekly women's magazines	21,0	23,2	22,1	20,7	20,4	22,0	21,2	22,1	20,5	19,1	18,4	23,7	23,0
Fortnightly women's magazines	6,8	5,9	5,4	6,8	6,5	7,4	6,7	8,1	5,7	6,1	7,7	6,1	7,7
Monthly women's magazines	3,6	3,6	2,9	3,3	3,6	5,4	3,8	3,6	3,3	3,0	3,8	3,7	3,3
Women's magazines	3,3	3,2	3,5	4,8	2,7	4,3	3,2	2,4	2,4	3,9	2,9	3,0	3,1
Cookery magazines	3,7	3,8	2,6	3,8	2,8	4,2	4,0	3,3	4,4	4,3	3,5	3,7	3,5
Parents' magazines	2,4	1,9	2,5	2,0	1,8	3,1	2,5	1,7	2,1	2,4	2,8	2,9	4,2
Health magazines	1,4	1,8	1,7	0,7	1,3	1,6	0,9	1,1	1,6	2,4	1,0	1,5	0,8
Youth magazines	4,8	5,1	4,3	4,6	5,5	5,0	5,8	6,6	5,9	3,8	5,5	6,1	3,7
Gardening magazines	3,9	4,3	3,4	3,7	4,1	5,3	3,7	3,4	2,9	2,9	4,4	5,1	3,9
Property, decoration	3,4	2,8	2,2	5,3	3,5	3,9	5,6	2,6	2,7	2,6	3,9	2,7	4,7
Building, renovation	1,4	1,3	1,4	0,7	1,9	1,5	2,1	1,0	1,5	2,2	2,2	1,2	1,2

Significances which reached 1 % in the analysis of the accumulated data of both surveys.
Significances which repeated themselves in both surveys.
positive   negative

Use of the media

Survey sample	Aged 14+ 13 283	Capricorn 837	Aquarius 909	Pisces 937	Aries 987	Taurus 928	Gemini 1021	Cancer 913	Leo 925	Virgo 909	Libra 812	Scorpio 820	Sagittarius 760
	⊘%	%	%	%	%	%	%	%	%	%	%	%	%
Building Society savings/mortgage mag.	7,5	7,3	6,9	7,6	8,3	9,1	8,6	8,3	6,2	8,8	8,2	7,9	7,5
D.I.Y. magazines	2,3	2,0	2,0	2,3	2,7	2,6	3,7	2,1	2,5	3,1	2,2	2,8	2,1
Erotic magazines	3,9	4,2	2,8	3,5	4,3	3,6	5,3	4,4	3,4	3,7	4,0	5,4	2,8
Men's magazines	1,4	1,2	1,1	2,2	1,1	1,1	2,1	1,4	1,8	1,8	1,6	0,8	1,3
Lifestyle, student magazines	2,4	2,1	2,3	2,2	2,7	2,8	1,8	2,3	2,8	2,5	2,9	2,8	2,2
City listings magazines	1,3	1,1	1,4	1,1	1,7	1,1	1,3	0,6	2,4	0,7	1,1	1,4	1,6
Car-buyers magazines	8,1	9,7	7,2	6,8	8,5	9,3	9,2	8,8	9,0	8,7	8,9	7,9	9,4
Car-club, company magazines	19,5	19,3	17,5	17,6	20,4	21,6	21,2	22,2	21,5	22,7	18,7	20,1	18,1
Motorcycle magazines	1,6	1,6	1,4	1,8	1,9	2,3	1,3	2,0	3,0	1,5	1,8	0,6	1,4
General sports magazines	6,1	5,5	6,6	6,2	8,2	4,8	5,2	5,2	6,5	7,3	6,1	5,9	6,6
Specialist sports magazines	3,0	2,8	3,0	3,5	3,9	2,8	3,0	3,8	4,3	3,5	1,7	3,0	3,8
Photography magazines	0,6	0,6	0,5	0,5	0,4	0,5	0,5	0,9	0,6	0,4	0,6	0,4	0,8
Consumer electronics	1,1	0,8	1,3	1,4	1,0	1,2	0,8	0,5	1,2	1,2	1,2	1,2	1,7
Nature, animal magazines	3,3	2,2	3,6	2,8	2,3	3,6	4,0	5,6	3,3	2,4	3,3	3,5	2,5
Science, culture magazines	6,7	6,3	7,3	6,5	7,1	7,0	7,3	6,7	7,2	6,2	7,5	5,5	7,0
Travel, holiday magazines	4,4	4,1	4,4	6,4	4,0	4,5	6,9	3,4	4,2	4,9	3,9	3,9	4,0
Customer magazines	9,5	12,6	11,3	9,3	10,3	11,5	8,3	9,4	8,9	9,6	9,6	9,5	10,0
National evening, daily newspapers	7,3	5,7	7,0	6,7	6,5	7,7	6,8	7,6	7,6	7,5	8,6	7,8	6,8

Significances which reached 1% in the analysis of the accumulated data of both surveys.
Significances which repeated themselves in both surveys.
☐ positive ☐ negative

Use of the media

Survey sample	Aged 14+ 13 283	Capricorn 837	Aquarius 909	Pisces 937	Aries 987	Taurus 928	Gemini 1021	Cancer 913	Leo 925	Virgo 909	Libra 812	Scorpio 820	Sagittarius 760
	⊘%	%	%	%	%	%	%	%	%	%	%	%	%
Regional evening, daily newspapers	75.2	72.2	76.2	75.1	76.1	77.3	78.9	76.6	75.0	75.4	77.5	75.3	78.7
	26.9	29.5	24.6	26.9	24.7	26.0	26.4	23.0	29.0	26.8	24.8	26.8	25.0
Free newspapers	75.4	76.2	76.7	78.8	76.2	77.5	74.8	76.5	74.4	74.3	72.6	78.8	77.5
Cinema	7.9	7.9	7.1	6.2	7.2	9.1	8.9	9.6	9.0	7.2	8.6	7.3	7.1
Radio advertisements – per hour	34.5	37.2	32.8	37.8	33.9	38.5	33.8	32.3	33.0	32.4	35.5	37.8	36.2
TV advertisements – Commercial channel	64.9	67.7	65.8	67.7	66.5	67.3	65.6	62.6	66.1	62.8	64.1	64.3	62.8
Posters	67.6	70.2	66.4	68.2	66.4	64.2	67.7	66.5	69.5	69.6	66.6	64.1	69.0
Public transport	23.6	26.3	24.2	21.1	21.3	21.8	21.8	24.7	25.5	22.5	22.6	20.0	22.4
Telephone directory	45.4	44.6	47.5	47.4	45.5	47.5	47.9	44.3	44.3	43.6	47.8	44.2	47.9
Telephone card	15.3	17.0	13.8	14.6	14.8	14.6	14.2	14.5	16.2	14.8	16.4	14.5	13.4
Magazines plus and TV plus	26.9	26.6	25.8	27.7	27.6	28.7	30.9	29.8	32.1	28.3	26.1	27.9	28.8
Magazines plus and TV minus	22.6	24.5	23.1	22.9	21.7	24.3	22.5	23.6	20.6	23.1	23.3	23.3	23.4
Magazines minus and TV plus	22.8	23.4	23.0	22.6	24.3	21.2	20.1	20.9	23.4	20.8	22.3	25.1	23.6
Magazines minus and TV minus	27.7	25.5	28.1	26.8	26.4	25.8	26.6	25.7	23.9	27.8	28.4	23.6	24.2
Above average range of magazines	31.3	34.2	29.8	32.0	33.3	33.4	34.7	35.5	31.3	32.3	34.3	32.4	34.3
Average range of magazines	38.0	37.3	39.1	37.8	37.1	37.9	36.7	37.5	39.1	39.0	34.7	39.3	37.4
Below average range of magazines	30.7	28.6	31.1	30.2	29.6	28.7	28.6	27.0	29.6	28.7	31.0	28.4	28.4

Significances which reached 1% in the analysis of the accumulated data of both surveys.
Significances which repeated themselves in both surveys.
positive   negative

Use of the media

Survey sample	Aged 14+ 13 283	Capricorn 837	Aquarius 909	Pisces 937	Aries 987	Taurus 928	Gemini 1021	Cancer 913	Leo 925	Virgo 909	Libra 812	Scorpio 820	Sagittarius 760
	∅%	%	%	%	%	%	%	%	%	%	%	%	%
Above average range of magazines	**31,3**	34,2	29,8	32,0	33,3	33,4	34,7	35,5	31,3	32,3	34,3	32,4	34,3
Average range of magazines	**38,0**	37,3	39,1	37,8	37,1	37,9	36,7	37,5	39,1	39,0	34,7	39,3	37,4
Below average range of magazines	**30,7**	28,6	31,1	30,2	29,6	28,7	28,6	27,0	29,6	28,7	31,0	28,4	28,4
Above average range of daily newspapers	**26,2**	28,2	26,4	26,7	27,0	24,2	26,9	27,6	23,8	26,9	29,2	25,4	30,8
Average range of daily newspapers	**31,6**	28,7	28,1	32,0	33,0	33,1	32,2	29,6	35,8	30,9	30,0	33,1	29,6
Below average range of daily newspapers	**42,1**	43,1	45,5	41,3	40,1	42,7	40,9	42,8	40,4	42,1	40,8	41,5	39,6
Above average range of TV watching	**31,8**	33,1	31,9	33,5	33,7	33,4	33,1	34,9	34,9	29,4	30,2	35,7	32,7
Average range of TV watching	**39,3**	36,6	38,9	37,8	39,8	40,0	38,9	38,1	40,1	40,2	40,3	40,1	41,7
Below average range of TV watching	**28,9**	30,2	29,2	28,6	26,5	26,5	28,0	27,0	25,0	30,4	29,4	24,1	25,6
Above average magazine reading	**29,6**	31,2	27,1	29,7	31,9	32,1	32,3	32,4	30,6	32,3	30,1	31,3	33,1
Average magazine reading	**40,0**	41,0	40,9	40,7	40,4	40,3	39,3	39,3	40,0	37,3	40,7	39,4	37,3
Below average magazine reading	**30,4**	27,8	32,0	29,6	27,7	27,6	28,4	28,3	29,4	30,4	29,1	29,3	29,6
Above average TV watching	**30,1**	30,6	30,6	32,1	31,3	31,4	31,2	31,8	35,4	27,5	29,0	30,8	32,4
Average TV watching	**39,2**	39,2	36,7	37,5	40,2	38,4	38,8	38,3	36,9	40,2	39,6	43,9	40,4
Below average TV watching	**30,7**	30,2	32,7	30,3	28,4	30,2	30,0	29,9	27,8	32,2	31,4	25,3	27,2

Significances which reached 1 % in the analysis of the accumulated data of both surveys.
Significances which repeated themselves in both surveys.
positive ☐ ☐ negative

Sociability, musicality

Survey sample	Aged 14+ 13 283	Capri-corn 837	Aquarius 909	Pisces 937	Aries 987	Taurus 928	Gemini 1021	Cancer 913	Leo 925	Virgo 909	Libra 812	Scorpio 820	Sagit-tarius 760
	∅%	%	%	%	%	%	%	%	%	%	%	%	%
I easily get to know new people	**55.5**	57.7	54.9	54.1	58.6	55.2	58.6	59.4	57.3	60.2	57.3	53.3	56.3
I sing in choir, musical society	**6.7**	5.6	7.4	6.9	5.1	6.2	6.9	7.5	7.3	6.1	7.5	6.2	7.9
I play an instrument	**13.1**	14.2	12.5	14.8	11.7	11.2	15.0	13.9	13.2	13.8	15.6	11.9	14.8
I often receive invitations	**43.0**	42.4	43.3	43.3	44.6	43.7	44.1	43.7	44.3	45.3	42.5	39.7	47.7

Significances which reached 1% in the analysis of the accumulated data of both surveys.
Significances which repeated themselves in both surveys.

positive   negative

Attitude to fashion, clothing

Survey sample	Aged 14+ 13283	Capricorn 837	Aquarius 909	Pisces 937	Aries 987	Taurus 928	Gemini 1021	Cancer 913	Leo 925	Virgo 909	Libra 812	Scorpio 820	Sagittarius 760
	⌀%	%	%	%	%	%	%	%	%	%	%	%	%
Denim clothes (almost) daily	47.7	45.8	49.7	50.8	51.0	46.2	49.8	53.2	52.9	45.5	49.3	51.2	50.3
I like buying clothes which are 'in'	31.2	30.7	29.5	28.5	31.7	34.2	34.5	34.3	32.5	31.1	31.9	31.4	35.1
Fashion conscious: women	5.3	6.2	5.5	5.1	6.2	5.2	5.3	5.0	5.7	4.8	6.4	5.4	4.1
Fashion conscious: men	2.4	3.0	2.5	1.5	2.1	2.8	2.3	2.1	3.0	2.8	2.3	1.6	2.0
I don't conform to fashion	32.6	32.4	33.6	29.5	32.7	31.8	32.8	30.1	33.5	33.5	33.3	29.7	30.2
Sports clothes, expensive brands	8.8	8.3	8.3	10.4	9.6	8.8	10.1	9.4	9.9	8.3	7.7	6.5	8.9
Dressmaking, sewing at least occasionally	12.2	12.3	13.3	13.8	10.6	13.1	12.5	10.0	12.6	12.4	11.5	12.4	13.5
Knitting, at least occasionally	16.5	18.3	18.0	18.2	14.8	17.8	17.7	15.9	15.3	14.9	18.0	14.6	20.0
Comfortable	82.9	83.2	83.4	87.5	84.1	84.7	83.6	84.5	85.4	82.9	85.6	83.7	86.9
Elegant	19.1	18.5	19.3	21.1	17.9	19.1	19.0	18.5	20.5	19.0	19.0	18.1	19.6
Discreet, low-key	31.0	32.7	30.9	33.1	30.3	32.3	34.9	30.1	30.0	33.4	29.3	30.5	33.9
Always latest trend	5.8	4.9	5.9	4.6	6.3	4.7	6.2	4.3	7.7	4.6	6.5	5.9	5.5
Discreet colours	36.7	35.8	37.5	37.5	34.1	38.3	38.0	35.0	39.6	40.0	32.6	34.9	41.4
Sporty	44.8	44.6	42.6	45.1	45.4	44.0	45.9	48.6	46.6	47.1	46.8	47.9	45.6
Timeless	39.9	41.2	40.0	42.3	41.7	43.3	41.3	41.0	40.3	42.0	38.1	41.2	40.3
Sexy	4.7	4.8	5.0	4.5	4.7	4.2	4.5	4.5	4.7	4.5	6.0	5.2	3.5
Casual, informal	45.8	46.3	44.2	48.3	49.9	45.5	47.8	51.0	50.4	48.0	44.0	43.8	49.1
Youthful	17.8	18.6	18.4	17.2	17.8	17.9	17.2	19.3	18.3	17.6	21.6	18.6	18.4

Significances which reached 1 % in the analysis of the accumulated data of both surveys.
Significances which repeated themselves in both surveys.
  positive   negative

Attitude to fashion, clothing

Survey sample	Aged 14+ 13 283	Capricorn 837	Aquarius 909	Pisces 937	Aries 987	Taurus 928	Gemini 1021	Cancer 913	Leo 925	Virgo 909	Libra 812	Scorpio 820	Sagittarius 760
	∅%	%	%	%	%	%	%	%	%	%	%	%	%
Practical, suitable	**59,1**	59.3	62.7	63.6	58.6	61.7	58.2	59.5	63.1	61.1	58.6	63.7	59.9
Fashionable	**27,7**	29.2	28.5	26.0	30.6	30.1	26.9	28.8	27.3	29.6	27.2	26.8	32.3
Loud, extravagant	**3,0**	2.3	3.7	2.6	3.3	2.7	2.8	2.9	2.4	3.4	2.6	2.8	2.9
Figure-hugging, tight	**6,3**	7.4	5.3	6.2	8.0	5.8	6.0	6.1	6.5	6.6	8.3	6.6	7.5
Vivid colours	**13,2**	12.3	13.1	11.4	16.0	13.0	14.4	11.9	16.0	12.8	12.4	13.1	15.6
Classical	**15,4**	16.4	15.7	15.2	16.3	14.6	14.7	15.0	14.3	17.7	15.4	15.4	15.0

Significances which reached 1 % in the analysis of the accumulated data of both surveys.
Significances which repeated themselves in both surveys.
positive [ ] negative

Smokers

Survey sample	Aged 14+ 13 283	Capri-corn 837	Aquarius 909	Pisces 937	Aries 987	Taurus 928	Gemini 1021	Cancer 913	Leo 925	Virgo 909	Libra 812	Scorpio 820	Sagit-tarius 760
	Ø%	%	%	%	%	%	%	%	%	%	%	%	%
Smokers, in total	**34.9**	33.2	32.9	33.8	36.6	33.3	34.1	34.0	38.1	33.8	34.0	35.7	36.7
Cigarette smokers	**30.1**	28.0	30.8	27.2	33.0	27.5	30.6	28.4	32.6	30.5	29.1	31.1	32.1
Mild cigarette smokers	**9.9**	8.4	12.3	9.3	12.0	9.0	9.1	8.6	9.9	11.9	10.0	8.9	10.7
Pipe smokers	**1.1**	1.8	1.1	0.5	0.7	2.6	0.5	1.4	0.8	0.9	1.5	1.1	1.2
Cut-price	**2.3**	1.1	1.9	1.9	2.3	2.3	2.5	3.0	3.1	2.2	2.9	2.4	2.2
Roll-up smokers	**4.3**	5.0	3.3	3.6	3.8	3.5	4.3	4.7	5.1	4.4	4.7	5.5	4.5
Strong cigarette smokers	**4.1**	5.4	2.3	3.5	3.0	3.7	3.7	4.6	5.0	4.7	3.3	5.9	3.7
Cigar, Cigarillo, Cheroot smokers	**1.4**	2.1	0.7	1.5	1.0	1.6	2.2	1.3	1.9	0.4	1.0	2.6	1.8

Significances which reached 1 % in the analysis of the accumulated data of both surveys.
Significances which repeated themselves in both surveys.
 positive   negative

Ownership of property and assets

Survey sample	Aged 14+ 13 283	Capricorn 837	Aquarius 909	Pisces 937	Aries 987	Taurus 928	Gemini 1021	Cancer 913	Leo 925	Virgo 909	Libra 812	Scorpio 820	Sagittarius 760
	∅%	%	%	%	%	%	%	%	%	%	%	%	%
Shares	7,3	6,4	7,1	9,1	8,3	6,5	7,9	7,9	6,9	9,1	8,6	6,8	7,1
Building land	5,0	5,4	6,1	5,9	4,3	3,2	6,7	5,0	6,1	5,2	4,1	4,2	5,6
Mortgage/Building Society savings contract	30,7	28,6	31,8	34,5	34,5	30,8	34,3	33,6	31,3	33,6	31,8	34,1	31,7
Mortgage above 40,000 DM	11,7	11,3	12,6	12,7	13,4	13,0	11,5	12,0	11,9	12,7	12,4	11,8	12,6
Owner-occupied flat	7,0	7,8	5,7	7,5	7,9	5,6	5,5	7,1	6,3	7,3	7,7	6,3	9,1
Holiday house, flat	1,5	1,5	0,9	1,9	1,8	1,2	2,1	0,7	2,1	1,4	1,0	1,6	1,6
Time deposit, investment	22,9	24,3	26,4	23,0	22,4	22,4	22,2	21,3	24,2	23,8	24,7	22,3	23,6
Fixed-interest bonds	11,3	12,1	12,7	12,3	12,3	10,9	11,0	12,9	10,4	11,4	12,3	13,4	10,2
Garden, vegetable garden	22,6	23,3	22,9	25,5	20,9	22,8	23,7	22,3	21,7	22,9	26,8	23,9	23,3
Garden, ornamental garden	36,8	37,1	37,5	38,2	38,5	40,7	38,3	39,3	36,8	38,3	33,8	38,9	37,0
Gold bars, coins	2,8	3,0	1,8	3,6	1,9	2,4	2,5	3,8	3,6	3,3	3,1	3,4	2,7
House, flat to rent	13,0	13,1	14,1	17,5	13,2	10,5	12,6	12,5	13,8	15,4	12,7	13,2	15,5
House, single family house	32,2	31,0	31,4	36,7	31,7	34,6	33,2	34,2	32,3	33,1	33,2	33,4	33,2
House, multiple dwelling	11,8	11,8	13,3	13,6	11,3	9,5	15,8	10,5	11,3	12,9	11,3	12,2	12,2
Investment, property bonds	7,0	7,5	8,3	6,0	6,6	6,8	8,3	7,1	8,4	7,9	6,7	6,5	8,8
Savings certificates	16,6	17,1	18,9	17,7	15,3	17,8	14,4	17,0	16,0	17,3	18,6	15,7	20,4
Savings agreement 624/936 DM	28,2	29,3	29,2	31,5	29,3	27,9	29,4	31,6	30,2	29,9	26,5	28,0	30,9
Company shares	2,3	2,9	2,3	2,2	2,4	1,7	2,1	1,7	2,7	3,3	2,0	1,9	2,9

Significances which reached 1 % in the analysis of the accumulated data of both surveys.
Significances which repeated themselves in both surveys.
positive   negative

Ownership of property and assets

Survey sample	Aged 14+ 13 283	Capricorn 837	Aquarius 909	Pisces 937	Aries 987	Taurus 928	Gemini 1021	Cancer 913	Leo 925	Virgo 909	Libra 812	Scorpio 820	Sagittarius 760
	Ø%	%	%	%	%	%	%	%	%	%	%	%	%
International Credit Card	17.3	17.1	16.1	17.4	16.1	15.1	15.9	15.4	17.1	17.4	18.8	16.1	16.7
Family insurance: legal liability	30.0	33.3	28.8	33.1	31.3	28.2	32.7	29.4	29.4	33.3	27.5	30.7	29.3
Personal liability ins. – without motor ins.	60.1	59.9	58.4	61.4	59.3	60.7	60.7	62.1	62.3	63.8	59.9	64.1	64.2
Household contents insurance	76.5	79.8	75.5	77.4	78.6	77.5	76.5	76.7	78.6	76.9	77.9	79.5	75.3
Private life ins. under 20,000 DM	16.8	15.8	17.8	18.1	15.6	20.1	18.0	17.6	16.2	18.1	17.6	18.6	16.8
Private life ins. above 20,000 DM	43.0	42.8	40.2	47.2	44.7	41.6	44.4	43.2	42.9	43.5	41.7	42.9	44.6
Private life ins. above 50,000 DM	19.0	18.8	18.9	20.4	19.4	17.8	18.9	19.9	18.9	21.4	18.8	18.7	21.0
Private accident insurance	42.9	46.2	42.0	46.6	42.7	42.5	45.9	46.7	41.7	43.6	44.2	47.3	46.5
Motor insurance: legal liability	24.0	25.8	22.9	27.3	25.6	26.4	24.5	25.6	25.4	25.7	23.9	25.9	26.3
Fully comprehensive motor insurance	31.5	34.9	34.5	33.5	32.1	29.7	32.3	33.1	30.6	32.8	32.2	31.3	31.7
Health insurance, private only	10.9	13.3	10.4	11.3	9.0	9.0	10.9	10.1	11.2	7.8	11.2	8.6	12.5

Significances which reached 1 % in the analysis of the accumulated data of both surveys.
Significances which repeated themselves in both surveys.
positive negative

Plans to purchase property, bonds, insurance

Survey sample	Aged 14+ 13 283	Capricorn 837	Aquarius 909	Pisces 937	Aries 987	Taurus 928	Gemini 1021	Cancer 913	Leo 925	Virgo 909	Libra 812	Scorpio 820	Sagittarius 760
	∅%	%	%	%	%	%	%	%	%	%	%	%	%
Take out Building Society savings contract	6.1	5.9	5.1	7.1	6.5	4.7	8.9	5.5	7.4	6.3	5.4	7.1	6.4
House/owner-occupied flat: build or buy	7.1	7.7	6.5	5.2	8.6	8.2	7.2	6.3	10.0	7.4	7.8	7.1	7.1
Modernise own house/flat	14.0	14.9	13.3	16.8	15.4	14.6	14.7	13.9	14.5	15.2	13.7	13.3	17.0
Renovate rented accommodation	20.1	22.0	22.3	19.0	19.9	21.8	20.7	21.4	18.6	19.6	22.2	21.9	20.8
Life insurance	4.7	4.5	4.3	4.1	4.2	4.3	5.7	5.4	5.7	4.6	5.1	5.1	6.4
Private personal liability insurance	3.4	3.7	2.5	3.6	3.6	2.6	4.3	3.3	4.5	3.6	4.0	3.6	4.6
Private health insurance	1.9	2.1	2.2	2.1	2.5	2.0	2.1	1.4	3.2	1.6	1.7	1.7	0.9
Legal liability insurance	3.8	3.4	2.8	4.8	3.5	4.5	5.2	3.3	4.8	3.9	4.8	4.2	4.0
Accident insurance	3.1	4.2	2.6	2.6	3.5	3.6	4.2	2.9	4.2	2.5	3.3	3.9	2.9
Taking out savings agreement	14.0	14.6	14.3	13.1	16.9	14.4	15.4	15.8	16.3	14.7	15.8	15.5	16.0
Buy savings certificates	5.2	5.5	6.6	4.9	4.9	5.4	5.2	5.7	4.7	6.1	5.9	4.6	6.2
Buy other bonds	7.4	8.2	7.9	8.8	7.3	6.9	8.3	7.6	8.0	9.1	8.3	7.9	7.7
Take out mortgage	2.2	3.1	2.8	1.3	2.4	2.2	2.0	1.7	2.5	2.7	2.9	2.5	2.4
Take out credit	3.4	3.1	2.3	3.2	3.7	2.9	4.0	3.9	3.8	3.6	4.4	2.9	4.0
International credit card	3.9	3.9	3.4	3.9	4.3	2.9	3.8	4.3	4.3	~ 4.1	5.6	4.3	5.4

Significances which reached 1% in the analysis of the accumulated data of both surveys.
Significances which repeated themselves in both surveys.
□ positive ▨ negative

Ownership of consumer goods

Survey sample	Aged 14+ 13 283	Capri- corn 837	Aquarius 909	Pisces 937	Aries 987	Taurus 928	Gemini 1021	Cancer 913	Leo 925	Virgo 909	Libra 812	Scorpio 820	Sagit- tarius 760
	⊘%	%	%	%	%	%	%	%	%	%	%	%	%
Computer: desktop or portable	24.8	28.6	26.0	24.1	22.7	24.0	26.5	27.8	28.7	26.9	26.6	24.0	28.7
Computer: portable, laptop	3.4	3.4	4.6	3.5	3.1	4.1	2.9	2.8	3.8	3.8	4.2	3.4	4.1
Answer machine	26.1	27.0	22.9	26.5	26.3	21.9	24.9	27.5	31.3	26.4	25.7	24.7	28.7
Mobile phone	6.2	5.6	5.7	6.6	6.7	4.8	5.9	6.7	6.6	7.3	7.7	5.9	6.4
Cordless phone	24.0	26.7	20.6	26.2	24.1	22.2	24.3	24.8	26.2	23.3	23.1	25.5	25.8
Fax machine	8.7	10.0	9.3	8.5	9.1	8.6	9.0	7.9	10.4	9.5	9.4	7.9	7.4
Car stereo: radio, cassette	43.9	43.7	44.0	43.6	50.7	43.8	45.3	46.7	46.6	42.9	42.0	46.8	44.6
CD player	54.9	55.3	56.0	56.7	56.1	51.5	55.5	55.4	56.2	55.7	55.6	53.7	57.3
Colour television, not portable	83.2	83.2	84.8	80.4	84.8	81.9	85.1	85.6	83.9	81.6	81.9	85.6	85.8
Colour television, portable	24.4	22.8	21.3	26.7	25.7	23.2	24.7	23.3	26.1	23.6	24.5	26.2	27.4
Hi-fi – cassette deck	48.1	48.5	45.7	47.8	49.1	44.3	48.2	48.1	52.0	47.9	47.5	49.7	52.3
Hi-fi – loud speakers	51.3	53.7	49.1	51.2	53.6	47.9	52.4	52.6	53.2	51.7	50.0	51.3	54.1
Hi-fi – amplifier/receiver	44.8	45.1	43.6	46.2	47.7	40.7	43.5	41.5	47.0	45.5	46.4	44.6	49.5
Hi-fi – tuner	35.9	35.6	32.7	34.8	38.0	32.7	37.3	36.9	40.1	37.5	34.6	34.3	39.9
Video camera, camcorder	16.6	15.7	15.5	15.3	15.0	16.0	19.1	20.9	16.3	17.0	15.7	17.1	22.6
Video recorder	65.5	65.3	63.2	64.5	67.8	59.1	68.3	69.3	68.7	64.9	63.2	69.5	69.7
Video equipment	6.5	6.4	6.0	6.2	5.4	5.8	9.5	9.0	5.4	6.9	6.8	6.4	8.0
Walkman: Sony or other makes	26.9	27.7	27.0	27.6	26.0	27.3	28.0	30.4	29.5	30.1	28.2	28.1	29.0

Significances which reached 1 % in the analysis of the accumulated data of both surveys.
Significances which repeated themselves in both surveys.
positive ☐ negative

Ownership of consumer goods

Survey sample	Aged 14+ 13 283	Capricorn 837	Aquarius 909	Pisces 937	Aries 987	Taurus 928	Gemini 1021	Cancer 913	Leo 925	Virgo 909	Libra 812	Scorpio 820	Sagittarius 760
	∅%	%	%	%	%	%	%	%	%	%	%	%	%
35mm camera (viewfinder)	35,5	32,9	33,1	39,5	35,8	36,0	36,2	35,6	36,6	34,6	35,8	34,9	34,7
Reflex camera	23,2	24,4	23,5	26,1	22,6	23,4	21,5	22,8	24,9	24,3	25,5	23,6	22,2
Fitted kitchen	61,5	61,3	62,7	64,3	61,9	59,6	59,3	60,2	60,9	63,5	58,3	60,0	60,3
Encyclopedia, high quality	17,7	20,5	18,2	18,9	16,7	15,2	17,9	19,0	15,9	16,1	18,9	20,4	21,8
Dishwasher	46,5	48,1	44,2	49,9	45,6	43,6	50,9	44,5	47,1	47,4	44,5	46,7	47,0
Prints, sculptures, paintings	10,1	8,7	9,9	13,2	10,9	8,3	10,1	7,4	9,3	8,7	11,2	11,4	10,3
Microwave oven	51,0	49,5	46,1	52,0	52,8	48,0	54,4	51,7	51,4	51,5	48,2	53,7	52,1
Furniture: high quality	10,6	10,9	10,1	11,8	11,1	9,1	9,9	9,5	10,8	9,4	10,6	11,6	10,4
Furniture: modern designer	6,0	7,1	5,7	6,6	5,6	5,2	6,1	4,3	5,2	6,0	6,7	6,6	7,0
Furniture: ready to assemble	34,5	32,3	32,3	35,7	35,0	33,0	36,5	36,6	36,3	33,1	36,4	34,6	38,9
Lawnmower: diesel/battery/electric	33,3	35,1	36,0	39,0	35,5	34,4	35,7	35,5	33,3	33,8	37,1	35,4	32,5
Women's accessories	27,5	29,0	25,7	28,1	28,7	27,5	25,3	26,5	28,7	27,4	28,4	27,7	29,9
Luxury wristwatch	6,1	6,5	5,8	6,1	6,0	5,3	6,4	6,1	6,5	6,7	7,6	5,1	7,1
Exclusive spectacles	10,8	10,8	12,8	12,5	9,5	11,4	10,2	10,3	9,5	11,0	12,6	10,3	13,4
Luxury fountain pen	2,9	3,2	3,3	2,3	2,6	2,2	2,9	3,0	3,3	3,5	2,7	2,4	2,9
Valuable luggage	3,6	3,0	3,6	4,3	3,4	2,4	3,6	2,7	3,5	3,3	4,6	3,5	4,2
Camper	1,7	1,7	1,1	2,3	1,1	1,7	1,5	1,8	1,8	1,9	1,5	1,5	1,9
Caravan/trailer	2,6	2,0	2,6	2,9	3,2	2,3	1,9	2,8	4,1	2,3	3,5	2,7	1,9

Significances which reached 1 % in the analysis of the accumulated data of both surveys.
Significances which repeated themselves in both surveys.
positive ☐ negative

Ownership of consumer goods

Survey sample	Aged 14+ 13 283	Capri- corn 837	Aquarius 909	Pisces 937	Aries 987	Taurus 928	Gemini 1021	Cancer 913	Leo 925	Virgo 909	Libra 812	Scorpio 820	Sagit- tarius 760
	∅%	%	%	%	%	%	%	%	%	%	%	%	%
Camping equipment	**13,8**	14,5	14,2	14,4	14,4	14,4	15,3	14,8	14,5	14,9	15,4	14,2	14,4
Mountain bike	**14,2**	14,1	17,2	16,1	14,1	13,7	14,8	15,4	14,5	15,9	14,5	15,1	16,6
Racing bicycle, sports bicycle	**17,9**	18,8	16,9	18,4	18,4	18,7	18,8	20,4	16,7	19,4	18,8	19,2	18,6
Sailing boat, dinghy	**0,9**	0,6	0,2	0,8	1,2	0,7	1,3	0,9	1,0	1,2	0,5	1,8	1,3

Significances which reached 1 % in the analysis of the accumulated data of both surveys.
Significances which repeated themselves in both surveys.
☐☐☐ positive ☐ negative

316

Plans to purchase consumer goods

Survey sample	Aged 14+ 13 283	Capricorn 837	Aquarius 909	Pisces 937	Aries 987	Taurus 928	Gemini 1021	Cancer 913	Leo 925	Virgo 909	Libra 812	Scorpio 820	Sagittarius 760
	⊘%	%	%	%	%	%	%	%	%	%	%	%	%
Computer: desktop or portable	7.7	8.7	6.4	7.8	8.6	7.5	9.1	9.1	7.6	7.8	11.2	6.4	6.7
Computer: portable, laptop	1.6	1.5	1.5	1.6	1.3	1.2	2.0	1.2	1.8	1.7	2.7	1.3	1.5
Answer machine	5.7	4.7	5.7	5.3	6.0	6.0	5.6	5.6	5.8	6.7	7.3	6.4	5.2
Mobile phone	2.1	3.0	1.4	1.7	3.0	1.4	2.4	1.7	3.1	2.2	1.7	1.6	2.1
Cordless phone	6.6	5.4	6.2	8.0	6.7	6.4	8.2	8.4	6.1	7.9	6.6	6.0	4.3
Fax machine	3.3	3.7	3.1	3.1	3.7	2.4	3.2	3.1	3.7	3.8	3.5	3.7	4.6
CD Player	3.9	3.9	4.0	4.7	4.1	3.6	3.5	3.9	5.3	3.1	3.2	4.6	3.0
Colour television, not portable	4.1	4.2	5.0	4.2	4.3	3.9	3.2	4.2	4.0	4.7	4.4	3.5	3.0
Colour television, portable	2.6	2.5	2.2	2.4	2.8	2.9	2.6	1.6	2.8	2.7	1.5	3.1	1.1
Hi-fi – cassette deck	1.9	1.7	2.2	1.9	2.3	2.0	1.5	2.0	2.1	1.9	1.8	1.4	1.5
Hi-fi – loud speakers	1.9	2.0	1.6	2.2	2.2	1.9	1.3	2.2	1.9	1.6	1.9	1.8	1.4
Hi-fi – amplifier/receiver	1.9	2.0	2.1	2.7	2.0	1.9	1.4	2.4	2.0	1.6	1.2	1.9	1.1
Hi-fi – tuner	1.5	1.1	1.5	1.7	1.8	1.0	1.1	1.9	2.4	1.5	1.7	1.7	1.3
Video camera, camcorder	5.5	4.6	5.4	6.0	6.5	4.1	5.9	3.9	7.7	7.3	5.2	5.7	5.3
Video recorder	5.7	6.0	5.2	7.0	6.8	4.6	4.8	6.7	6.0	6.5	6.1	6.0	4.8
Video equipment	1.2	0.7	1.0	1.3	0.6	0.4	1.4	0.6	2.1	1.3	0.6	1.5	1.0
Walkman: Sony or other makes	1.1	1.1	1.0	1.4	1.0	0.7	1.0	1.3	0.9	1.6	0.8	1.1	1.0
35mm camera (viewfinder)	1.7	1.7	1.8	2.0	1.0	2.4	1.5	2.8	1.7	2.3	1.8	2.2	1.3

Significances which reached 1% in the analysis of the accumulated data of both surveys.
Significances which repeated themselves in both surveys.
☐ positive ☐ negative

Plans to purchase consumer goods

Survey sample	Aged 14+ 13 283	Capri-corn 837	Aquarius 909	Pisces 937	Aries 987	Taurus 928	Gemini 1021	Cancer 913	Leo 925	Virgo 909	Libra 812	Scorpio 820	Sagit-tarius 760
	⊘%	%	%	%	%	%	%	%	%	%	%	%	%
Reflex camera	2,1	1,8	2,6	2,3	3,4	2,5	1,7	2,3	2,0	1,3	1,0	1,8	2,4
Fitted kitchen	5,0	4,9	5,6	5,2	6,0	6,0	4,6	4,8	5,4	4,6	4,7	6,0	5,7
Encyclopedia, high quality	1,1	1,5	1,1	0,9	0,8	1,0	1,6	1,3	1,0	1,0	1,3	0,7	0,7
Dishwasher	5,8	5,6	4,3	7,0	6,1	6,0	5,1	6,6	6,1	4,8	6,8	7,4	6,1
Prints, sculptures, paintings	1,2	1,4	1,2	0,9	1,1	2,3	1,3	0,9	1,3	1,1	1,7	0,5	1,5
Microwave oven	5,3	5,1	5,2	5,0	4,5	6,2	4,6	5,9	5,3	6,4	6,0	3,5	5,3
Furniture: high quality	1,1	1,9	0,6	1,6	0,9	1,3	0,4	1,1	1,3	1,1	0,5	0,9	1,0
Furniture: modern designer	1,5	1,9	1,5	1,4	1,1	2,2	2,1	1,5	1,4	1,4	1,1	1,6	1,2
Furniture: ready to assemble	2,6	3,0	2,9	3,3	2,5	2,6	2,7	3,6	2,0	2,4	3,3	3,0	2,3
Lawnmower: diesel/battery/electric	1,6	1,7	0,5	1,5	1,9	2,1	2,1	2,3	0,9	2,3	0,7	1,8	1,4
Women's accessories	2,9	3,1	2,9	2,8	2,8	1,8	3,1	2,7	2,3	2,7	5,0	2,7	3,1
Luxury wristwatch	0,8	1,5	0,7	0,9	0,6	0,8	0,5	0,8	0,8	0,6	0,6	0,4	0,6
Exclusive spectacles	1,3	1,6	1,3	1,2	1,6	1,1	0,9	0,9	2,5	1,3	1,1	1,1	1,4
Luxury fountain pen	0,3	0,6	0,4	0,5	0,2	0,3	0,3	0,2	0,6	0,4	0,1	0,6	0,0
Valuable luggage	0,4	0,8	0,4	0,6	0,3	0,1	0,3	0,5	0,3	0,1	0,7	0,7	0,2
Camper	0,5	0,5	0,2	0,3	0,1	0,4	0,6	1,0	0,9	0,3	1,2	0,4	0,4
Caravan/trailer	0,5	0,2	0,3	0,6	0,4	0,4	0,8	0,1	0,9	0,4	0,6	0,7	0,8

Significances which reached 1 % in the analysis of the accumulated data of both surveys.
Significances which repeated themselves in both surveys.
  positive   negative

318

Car and motorcycle drivers, driving habits

Survey sample	Aged 14+ 13 283	Capricorn 837	Aquarius 909	Pisces 937	Aries 987	Taurus 928	Gemini 1021	Cancer 913	Leo 925	Virgo 909	Libra 812	Scorpio 820	Sagittarius 760
	⌀%	%	%	%	%	%	%	%	%	%	%	%	%
Car driver	64.7	61.7	61.6	69.1	68.1	60.9	64.2	65.7	64.2	69.8	63.1	67.9	68.3
H.G.V. driver	11.0	10.8	8.9	12.2	12.6	12.8	11.8	12.3	13.2	11.3	11.2	11.2	10.5
Motorcyclist (above 80cc)	4.3	3.5	3.5	4.6	3.3	4.1	5.3	6.1	5.0	5.3	5.4	4.5	4.0
Motorcyclist (below 80cc)	2.0	2.4	1.7	2.4	2.2	1.0	2.4	3.0	2.5	2.3	1.6	3.0	1.9
Scooter	2.1	1.9	2.4	2.2	2.0	2.8	2.4	2.6	2.2	2.4	2.4	1.9	2.8
Moped	3.1	3.1	2.5	4.1	2.8	3.6	2.0	4.3	4.4	3.8	3.3	3.3	3.1
Frequent driver: 20,000km and more	10.6	12.4	10.1	10.7	11.7	11.0	11.1	9.2	10.3	10.0	11.6	12.7	11.4
Moderate driver: 10–20,000km	28.9	25.7	24.5	33.0	30.5	26.8	29.3	30.3	28.2	31.8	28.1	31.7	28.8
Infrequent driver: under 10,000km	20.9	20.9	23.8	22.0	21.4	19.3	21.3	21.8	22.0	21.5	20.6	19.0	24.8
Interested car experts	6.6	7.3	7.8	7.8	6.2	7.1	8.1	7.7	8.4	5.4	6.6	5.7	6.6
Environmentally committed car drivers	12.2	11.0	9.5	13.4	11.2	13.2	12.7	13.1	12.5	14.8	11.7	14.8	14.1

Significances which reached 1 % in the analysis of the accumulated data of both surveys.
Significances which repeated themselves in both surveys.

positive ☐ negative

Car, motorcycle ownership, makes, plans to purchase

Survey sample	Aged 14+ 13 283	Capricorn 837	Aquarius 909	Pisces 937	Aries 987	Taurus 928	Gemini 1021	Cancer 913	Leo 925	Virgo 909	Libra 812	Scorpio 820	Sagittarius 760
	∅%	%	%	%	%	%	%	%	%	%	%	%	%
Car (themselves drive)	60,5	59,0	58,4	65,9	63,6	57,2	61,7	61,3	60,7	63,3	60,3	63,7	64,9
Second car (themselves drive)	7,6	8,4	7,4	8,3	8,8	8,2	7,0	7,0	7,1	7,7	8,4	8,8	7,7
Used car (themselves drive)	31,4	28,5	28,8	32,6	33,9	28,4	33,7	32,2	33,6	33,5	30,5	32,7	32,3
New car (themselves drive)	28,8	30,5	29,3	33,1	29,3	28,1	27,8	29,1	26,8	29,6	29,5	30,7	32,3
Car of more than 90HP (themselves drive)	16,9	19,5	16,7	17,6	17,2	14,7	16,5	16,0	19,0	15,5	16,8	18,0	18,2
Two or more cars in household	26,1	26,6	26,7	28,8	28,9	27,0	26,8	28,3	28,0	25,5	26,6	29,2	30,7
Audi	3,4	2,9	3,4	3,3	3,8	3,3	3,3	2,8	4,5	3,4	3,0	4,3	3,5
BMW	3,3	4,4	3,2	3,1	2,8	2,6	3,3	3,6	3,3	3,2	4,6	3,4	2,5
Ford	6,6	5,9	6,3	7,4	7,2	5,5	7,1	8,0	5,4	5,7	7,3	9,3	4,8
Mercedes	4,2	4,4	3,1	4,6	4,5	4,4	4,5	3,5	5,1	4,6	3,4	4,2	5,1
Opel	10,9	9,3	10,7	13,7	10,5	10,6	10,2	11,3	11,3	11,6	10,0	10,8	13,0
VW	15,0	15,2	13,3	17,6	16,2	14,5	15,0	14,0	13,8	17,1	15,2	13,6	14,9
Italian makes	1,9	1,6	1,9	1,9	2,3	1,1	2,0	1,7	2,0	2,4	2,2	1,9	2,4
French makes	4,8	4,2	4,8	4,8	4,2	6,0	5,4	4,9	4,4	4,9	5,5	4,7	4,8
Japanese makes	7,0	7,0	6,4	6,3	8,2	6,4	7,0	8,9	7,3	8,0	5,8	7,2	9,2
Used cars	9,5	8,5	11,1	9,8	11,6	10,1	9,1	11,9	10,3	10,1	10,9	10,4	10,6
New cars	6,0	6,3	7,6	6,2	6,8	4,7	6,8	4,4	6,4	6,6	7,0	6,8	7,1
Motorcycle over 80cc	1,6	2,5	1,5	1,7	1,4	1,6	1,2	1,8	2,6	1,0	1,5	1,3	1,4

Significances which reached 1% in the analysis of the accumulated data of both surveys.
Significances which repeated themselves in both surveys.
positive [ ] negative

Foodstuffs bought in the last 14 days by those surveyed

Survey sample	Aged 14+ 13 283	Capricorn 837	Aquarius 909	Pisces 937	Aries 987	Taurus 928	Gemini 1021	Cancer 913	Leo 925	Virgo 909	Libra 812	Scorpio 820	Sagittarius 760
	⊘%	%	%	%	%	%	%	%	%	%	%	%	%
Baby food	3,2	2,4	3,2	3,2	2,5	2,7	3,9	4,1	3,0	2,0	3,7	3,6	3,9
Organic fruit, vegetables	13,4	12,9	12,3	13,1	11,8	14,0	12,5	13,4	12,4	14,8	12,7	14,2	15,7
Diabetic food	5,4	6,5	5,2	6,1	5,0	5,6	5,0	5,7	5,9	4,3	5,1	5,3	6,2
Family pack of ice, deep frozen	17,9	16,6	22,2	18,0	17,4	19,8	20,2	17,2	19,9	15,9	14,1	16,4	23,6
Gourmet specialities	12,0	13,5	10,5	14,2	14,2	10,7	10,8	11,6	11,6	12,2	13,5	11,6	12,4
Ready-to-serve meals, in total	39,8	38,2	37,6	39,7	39,6	41,1	39,5	38,8	36,9	40,7	43,0	39,0	42,9
Ready-to-serve meals for microwave	6,6	5,5	7,2	6,9	6,1	6,1	6,1	7,3	5,0	5,5	7,5	6,2	7,1
Ready-to-serve meals, frozen	19,2	19,3	19,7	20,7	18,8	18,9	18,0	18,4	16,6	18,8	21,0	17,3	21,9
Ready-to-serve, other	9,0	9,4	9,7	8,8	9,1	8,1	7,7	7,9	9,3	9,5	8,6	8,4	8,5
Instant soups	23,7	23,7	22,4	23,6	23,1	24,4	24,2	23,1	21,9	23,6	24,4	26,3	25,0
Fish, fresh	21,6	22,6	22,5	22,5	19,7	21,1	21,4	19,9	23,9	21,8	20,0	21,9	22,5
Fish, deep frozen	17,3	16,4	17,7	16,4	15,8	19,1	19,6	17,5	15,7	15,5	19,3	16,3	19,6
Poultry, deep frozen	21,8	20,2	21,8	19,7	23,1	24,8	22,3	21,8	22,6	21,7	20,4	24,4	22,5
Bottled condiments, sauces, ketchup	24,7	29,3	21,9	24,5	24,6	26,1	25,7	26,5	26,7	25,4	24,0	25,5	24,2
Cough drops	19,2	20,6	19,3	19,3	19,4	20,7	20,5	22,6	19,2	19,8	20,9	21,9	20,4
Low calorie food	9,7	12,3	10,7	9,7	10,3	9,9	10,5	9,0	8,7	8,3	10,5	10,5	11,0
Chewing gum	22,5	22,9	22,8	20,6	23,8	19,7	21,6	27,2	25,5	25,7	24,0	23,9	23,0
Snack biscuits, salted	29,2	28,6	31,3	31,9	28,8	29,6	32,1	29,0	29,3	30,5	28,6	27,3	30,9

Significances which reached 1 % in the analysis of the accumulated data of both surveys.
Significances which repeated themselves in both surveys.
☐ positive ☐ negative

Foodstuffs bought in the last fortnight by those surveyed

Survey sample	Aged 14+ 13 283	Capricorn 837	Aquarius 909	Pisces 937	Aries 987	Taurus 928	Gemini 1021	Cancer 913	Leo 925	Virgo 909	Libra 812	Scorpio 820	Sagittarius 760
	⊘%	%	%	%	%	%	%	%	%	%	%	%	%
Snack biscuits, sweet	14,1	14,5	15,8	14,9	13,7	13,4	14,9	14,8	14,1	14,3	14,1	13,8	14,5
Crispbread	22,9	21,9	23,5	23,4	21,8	26,2	23,2	22,7	19,0	21,7	24,6	25,9	22,1
Muesli bar	9,7	7,8	9,9	8,9	11,9	9,6	9,5	10,7	9,8	11,0	8,4	10,4	10,4
Peppermint drops, sweets	5,3	5,5	5,3	5,4	5,8	5,4	5,2	5,4	4,1	5,6	3,9	4,3	6,5
Pralines	11,5	14,1	10,5	9,4	8,5	11,0	13,5	11,3	10,9	10,9	13,3	10,3	12,2
Custard, mousse	19,9	21,0	18,1	18,3	18,2	21,2	23,1	22,0	20,3	18,5	21,2	21,5	22,2
Chocolate, full milk, butter	34,5	41,8	36,3	33,7	31,1	36,0	37,6	32,1	34,2	32,6	38,1	35,2	39,4
Chocolate, filled	12,8	14,5	12,6	12,3	11,6	14,6	11,9	12,4	10,5	13,6	17,1	13,3	11,9
Chocolate bars	24,1	26,3	22,4	22,4	24,9	25,6	23,2	26,2	25,6	23,0	26,6	26,1	26,3
Salt	21,5	26,4	22,2	19,7	20,7	23,0	18,9	21,0	21,7	21,2	18,4	23,5	25,8
Sweetener	12,3	10,5	11,6	12,1	11,0	13,9	12,8	11,0	11,2	13,4	14,9	11,8	13,4

Significances which reached 1 % in the analysis of the accumulated data of both surveys.
Significances which repeated themselves in both surveys.
positive [ ] negative

Drinks bought or drunk in the last fortnight by those surveyed

Survey sample	Aged 14+ 13 283	Capri-corn 837	Aquarius 909	Pisces 937	Aries 987	Taurus 928	Gemini 1021	Cancer 913	Leo 925	Virgo 909	Libra 812	Scorpio 820	Sagit-tarius 760
	Ø%	%	%	%	%	%	%	%	%	%	%	%	%
Aperitifs	3,3	4,6	2,7	3,1	3,1	2,1	3,3	2,4	2,4	3,2	4,3	4,4	3,2
Beer, in general	57,6	56,0	57,5	57,4	59,8	56,3	57,1	59,8	57,4	56,3	59,2	60,0	56,3
Beer, low-alcohol, alcohol-free	8,3	8,7	8,2	8,7	8,0	8,8	8,1	8,5	7,1	8,6	8,9	9,6	8,5
Bitter lemon etc.	7,7	7,6	7,1	7,1	7,4	7,3	8,1	8,4	6,4	7,8	9,2	6,9	9,0
Champagne	3,8	4,2	3,4	4,5	5,1	4,0	2,6	3,0	3,5	4,1	5,0	3,6	3,7
Cola-drinks	38,5	40,7	37,1	35,3	42,1	36,1	37,8	39,9	37,9	38,5	39,8	40,8	39,1
Cream sodas	5,3	4,5	5,7	5,4	4,6	4,3	4,4	6,1	6,5	4,9	6,5	6,0	5,0
Fruit juice (100%)	47,7	49,7	50,3	49,5	44,3	47,9	49,0	47,6	47,7	50,1	48,4	49,8	48,6
Fruit nectar (under 100%)	31,5	31,4	33,0	32,9	30,4	33,4	36,0	34,4	30,6	27,9	30,1	35,6	28,4
Gin	1,1	1,2	1,4	1,5	1,5	0,7	1,1	0,6	1,4	0,7	1,0	0,7	1,0

Significances which reached 1% in the analysis of the accumulated data of both surveys.
Significances which repeated themselves in both surveys.
☐ positive ☐ negative

Drinks bought or drunk in the last fortnight by those surveyed

Survey sample	Aged 14+ 13 283	Capricorn 837	Aquarius 909	Pisces 937	Aries 987	Taurus 928	Gemini 1021	Cancer 913	Leo 925	Virgo 909	Libra 812	Scorpio 820	Sagittarius 760
	∅%	%	%	%	%	%	%	%	%	%	%	%	%
Herbal liqueurs	7,8	7,1	7,5	8,8	8,3	6,7	7,3	8,2	5,8	8,6	8,2	8,7	8,0
Liqueurs	10,2	9,8	10,7	9,9	10,2	11,0	9,9	11,7	10,6	10,3	11,1	12,1	10,8
Lemonade	31,7	32,4	29,6	29,7	32,9	32,6	33,8	35,4	32,2	31,2	32,3	33,5	33,6
Bitters	9,0	10,5	9,6	8,4	8,9	7,9	9,2	10,2	8,6	7,3	10,0	8,8	8,9
Milk shakes	17,7	16,9	19,3	17,5	18,7	16,3	18,5	14,7	17,7	20,8	18,4	19,3	19,3
Mineral – soda-water	79,4	78,4	79,0	80,9	80,6	82,0	77,0	78,6	80,0	80,2	78,4	80,2	82,2
Fruit schnaps	7,1	5,6	8,3	7,5	6,9	8,5	6,2	6,0	7,7	7,6	7,2	7,4	5,2
Rum	3,2	2,4	2,6	3,2	4,1	2,3	2,8	4,9	4,1	4,1	3,0	3,8	2,8
Schnaps	12,3	10,0	11,5	13,1	12,4	10,6	13,2	12,2	12,0	13,5	13,1	16,4	10,7
Sparkling wine	28,4	29,9	28,8	30,3	27,7	28,0	27,4	30,4	28,4	31,0	31,9	29,0	27,7
Sherry, port	4,7	4,8	4,4	5,3	4,6	4,7	4,2	4,4	4,8	4,1	4,7	4,9	4,1
Sports drinks	6,3	7,1	7,8	5,9	7,3	5,7	5,9	7,7	6,8	5,2	6,0	5,9	5,0
Wine, in general	46,5	48,4	49,3	49,4	47,6	47,4	46,7	46,7	44,4	48,0	48,9	44,9	48,4
Wine, red	24,0	25,5	24,9	26,1	25,7	22,1	23,7	25,1	23,5	23,4	26,1	23,6	25,6
Wine, white, dry	23,2	24,9	23,8	26,4	23,6	24,0	23,7	23,2	22,6	24,0	24,3	21,2	19,8
Wine, white, not dry	15,2	15,4	15,9	14,2	15,0	12,3	16,2	15,7	13,1	15,3	18,1	14,8	15,9

Significances which reached 1 % in the analysis of the accumulated data of both surveys.
Significances which repeated themselves in both surveys.
positive   negative

Drinks bought or drunk in the last fortnight by those surveyed

Survey sample	Aged 14+ 13 283	Capricorn 837	Aquarius 909	Pisces 937	Aries 987	Taurus 928	Gemini 1021	Cancer 913	Leo 925	Virgo 909	Libra 812	Scorpio 820	Sagittarius 760
	Ø%	%	%	%	%	%	%	%	%	%	%	%	%
Foreign brandies, cognac	4,7	5,5	6,3	5,4	3,9	3,7	3,9	4,8	5,4	4,7	4,6	4,9	4,5
German brandies	10,6	11,9	12,7	11,0	10,2	9,6	10,0	11,4	10,2	12,1	10,4	10,1	11,4
Whisky	5,8	5,7	5,8	4,6	6,4	5,5	5,2	5,4	6,3	5,3	6,1	5,9	7,1
Vodka	4,5	5,2	4,1	4,8	5,8	4,0	4,1	4,6	4,3	3,8	3,2	5,3	3,1
Spirts, high proof	34,0	34,4	33,9	34,2	34,4	31,9	32,7	33,0	33,7	36,0	34,7	36,5	31,7

Significances which reached 1% in the analysis of the accumulated data of both surveys.
Significances which repeated themselves in both surveys.
positive   negative

Purchase of books

Survey sample	Aged 14+ 13 283	Capricorn 837	Aquarius 909	Pisces 937	Aries 987	Taurus 928	Gemini 1021	Cancer 913	Leo 925	Virgo 909	Libra 812	Scorpio 820	Sagittarius 760
	Ø%	%	%	%	%	%	%	%	%	%	%	%	%
Book club, readers club: member of	10.3	10.9	8.4	10.0	12.2	9.8	12.5	11.2	9.8	9.0	11.6	9.5	12.3
Purchase 10 or more books	12.1	14.9	11.0	11.5	12.6	11.1	13.3	11.6	12.8	11.1	14.9	11.5	15.3
Purchase 1-9 books	39.8	41.5	41.9	40.8	39.0	39.5	39.2	41.2	39.1	40.6	36.8	41.6	37.7
Purchase of paperbacks: £5 or more	12.2	13.2	11.2	12.0	12.6	11.7	14.1	12.2	11.9	12.2	13.6	10.3	10.4
Purchase of hardbacks: £12 or more	20.5	20.5	20.8	22.4	19.7	19.4	22.6	21.0	21.0	20.5	22.6	17.5	21.9
Reading: daily	15.5	16.7	18.2	15.3	17.3	16.3	15.1	17.6	15.7	12.9	17.2	14.3	18.7
Reading: several times a week	19.0	17.8	20.1	19.7	18.3	17.2	19.5	18.1	18.8	20.8	18.2	17.9	19.9
Reading: once a week	11.1	11.4	9.1	11.0	9.6	12.9	11.0	11.0	12.0	9.6	11.7	11.3	10.0
Reading: once a fortnight or less	54.5	54.1	52.7	54.0	54.7	53.6	54.4	53.4	53.5	56.7	53.0	56.5	51.4

Significances which reached 1% in the analysis of the accumulated data of both surveys.
Significances which repeated themselves in both surveys.
positive ☐ negative

Purchase of visual and audio recording materials

Survey sample	Aged 14+ 13 283	Capri-corn 837	Aquarius 909	Pisces 937	Aries 987	Taurus 928	Gemini 1021	Cancer 913	Leo 925	Virgo 909	Libra 812	Scorpio 820	Sagit-tarius 760
	⊘%	%	%	%	%	%	%	%	%	%	%	%	%
Amateur photographers	58,5	58,1	56,8	60,1	60,5	59,9	58,4	62,5	60,1	58,9	60,2	60,1	60,9
A. photo.: purchase of colour film	52,5	52,2	51,6	54,4	53,6	53,9	52,2	55,9	55,2	54,5	53,4	55,1	55,7
A. photo.: purchase of colour slide film	6,7	6,8	5,0	7,4	6,8	7,2	7,5	7,0	5,5	5,8	7,8	5,8	7,1
A. photo.: purchase of B&W film	1,6	2,2	1,5	1,5	1,6	1,1	2,0	1,5	1,8	1,4	2,1	2,4	1,4
A. photo.: purchase of 10 or more films	9,0	11,2	7,8	9,8	8,5	9,9	9,7	10,8	8,7	9,1	11,0	10,1	10,9
A. photo.: purchase of 1–9 films	46,8	44,8	46,9	47,3	49,3	47,6	46,0	48,1	49,1	46,6	46,3	47,2	47,7
Records, cassettes	11,4	12,4	10,6	10,7	12,2	12,1	14,1	12,0	14,1	10,7	10,7	8,9	11,3
CDs	38,3	41,0	36,4	39,0	39,0	35,2	40,7	38,8	42,1	36,1	40,4	39,9	40,5
Video cassettes	34,0	35,2	32,6	34,0	33,7	29,5	38,0	36,7	37,3	32,3	33,9	36,2	36,3

Significances which reached 1 % in the analysis of the accumulated data of both surveys.
Significances which repeated themselves in both surveys.
positive ☐ ☐ negative

Health-conscious, self-medication, -treatment

Survey sample	Aged 14+ 13 283	Capricorn 837	Aquarius 909	Pisces 937	Aries 987	Taurus 928	Gemini 1021	Cancer 913	Leo 925	Virgo 909	Libra 812	Scorpio 820	Sagittarius 760
	⊘%	%	%	%	%	%	%	%	%	%	%	%	%
Allergies, hay fever	2,5	3,0	3,0	3,0	2,4	1,4	3,3	1,6	2,0	4,2	2,3	2,4	3,3
Tranquillizers	5,6	3,8	6,8	5,3	6,8	5,6	4,4	4,8	6,1	6,7	6,4	5,2	5,3
Blood-pressure: reducing	3,1	2,6	2,4	2,6	3,3	3,0	1,8	2,3	2,4	2,5	4,9	2,1	3,7
Blood-pressure: raising	1,1	0,6	1,1	1,0	0,3	1,2	0,7	1,1	2,0	1,0	0,5	1,1	1,5
Mouthwash	11,8	10,7	11,2	13,0	12,1	10,0	11,7	13,5	11,9	12,4	15,8	11,3	13,6
Cod liver oil (capsules)	1,4	1,1	1,0	2,5	1,0	1,2	1,8	1,1	2,7	1,0	0,7	1,3	1,9
Geriatrika – anti-ageing	2,3	1,9	3,7	0,9	2,2	3,0	2,6	3,0	2,4	2,7	3,0	1,1	1,9
Essential oils	6,5	5,7	7,1	7,6	5,3	6,1	7,7	6,4	7,3	7,3	7,0	5,3	7,4
Skin complaints – fungal	2,2	2,1	2,7	2,2	3,1	1,9	2,4	2,7	1,8	2,4	2,1	2,5	1,8
Heart, circulation – medicines	5,0	4,8	6,2	4,2	4,7	4,4	4,5	4,3	6,0	4,4	6,5	5,0	4,3
Cough mixture, drops	18,5	17,8	18,9	19,1	17,7	16,9	18,2	20,6	20,3	17,8	19,5	17,6	20,0
Sciatica, rheumatism, pains in the joints	8,8	8,7	10,3	8,3	9,0	8,4	8,2	7,7	10,7	9,0	10,1	8,2	9,4
Garlic products	9,0	11,8	7,7	9,1	8,5	8,9	10,0	8,8	8,9	7,3	10,2	8,6	7,8
Stomach, liver, gallbladder problems	5,6	6,0	4,8	6,5	5,1	5,1	5,8	6,3	5,8	5,5	5,5	5,2	4,7
Massage oil	4,8	5,7	4,9	6,7	4,7	3,7	4,4	6,1	3,9	5,1	3,8	5,2	5,3
Mistletoe products	1,8	2,6	2,5	2,1	1,7	1,7	1,4	1,7	2,2	0,8	1,8	1,5	2,0
Renal, bladder problems	2,2	1,5	2,9	2,5	1,6	2,8	1,8	1,5	2,2	1,5	3,4	1,6	3,3
Sleeping pills	4,2	4,4	4,5	2,5	3,1	3,4	2,7	2,8	2,9	4,6	5,5	3,7	6,0

Significances which reached 1 % in the analysis of the accumulated data of both surveys.
Significances which repeated themselves in both surveys.
▨ positive ☐ negative

Health-consciousness, self-medication, -treatment

Survey sample	Aged 14+ 13283	Capricorn 837	Aquarius 909	Pisces 937	Aries 987	Taurus 928	Gemini 1021	Cancer 913	Leo 925	Virgo 909	Libra 812	Scorpio 820	Sagittarius 760
	⌀%	%	%	%	%	%	%	%	%	%	%	%	%
Slimming products	1.1	0.7	1.3	1.5	1.5	1.2	1.1	0.7	1.1	0.9	1.0	0.4	1.5
Painkillers, toothache, headache	37.2	35.9	40.4	37.5	37.8	37.5	38.0	39.4	36.5	42.2	35.2	38.6	37.5
Painkillers: sore throat	21.2	19.7	21.1	22.9	20.4	19.6	19.9	22.0	22.8	20.6	24.8	22.0	24.8
Cold medicine	21.7	21.0	21.7	21.9	22.0	20.3	20.5	24.1	23.0	19.9	23.4	24.7	22.6
Prevention of sports injuries	9.1	8.2	10.2	10.4	10.4	7.7	10.9	10.7	9.8	11.1	9.3	7.3	13.3
Tonic	4.6	4.1	5.2	4.4	5.1	4.4	4.9	5.6	4.4	4.3	5.1	4.6	5.5
Bad skin (spots, acne)	4.5	5.7	4.7	4.9	4.6	3.6	4.1	5.3	5.1	4.2	5.4	5.0	5.5
Veins (ointment, pills)	3.9	5.3	2.7	5.1	4.7	3.4	4.7	3.6	3.2	4.6	4.4	2.6	5.3
Digestive products	6.4	7.7	5.6	7.9	5.1	6.0	4.2	6.5	5.9	6.0	6.0	6.2	7.5
Vitamin-drinks, -tablets	24.3	23.9	26.2	21.9	24.9	24.6	26.2	25.4	26.4	27.0	25.7	26.3	28.3
Ointment	9.6	9.5	8.6	11.8	9.2	9.4	8.3	12.5	12.0	8.7	12.5	10.2	8.7
Very concerned about health	24.9	25.0	24.4	24.8	26.7	23.2	27.2	24.4	26.4	24.2	24.8	25.6	26.4
Organic – health food store: at least once a month	15.7	18.1	16.5	18.7	15.1	14.3	13.5	12.6	16.8	16.5	15.5	14.6	16.0
Self-treatment – if not too serious	58.4	58.9	60.6	57.8	61.3	57.9	60.9	59.6	60.0	59.4	56.9	56.5	63.7

Significances which reached 1% in the analysis of the accumulated data of both surveys.
Significances which repeated themselves in both surveys.
☐ positive ☐ negative

Purchasing behaviour: sole or main decision-makers

Survey sample	Aged 14+ 13 283	Capricorn 837	Aquarius 909	Pisces 937	Aries 987	Taurus 928	Gemini 1021	Cancer 913	Leo 925	Virgo 909	Libra 812	Scorpio 820	Sagittarius 760
	Ø%	%	%	%	%	%	%	%	%	%	%	%	%
Alcoholic drinks	61.5	61.2	61.3	64.5	60.4	58.0	63.8	62.2	62.5	66.0	59.8	62.0	61.2
Car	52.9	51.0	50.2	56.0	57.3	51.1	53.1	51.5	54.8	56.4	51.5	54.9	55.0
Mortgage/Building Society savings contracts	39.2	38.1	38.1	41.6	41.1	39.6	41.0	43.1	40.8	42.3	36.2	40.3	39.8
TV, video equipment	65.6	64.4	60.9	67.5	66.1	67.8	64.0	67.2	66.5	66.2	63.6	65.8	70.3
Garden	42.8	40.4	45.5	46.5	43.7	44.0	43.8	42.0	41.6	42.8	42.4	42.8	44.1
Financial investments	62.1	60.3	59.0	65.1	63.2	63.7	60.5	63.7	63.5	67.3	61.8	62.8	67.6
Men's cosmetics, aftershave	56.5	56.3	56.4	54.3	59.0	55.1	55.5	57.4	58.0	57.3	54.9	56.0	53.7
Hi-Fi equipment	54.8	54.2	52.6	56.2	55.7	56.3	53.5	57.5	54.0	54.1	53.4	52.5	58.0
Cameras, lens, equipment	50.0	47.1	45.9	52.0	50.7	49.3	48.4	49.9	53.7	48.9	48.1	52.1	51.7
Kitchen appliances, large, electric	62.3	58.7	60.8	63.6	61.1	62.9	60.1	62.0	63.1	59.4	61.9	62.3	66.4
Furniture, furnishings	69.9	66.1	67.7	70.9	69.8	71.7	68.9	67.9	70.9	70.4	70.9	70.4	72.2
Women's perfume, toilet water	56.7	57.2	58.6	56.6	56.2	57.0	58.3	57.9	55.3	55.0	57.0	54.7	61.9
PC or other large DP equipment	19.3	20.3	18.7	18.8	19.8	19.9	19.5	20.9	21.4	21.7	20.1	16.2	19.9
Holiday plans	67.3	63.4	65.2	71.4	72.3	66.4	69.2	69.0	65.5	71.1	64.1	65.0	71.6
Insurance	65.8	63.8	61.7	66.8	65.8	68.0	66.5	67.0	67.4	72.5	59.7	66.0	68.8

Significances which reached 1% in the analysis of the accumulated data of both surveys.
Significances which repeated themselves in both surveys.
positive ☐ ☐ negative

INFORMATION
ON THE
INVESTIGATIVE DESIGN

1. Duration of study

Autumn 1995:	22 September– 9 December 1995	IfD Archives Survey 6020
Spring 1996:	13 February– 27April 1996	IfD Archives Survey 6026

Fieldwork was conducted exclusively by trained interviewers from the Allensbach Institute.

2. Sample

Sample drawn using the quota selection procedure.

13,283 respondents in total, of whom 10,758 supplied their dates of birth.

The sample was biased to increase subsample sizes and thus improve accuracy in the segment of the population age 14–59, which is especially targeted by market and media analyses.

Unweighted sample size		Weighted sample size
13,283	Total respondents	13,185
10,866	Age 14–59	9,665
2,417	Age 60 +	3,520
6,319	Men	6,261
6,964	Women	6,924
6,696	Autumn 1995	6,593
6,587	Spring 1996	6,592

By means of factorial (iterative) weighting, the values were adjusted to the extrapolated figures from the official statistics on gender, age groups, size of households, size of administrative districts, and regions.

INFORMATION ON THE ACCURACY
OF REPRESENTATIVE SURVEYS
(TOLERANCE LIMITS OF THE RESULTS)

Percentage figures ascertained in representative surveys conducted according to the sampling principle may differ within specified tolerance limits from the percentages actually present in the total universe.

The magnitude of the tolerance limits depends in each case upon the sampling method used, the sample size, and the percentage rate of occurrence for the characteristic under investigation. For decades, it has been debated whether tolerance limits may only be calculated for samples drawn according to the random sampling principle, or whether they can also be applied to samples designed using the quota method. This question cannot be answered by theoretical arguments, but only by empirical data. In practice, both the random and quota methods are subject to error. Assuming they are applied correctly, however, all the evidence thus far indicates that the random and quota methods are equally valid and equally suited to the calculation of tolerance limits for the percentage values found on this basis. More detailed information can be found in: E. Noelle-Neumann and T. Petersen, *Alle, nicht jeder: Einführung in die Methoden der Demoskopie* (Munich: dtv, 1986, pp. 263–276). Corresponding tables of tolerance limits consider the size of the sample and the percentage at which the relevant characteristic occurs. The following table shows the extent to which a percentage figure *p* obtained from a representative sample of *n* people may deviate from the actual value, with a 95 per cent probability.

Statistical tolerance limits
(95 per cent confidence level)

Statistical level of tolerance
(reliability 95%)

No. of people in spot check	p = Percentage share of sample									
	50 50	45 55	40 60	35 65	30 70	25 75	20 80	15 85	10 90	5 95
100	9,80	9,75	9,60	9,35	8,98	8,49	7,84	7,00	5,88	–
150	8,00	7,96	7,84	7,63	7,33	6,93	6,40	5,71	4,80	3,49
200	6,93	6,89	6,79	6,61	6,35	6,00	5,54	4,95	4,16	3,02
300	5,66	5,63	5,54	5,40	5,19	4,90	4,53	4,04	3,39	2,47
400	4,90	4,88	4,80	4,67	4,49	4,24	3,92	3,50	2,94	2,14
500	4,38	4,36	4,29	4,18	4,02	3,80	3,51	3,13	2,63	1,91
1000	3,10	3,08	3,04	2,96	2,84	2,68	2,48	2,21	1,86	1,35
2000	2,19	2,18	2,15	2,09	2,01	1,90	1,75	1,56	1,31	0,96
5000	1,39	1,38	1,36	1,32	1,27	1,20	1,11	0,99	0,83	0,60

Number of respondents in sample = *n*
p = percentage at which the characteristic occurs

Explanation: Assuming that a representative survey of *n* = 2,000 people determines that 80 per cent of these people are familiar with a particular product: by finding the point where the line *n* = 2,000 crosses the column *p* = 80, we see

that this result must be viewed within a tolerance limit of +/–
1.75 per cent. The actual figure, which would be found if the
entire population were surveyed, is thus located with a 95
per cent probability somewhere between the limits of 78.25
per cent and 81.75 per cent.

When using tolerance tables, it must be remembered that not
all values between the limits are equally probable. Rather,
the actual value found is the most likely, as the Gaussian bell-
shaped curve plainly shows.

Comment: The gap in the top corner of the table results from
the fact that the standard error cannot be expressed as a single figure in these cases. The table opposite assumes that the
binomial distribution followed by the proportions can be
approximated by a normal distribution.

When the percentage occurrence of a characteristic
approaches 0 per cent or 100 per cent, the binomial distribution becomes noticeably asymmetric and departs from the
normal distribution. In other words, the margins of error
upwards and downwards taken on different values.